Reiner Schürmann
Selected Writings and Lecture Notes

Reiner Schürmann

The Place of the Symbolic

Essays on Art and Politics

Edited by
Kieran Aarons and Nicolas Schneider

DIAPHANES

Reiner Schürmann
Selected Writings and Lecture Notes

Edited by Francesco Guercio, Michael Heitz,
Ian Alexander Moore, and Nicolas Schneider

1st edition
ISBN 978-3-0358-0434-8

Layout: 2edit, Zurich
Printed in Germany

www.diaphanes.com

Table of Contents

Symbolic Difference

It is not self-evident that God and the world, friendship and love, owe any allegiance to words. On the shore of a lake surrounded by pine trees, I say "this lake is surrounded by pine trees." As soon as the words are spoken, immediacy is lost. Wherever I turn, words are already there.

The technician rejoices at this. It is by means of words that he organizes, transforms, and fabricates what he calls the universe of things. In contrast, he who faces not a world of things to dominate, but a human being to know and love, will already deem the assistance of words to be more ambiguous: through words, indeed, he must dissect the unsayable into consonants, vowels, and syllables. The perfectly taciturn person neither knows nor loves anyone.

Faced with this invasion, man may take flight: perhaps the lake then becomes a lake for us, once again, and nothing more, and God becomes God, once again. However, if nothing is worth being said or thought at the edge of the lake, beneath the gaze of God, then emptiness itself, this saying and thinking all, will not be abolished *qua* emptiness: if emptiness has the last word, then it is not emptiness. Similarly, if pure feeling has the last word, then it is not pure feeling.[1] It is when the army of words appears to be a useless, bothersome carcass and residue, that the danger is the most treacherous. In order to attain either pure undergoing or experiencing, or vacuity, or any other non-word, the vehicle will still be the speakable, if only a shout: "Silence!" Immediacy will be a continuous victory over words, within words.

The questioning of language will then strive to retrace the steps, going backwards along the course of a privileged speaking: that which establishes a new way of existing in the listener. Symbols do this. They are plenary words, full of meaning and inciting power, addressed to existence. This addressing alone allows for a renewal of the traditional problematic of meaning: the structure of the call in language, the reception of meaning, and solicitation by symbols:

---

1 See Friedrich Schleiermacher, *Glaubenslehre* (Leipzig: A. Deichert, 1910–), §5.

these are the first three cardinal points which orient the understanding of words. The fourth cardinal point will be their monstration. Symbols are a region of speaking which shows being. Symbols are given (*donné*). The apprenticeship of hearing is ordered (*ordonné*).

After briefly recalling this preexistence of symbols, I shall indicate the two types of reading which rest on this given; the discrimination between the two will precisely follow from a certain understanding of meaning. After thus delimiting the symbol within our language, the task will be to attempt to delimit the ontological locus of the symbol. Finally, I will return to existence in order to discern in it the efficaciousness of the symbol in a human life. The narrative of Francis of Assisi's conversion will in some sense serve as a material for my reflection. This narrative will assist one in thinking the symbolic difference.

I. The Symbol, a Given

Water is a reality: every year it attracts millions of city-dwellers who come to renew themselves through contact with it; it is a word: the "water" of which poets of all ages speak, whether their world-view is directly aquatic-like that of Thales of Miletus-or not. Water is given to the fatigue of our body, to our cosmogonic imagination, to our oneiric unconscious. We are entitled to attempt to grasp this given by formulating a series of propositions, all of which begin with "Water is ..." Water is life, "water heals, rejuvenates, ensures life."[2] It flows from fountains of youth and is preserved in flasks of the water of life. Water is hence also the origin. The world, in the beginning, emerged from primordial waters. In Indian iconography,[3] in Neoplatonic systems,[4] in Christian mysticism,[5] the aquatic imagination seems to

2 Mircea Eliade, *Traité d'histoire des religions* (Paris: Payot, 1953), 172.

3 Ibid., 170.

4 Diadochus Proclus, *The Elements of Theology*, ed. E.R. Dodds (Oxford: Clarendon Press, 1933), e.g. propositions 25–26, 152, 174.

5 Meister Eckhart, *Die Deutschen und Lateinischen Werke* (Stuttgart: W. Kohlhammer, 1936–), vol. 2 of the Latin works, 21, #16: Eckhart speaks of the "ebullitio" or "liquefactio" of all things from their "ground."

have led the mind to the intuition of causality. Water, which washes away what is soiled, returns man to the purity of his origin. To take a bath is to have a premonition of totality.[6] From here, the association of ideas moves on easily to fecundity and sensuality. Like the ocean, woman is fecund. Shells, because they come from the sea and bring to mind the vulva, symbolize the return to the mother's breast; in some funerary rites, one scatters them along the path leading from the house of the dead one to the cemetery, or to the bottom of the grave.[7] Water, because it thus conjures up death, horrifies. Stagnant water is "dead,"[8] it is the shapeless procession of Ophelia and the Unknown Woman of the Seine. It is even a powerful invitation to commit suicide by drowning.[9] Water is deceitful, unfathomable, and threatening—feminine. Loreley is the ally of the reefs in the Rhine.

I should like to suggest another constituted symbolism, as rich as that of water: the symbolism of wandering. Parsifal in search of the Grail "is" wandering. The multiplicity of Wolfram von Eschenbach's sources[10] shows how popular these narratives of the great quest were. The young knight, *tumb*, leaves his mother, in search of a community of saints (perhaps the Parfaits, the Cathars of Montsegur); he arrives there without any trouble, but does not recognize the gift made to him. He is excluded from their company and begins his wandering proper, the period of apprenticeship which will lead him back, much later, to the same castle of the Grail. Parsifal: someone fallen from grace (*hors-la-grace*), both divine and social grace, or better, fallen from the origin (*hors-l'origine*), who remembers the happiness he failed to attain and works at a second coming of its proximity. The identity glimpsed, then lost "for nothing," is also identity promised. Wandering experiences the origin as the site of provenance and as immanence: "the perfection of paradise, root and spray of flowers at once; it was a thing called the Grail,

---

6 G.W.F. Hegel, *Theologische Jugendschriften* (Tübingen: Mohr, 1907), 319.

7 Mircea Eliade, *Images et symboles* (Paris: Gallimard, 1952), 180.

8 Gaston Bachelard, *L'eau et les rêves* (Paris: PUF, 1968), 89.

9 The most beautiful literary depiction of this attraction is James Baldwin's *Another Country* (New York: Dell, 1962), at the end of chapter 1.

10 Friedrich Panzer, *Gahmuret. Quellenstudie zu Wolframs Parzival* (Heidelberg: Carl Winter, 1940).

the overflowing of all earthly blessing (*erdenwunsches überall*)."[11] These themes never run dry in German literature, but they reach their apex after the French Revolution, during the years of political disarray in Europe which led to the emergence of German Romanticism. The Romantic soul wanders through social, religious and intellectual decomposition. It mainly produces fragments, the only literary form which is suitable for its experience. Against the judgment of generalized dislocation, it brings to bear a great unitary dream. It poetizes its ruins, with a view to restoring lost harmony. Novalis' thought is the passionate quest of undividedness. "Where are we going, then? Always towards the homeland."[12] The primitive age will be reborn "from below," far from reason and its overly crude light. The song of totality can only be a Hymn to the Night. The night is full of reminiscences, it contains or shelters the only reminiscence—that of the origin, to which only the dreamer has access. This vanished origin is the carnal delight of Sophie (the dead mistress), the old order of Europe, and salvation in Christ, all at once. "Its sensual religiosity, its Christian eroticism"[13] drove Novalis to escape from the world. He accedes to the more real world of the imagination, where the blue flower blooms.[14] In many ways, the quest for the flower resembles the quest for the Grail: to find it is to be granted access to the intimacy of those who "know," to be united with the depths or ground of the world (the term "Weltfrömmigkeit" appears) by overcoming the painful split between the dream and the everyday. "The world becomes a dream, the dream becomes a world."[15] A future existence lies dormant within present existence. Romantic wandering is wholly fascinated with this unity which it glimpsed in dreams. This allows the nostalgia of a return to the origin to take root in these authors. To have glimpsed the blue flower is to know the universe through initiation; it is the principle

---

11 Wolfram von Eschenbach, *Parzival*, ed. Wilhelm Stapel (Munich: Langen Müller, 1950), chapter III, 2.

12 Novalis, *Fragmente* (Dresden: Wolfgang Jess, 1929), ed. Minor III, 365, 224.

13 Vladimir Jankélévitch, "Le Nocturne," in *Cahiers du Sud* (May–June 1937), 81.

14 Novalis, *Hymnen an die Nacht, Heinrich von Ofterdingen* (Munich: Goldmann, 1958), 43–44.

15 Ibid., 149.

of unity between all of its elements. It allows one to communicate immediately, intimately, with all things. It transposes one beyond oppositions.

It is not enough to repeat that with which most authors agree: all symbolisms, in one way or another, speak of the origin of man and the world. Both of the symbolisms I sketched form a one-piece fabric. We must now turn our gaze to this fabric as a whole. The practices and dreams I mentioned are connected amongst themselves by something. Once they are removed from the behavior or discourse which encompasses them, they say nothing more. The symbolic given is a homogeneous plurality of elements which call on one another to constitute an autonomous system of relations. Moreover, the cultural domain from which one selects these "facts" matters little, for the internal dependencies follow simple rules which are always the same. Mircea Eliade has already spoken of the aquatic "system."[16] The elements are quantitatively limited and qualitatively stable. Their chart may be drawn up, and if an element is lacking, it may be reconstituted. "Models" may be constituted.[17] All this is well known. It is clear that the structuralist method draws one away from the experiences of water or wandering themselves. This is even its avowed goal. Our question, in contrast, shall be: which understanding of being comes together when we commune with symbols? What is the force of wandering, what is its knowledge? Because on the one hand, participation in symbols is lived as a reception of knowledge, and on the other hand, this latter is precisely not received as an entity which is autonomous from internal dependencies, or as a model. Our question starts from the *meaning* of symbols. The model is a convention among scientific minds working on the same region of knowledge; an invariable, intelligible convention which allows for communication between researchers, but is void of meaning. But one does not agree on symbols, for they summon us. Thereby, they distinguish themselves from all that the natural sciences or human sciences call by the same name. Symbolic speech, as I mentioned, is to be under-

---

16 Mircea Eliade, *Traité d'histoire des religions,* §73.

17 Claude Lévi-Strauss, *Anthropologie structurale* (Paris: Plon, 1958), 306.

stood as reception of meaning, not as convention. Every celebration which includes a water ritual, every uprooting which makes one "go away in order to learn," makes use of a certain understanding of language. The latter is received as something given. Between the formalized symbols, "full of language,"[18] there is pure equivocity.

If scientific formalization cannot satisfy the desire for full, plenary understanding, as promised by the symbolic fact, if the attitude of neutrality towards the problem of meaning is unbearable when one is faced with this promise, the agreement must be recomposed. The cloth which brings together the "facts," which I mentioned in the beginning, gives itself through them, even as it withdraws. It is the object of the prayers and songs of the worshippers of the oceanic Magna Mater, or of those who sing of the Grail and the blue flower, even though they do not inquire into this cloth for itself. It is the unthought of the symbolism. Words and things are joined in it, set into motion by the feast, assembled in the poem, brought close to the heart of man by the solemn narrative of the ancient presence of the origin. It is the rhythm of the agreeable dance with its holy icons, and it is the breeze on Mount Carmel in which the Ineffable wraps itself in order to silence its name. Close and distant at once, unthought in the midst of gestures and speech, after the fashion of "He whose oracle is in Delphos," it "neither states nor conceals, but beckons."[19] The meaning-bearing cloth is present-absent, like the mystery.

Mystery restores a reference at the heart of the symbolism, a reference to that which the "facts" are not, which is greater than they are. If water *is* life, the mother is the plenitude of forms, purity, and the outcome to which wandering leads *is* grace found again, the identification with the cosmic depth—then water and wandering speak of something which they both are, and which one must recognize. The proximity of mystery enables them to be that which they are not in and of themselves, but that which they become in addition, as a surplus. Proximity is too close to be recognized, unless man decisively places himself in the hands of symbols. In all symbolisms, this call, summons, reprimand (*apostrophe*) stirs

---

18 Paul Ricœur, *De l'interprétation* (Paris: Seuil, 1965), 39.

19 Heraclitus, Fragment 93, in Diels-Kranz, *Fragmente der Vorsokratiker* (Berlin: Weidmann, 1934).

hearts and crowds. The mystery then reveals itself to be the celebrated Homeland. The *Geheimnis* is the *Heimat*.

The mystery is the homeland—this formulation is only meaningful in the resolute fulfilling of the 'giving over of oneself' to the senses, which appears in symbols. It is not a philosophical thesis. It says that proximity will be thought as a stable presence, as long as that which makes it proximal, the other trait of the present, is not also experienced as distant. The full, plenary hearing of symbols is thus the condition of the manifestation of the mystery. The reflection on meaning only bears one fruit here: it brings to light the symbols as traces of the inseparable advent and departure of the signifying fabric. It parts ways with the "philosophy of meaning" in that it points to an opening. It thinks this opening for itself, insofar as it lets that which appears within it, appear. In other words, it thinks a difference. Our concern in what follows will be whether this difference can be reduced to the mere relation between symbols and their meaning, or whether it evokes a differing other.

One last step remains to be taken, in this meditation on the symbolic given. Indeed, what is the consequence for a better understanding of language, if man's relation to the symbol is essentially characterized by the reception of meaning? What occurs in language, understood in this fashion? To be sure, it is an invitation—to swim, to libations, to wander, etc. But something already occurs in this invitation. It brings together (*dichtet, verdichtet*) man and symbol; it constitutes man as poet (*Dichter*). Heidegger sometimes refers to this approach of the present-absent in language as the *Geviert*. Poetic saying, he writes, brings together earth and heaven, the mortals and the divine. Our attention need not be focused on these four words themselves, but rather on the event of their uniting insofar as it occurs in symbols. I shall not discuss Heidegger's critique of the symbol.[20]

Jean Beaufret translates *Geviert* as "Quadriparti" (the fourfold).[21] Now, the term "Geviert" does not refer to "parts" or "folds"; nor does Heidegger have any special attachment to the number four.

---

20 Martin Heidegger, *Unterwegs zur Sprache* (Pfullingen: Neske, 1959), 15; *Vorträge und Aufsätze* (Pfullingen: Neske, 1954), 154.

21 Martin Heidegger, *Essais et conférences* (Paris: Gallimard, 1958).

The *Geviert*, first of all, is the feast of language, the game in which the elements I mentioned come together. One could hence translate the term as "quatuor" or "quartet," for the game brings together four players. *Geviert* or *Viertung*, secondly, means the intersection of two naves in a church, a point of luminosity, because it is topped with a dome and a lantern, and is a point which provides a full view, because it is the center of the four wings of the edifice. The *Geviert* is the heart of the cathedral, a good place to dwell. This must be the site of altar of the Saint (*der Heilige*) who heals (*heilt*), and, by restoring integrity (*das Heile*), gives salvation (*das Heil*). This is the point where the house welcomes those who come together in it. Instead of conveying a sense of this gathering into a point of light and a center in which architectonic lines and spaces come together, "fourfold" makes one think of a quadrature or a division into four pieces. Lastly, *Geviert* is a term, less frequent nowadays, which refers to dimensions: one still speaks of a *Gevierthof*, that is, the courtyard around which, and in relation to which, the four buildings of a farm are oriented. *Geviert* then means the four regions of the world, the cardinal points which are rendered close in the thing.[22] The famous examples of the bridge and the jug[23] precisely speak of things whose *ronde* rolls the four regions of the world into a circle. Far from cutting the world into parts, the *Geviert* brings the game of the world together: it summons and it gathers.

Man's symbolic speaking has always summoned and gathered. Man has always been a poet. There has always been one poem: the sole poem that no troubadour will ever exhaust, the originary poem, the feast of gods and men, the sacred.[24] The sacred itself strikes up the hymn of the ancient surging-forth, it speaks the poetic word which can bring men together, beside their origin. The word which gathers is the event of the sacred. Meaning comes about when poetic saying corresponds to the primordial poem, by summoning the Four in the event of a sudden lighting.

---

22 Heidegger, *Vorträge und Aufsätze*, 163 ff.

23 Ibid., 152–155, 163–181.

24 Martin Heidegger, *Erläuterungen zu Hölderlins Dichtung* (Frankfurt: Klostermann, 1951), 139: "Dies im voraus Öffnende ist das Heilige, das unvordichtbare Gedicht."

Three steps have been taken thus far, in our examination: we moved from the investigation of the given to an inquiry into its meaning, and in the end, the meaning of symbols compelled us to turn to mystery and the sacred, as events of the coming in language of that which is close and far away, of that which beckons. However, the symbol is more than a manifestation, and it exceeds the frame of language. We are now in a position to enumerate some of its characteristic traits:

—as a primordial poem, that which is symbolized (which the symbol refers to) manifests and hides itself at the same time;

—as a path which opens onto the sacred, the symbol heals and restores integrity;

—etymologically, *symbolon* (*symballein*) referred to an object serving the purpose of recognition, made up of the two halves of a broken clay tablet, which each of the partners in a contract kept, and which needed only to be "brought together," "thrown together," in order to verify an agreement that had been made, or bonds of hospitality that had been established;

—grammatically, it is a noun, a word, not a phrase or a narrative. This distinguishes it from the *myth*, of which it is an element;

—the symbol, as an element of language, refers to a second meaning; it hence resembles the *allegory*. But the latter says something so that one can understand something else, which is not said. It is an oratorical artifice in which there is no continuity of meaning from the signifier to the signified. The symbol, on its part, already bears the second sense within it, discourse cannot step beyond the symbol;

—as a reality, an object, the symbol realizes that which it means. In this way, it differs from the *metaphor* which annihilates itself in its function of referral to a meaning which lies beyond it;

—the symbol is naturally the bearer of a double meaning, not artificially, like the *analogy*. The relation of participation between an imperfect being and a perfect being is constructed through the widening of meaning from, and deficient similarity to, the inferior being. Such a construction comes after the entity, whereas the symbol contains a double meaning which makes it be both itself and the other;

—Karl Jaspers speaks of the "ciphers" of transcendence, in which existence reads its intrinsic possibility of renewal. The all-embracing, which draws back from any direct communication, only concerns me insofar as I exist in a new way; I only begin to exist in this way when I open myself to the all-embracing. The locus of the possible thematization of this intertwining of transcendence and existence is the reading of ciphers. This impact of ciphers on existence, in light of its conversion to transcendence, is to be retained; but the symbol differs from ciphers insofar as it realizes the presence of the symbolized, which Jaspers denies;[25]

—the symbol "is" that which it means, it is not content to reflect it or resemble it, like an image.

The symbol is different from the myth, the allegory, the metaphor, the analogy, the cipher, and the image, and yet it belongs along with all of these to the same genus. The generic concept is the "sign." A sign is an object or event which is ordered in accordance with another object or event, in such a way that the perception or representation of the sign also brings about that of the object coordinated with it. The modes of this coordination vary. The different species within this genus are diversified according to the relation of meaning they establish. Every sign is a present manifestation (i.e., one which is immanent to existence or to its speaking) of a non-present which transcends existence and its speaking. Significance is only natural to the symbol, as well as to the myth which is made up of symbols. The symbol is the most signifying sign. But there is something prior to its significance.

II. The Ontological Locus of the Symbol

1. Meaning and Language

The exploration of this preamble must begin with a reflection on understanding. Like any other region of language, the symbol does

---

25 Karl Jaspers, *Der philosophische Glaube angesichts der Offenbarung* (Munich: Piper, 1963), 157: "Chiffer sei Sprache des Transzendenten, das nur durch Sprache, nicht durch die Identität von Sache und Symbol im Symbol selber zugänglich ist."

not exist outside of human understanding. Man is the being who can understand or hear (*entendre*). A growing abandonment, a faculty of hearing prepare the ringing out of words in man. Man is the being who has already understood that something in words wishes to accede to hearing. He cannot remain indifferent to words, for they are bearers of a demand. Primitive familiarity with words manifests itself in their demanding acceptance or refusal: they demand an answer. An interlocutor's absent-mindedness before it is a lack of politeness, is an untruth. The truth is that man can and must hear, that he cannot not hear.

Fundamentally, saying comes forth in a back-and-forth motion. Speaking is essentially speaking "with," *logos* is in essence a dialogue. The *legein* will only be full, plenary, when speaking is gathered up. Listening brings together. The interlocutors come together in what is said. In such a gathering, a sudden clarity is expected, possible, begged-for. Then words show themselves in their essence, which is an event, an occurrence. As such, they rule over the fate of a man. Their coming forth, always unforeseeable, reveals the highest possibilities of being human to man. As a being capable of listening, man is given over to the occurrence, the 'happening' of words, in order to hear himself say his human truth.

But if his truth comes to him thus, in a sudden invasion of words, then man recalls something in them. An ancient horizon is newly opened. Words which had grown dull discover their childhood and give forth a meaning which slides easily towards forgetting. Man then replies: "I see," "Yes," "I have understood."

The phenomenon of understanding thus manifests a truth which was always known but was buried in everydayness, a truth which returns from oblivion to spread a new light, which is actually not new. It is the most ancient light under which man thinks and speaks, each time, inasmuch as he thinks and speaks. The event of understanding shows the advent of the most ancient clarity. It is the work of no one. The light which enables me to understand what another says is not my doing. And the same light which gives words the power to be said was not brought about by speaking. The new horizon which brings man and words together is the event of a beyond, behind them, withdrawing itself. Words are not transparent of themselves; nor is man a listener of or to himself. An unthought, the forgotten beyond, comes to light in understanding: the light of day in which words come forth for hearing. It is this day which must be thought. It is experienced as something given. It is the clarity which enables words to be understood, and man to heed, attend, hear. This double giving is felt to be one and the same gift, always behind us, never given over to us. In line with what was said earlier, it appears as the giving of meaning.

It is remarkable that Hans-Georg Gadamer arrives at a point where he questions himself, regarding the unfolding of meaning, when he addresses the ontological dimensions of hermeneutics, according to the guiding thread of language.[26] He then forgoes the expressions "pre-understanding" and "prejudice" which had served as his guidelines up until then, for they seem to be overly connected to a metaphysical context of an interpretation aiming at representing a monument of the past to itself. Thus there is a reversal in the thinking of *Truth and Method.* Until this point, starting from a vague, curious approach called pre-understanding, a bridge was thrown across the distance of time, for an ever-improving understanding of the monument in question. The reversal is a "rendering concrete" of what Gadamer, from the outset, had called effective-historical consciousness (*wirkungsgeschichtliches Bewusstsein*), a "speculative" rendering concrete, he specifies, for like a mirror (*speculum*), sensible (i.e., meaningful) understanding reflects the words of the ancient text. Speaking and understanding, Gadamer writes, are unfoldings of meaning

> insofar as the finite possibilities of the word tailor it to the meaning which is intended, as if it were heading in the direction of the infinite. S/he who has something to say searches for, and finds, the words by means of which s/he will be understood by another ... To say what one wishes to say, to make oneself understood, gathers up in the unity of the finite thing which is said, and an infinite which is never said. It is only in this way, therefore, that this infinite can be understood.[27]

---

26 Hans-Georg Gadamer, *Wahrheit und Methode* (Tübingen: Mohr, 1965), Part III.
27 Ibid., 444.

For Gadamer, then, the statement of the definite content, which disfigures meaning, is opposed to the intention or aim of meaning which always refers to a totality, an infinity of the unsaid beyond what is said. This opposition resembles that which emerged earlier, between the manipulation and the reception of meaning: the manipulated meaning, the definite content of the statement or the text, contains no reference to something greater than itself. On the other hand, to think meaning as an infinite totality beyond what is said, glimpsed through or from the surface like something unsayable, is to make heard that which grants words their power of affirmation. The issue is no longer, then, to read a text in order to come as close as possible to the thoughts and feelings of an author, but to accept, to agree to (*agréer*) the meaning within the words which ring out, which however does not reside in them—rather, they reside or ring out therein. The words flow from this meaning, and their only goal is to make it appear. Listening, attending to meaning is the welcoming of that which makes an understanding possible, not a specific understanding, but the power of understanding in general. The text or the discourse relates to meaning in a "speculative" fashion: they reflect its totality and shatter it.

Thus Gadamer, I believe, takes leave of the sciences of interpretation ("the sciences of the objectifications of life, retranslated into the vitality of the present spirit"—Wilhelm Dilthey). The hermeneutics of historical consciousness is dependent on the hermeneutics of meaning as a condition of its possibility. In this realm, every methodology can only be termed hermeneutical in a derivative manner. The meaning which manifests itself in the event of understanding requires an autonomous interpretation. It will proceed by means of circumscription, glimpsing from the surface, and suggestion. It lacks an object, for the second meaning, at issue here, is not connected to any object. Only the immediate, primary meaning, the vehicle of a variety of information, is the grasping of an object. Between the manifest meaning and the hidden meaning, there is equivocity. The double meaning appears as a tear in language. The tear or rift is essential to language, for it conceals itself even as it unconceals the contents. The second meaning unfolds itself in the difference of the present-absent. That which is rendered present by language's saying, namely, the world of things and their senses, conceals the second meaning with its appearing; this is so, necessarily. The most familiar is the most difficult to hear. Language refuses its essence, significations conceal meaning. Interpretation requires a new thinking.

Language is the sum of our relations to that which is, within a space of originary clarity, and the modes in which the latter gives itself to us. It is the close dwelling, so far away that it is forgotten in its essence. In the middle of propositions and inquiries, it keeps silent. The new thinking is the thinking of the mystery of language. The light as possibility, which makes one speak and allows one to understand, gives one understanding, beckons to us through words. It is thus literally senseless to move through language without meditating on the hiding-showing behind and within clear and distinct, definite and communicable statements. Along with this mystery, immediacy shall be conquered, a second naïveté beyond the work of hermeneutics.

The question then arises, whether language does not give itself to man, in one of the regions of its unfolding or deployment, in such a way that the conquest of the immediacy of the second meaning is explicitly thematized therein. In other words, it belongs to the essence of language that it conceals its truth, as an originary condition of its possibility, even as it unconceals true words. The second meaning withdraws behind the evidence of the first meaning. Is there a region of language which is defined precisely by this concealment-unconcealment? It would have to be an inviting region which, once thought in its totality, would make the question of double meaning and mystery emerge on its own account.

The region of language whose structure is determined by double meaning and mystery is the symbol. Every word or utterance that says more than itself, that explicitly refers to something beyond itself, is symbolic. Thus water is more than the liquid element: it is the matrix and the origin of the world. And wandering is more than an unstable succession of impromptu displacements: it is the loss and promised recovery of the origin. To think the symbol in its truth is to receive it in a hearing which is open to the second meaning. The symbol, the region where language gives its own essence over to be explored, is the resonance of an originary speech which cannot be grasped as a meaning of things, but which makes a gift to thought of the primitive rift where the thinkable appears. The symbol is the glare of language which makes its own revelatory power shine. The symbol is the very movement of the primary meaning which introduces the new thinking into its own dwelling. It is the speech of the origin of understanding, through which the essence of language beckons to us.

Martin Heidegger emphasizes that the word "symbol" has been invested with a scientific or artistic resonance which makes it either into a human convention, or into a thickness added onto speech, which strictly speaking does not belong to it. I have already eliminated these two deviations. Heidegger circumscribes what I am calling the symbol with four words: *Gebärde, Wink, Brauch,* and *Spur.* Attending to these words will assist us in preparing the way for the decisive step of our undertaking, i.e., determining the ontological locus of the symbol.

a) Gesture. In Heidegger's dialogue with a Japanese, his interlocutor speaks of *Nô* theater. He imitates one of its gestures (*Gebärde*), carried out on the empty stage, which, by means of a simple motion of the arm and the hand, makes a mountainous landscape appear in front of the audience. In such a gesture, that which is evoked is borne towards us: "Gesture is the gathering of a bearing."[28] What is it that is gathered or harvested thus? That which bears language so that it gives itself to us. But this is empty. The gesture beckons from that which is bare. It reaches us from that which unfolds and "which we attempt to think as the other of all that is present or absent."[29] Emptiness unfolds itself; the gesture gathers up into an unmeasurable unity the hill and the valley, the forest and the lake. That which brings them together is nothing, it comes from nowhere. But it brings them together. Elsewhere, Heidegger writes about this unity of emptiness, of this nothingness, which he says is essentially different from the objects analyzed by the sciences.[30] Nothingness is

---

28 Heidegger, *Unterwegs zur Sprache,* 107: "Gebärde ist Versammlung eines Tragens"; "A Dialogue on Language," in *On the Way to Language,* trans. Peter D. Hertz (New York: Harper & Row, 1971), 18.

29 "[J]enes Wesende nämlich, das wir als das Andere zu allem An- und Abwesenden zu denken versuchen" (ibid., 108); translation, 19 (modified).

30 *Was ist Metaphysik?* (Frankfurt: Klostermann, 1963), 45.

That which cannot be analyzed or explained, which makes a gesture. It is remarkable that this meditation on the gesture is located in a dialogue. Where two men who are able to listen together take the path which leads to essential thinking, the origin beckons.

b) Sign. In the same dialogue, the untranslatable term *Wink* appears. *Winken* means "to signal"; but as I have shown, the term "sign" is a generic concept. Consequently, I will use the term *Wink*. The Japanese tries to translate a term from his language which expresses the very emergence or surging-forth of speaking. The fundamental trait of this expression is the *Wink*. A man leans his head forward; thus, in the advent of language within words, something capital manifests itself as a leaning forward. This trait is as enigmatic as the "message of the lightening concealing."[31] The *Wink* points toward a long way still to be traveled. Yet it does not come to us from a far-off hermeneutician: That which beckons or signals to us invites us to go towards that which is closest, to the source of speaking and thinking. This source gives itself as the essence of language, but it refuses to give itself up, in words. It sends an invitation to thinking: men respond to the *Wink* of the nearby proximity, which comes to those who speak, as if from somewhere else.

c) Use. *Brauch* in everyday usage means the use, the enjoyment of that which one needs. To use something is "to delight in it and thereby to acquire the habit of it."[32] This term thus recalls the Latin verb *frui*, which means *praesto habere*, to let that which is present be present. To make use of something refers to a making which preserves: the person who makes use of something places it under the essential guard of what it is. Thus s/he maintains it in a presence. Conversely, the relation s/he who uses has to the thing that is present in the image, is a letting-unfold, in such a way that s/he who enjoys the right to use something, holds and protects it in his or her hand. Use makes it remain in the tear of the present-absent.

---

31 *Unterwegs zur Sprache*, 141: "Der Wink aber ist die Botschaft des lichtenden Verhüllens."

32 Martin Heidegger, *Holzwege* (Frankfurt: Klostermann, 1963), 338: "einer Sache froh sein und dergestalt sie im Brauch haben … 'Brauchen' besagt demnach: etwas Anwesendes als Anwesendes anwesen lassen, … etwas seinem eigenen Wesen aushändigen und es als so Anwesendes in der wahrenden Hand behalten."

That which is there, and according to its being there, in a manner which differs, depending on the user who makes it present, is introduced into *Dasein* by a treatment which does not stem from it, which remains in absence, and over which it has no control. It is not that the present is maintained in its presence by some invisible cause: the relation of use is not a causal relation, but a relation which lets it appear. To say that language makes use of words means that it keeps them under its essential clarity. Language sheds light on words in order that man can recognize them in the there of their understanding. Words only give themselves over to man's use because language has always taken them up in its usage.

d) Trace. That which does not appear leaves behind the trace (*Spur*) of its advent in that which does appear. Thinking is called on to walk, in an always renewed fashion, along the traces it must cross in order to preserve them as its own. The man of the new thinking ceaselessly returns to these traces, but they are never ceded to him proper.[33] They are the traces of the Other of things, the Other of words, in words. They belong to That which traced them. It falls upon the man who walks along these traces to say what was experienced according to their display.[34] A trace of this sort is a path which leads nowhere: the origin of language towards which the trace leads, is neither in a beyond nor somewhere in particular. The trace leads to this emptiness, which showed itself in the nakedness of space where speaking becomes possible. The song of the poet who celebrates the steps of the gods, rises from the trace they left behind: "The poet … in his song, goes forth riveted to the trace of the gods who fled."[35] The gods are no longer, yet this does not mean that if their trace is read, it leads from the there to the beyond. The poet sees an *archē*-writing behind and within all the lines from which the world is woven, even if they are only a

---

33 [Here the author plays on "revenir à" as returning to, and "revenir" as something rightfully attributed or ceded to someone.—Trans.]

34 *Holzwege*, 194–195: "Doch ist jedem Denkenden je nur ein Weg, der seine, zugewiesen, in dessen Spur er immer wieder hin und her gehen muss, um ihn endlich als den seinen, der ihm doch nie gehört, einzuhalten und das auf diesem Weg Erfahrbare zu sagen."

35 Ibid., 251: "Dichter in dürftiger Zeit sein heißt: singend auf die Spur der entflohenen Götter achten. Darum sagt der Dichter zur Zeit der Weltnacht das Heilige."

matter for science, in the case of modern man. The god who does not appear, who is lacking amongst his people, leaves the sparks of his light in language. The task of the new thinking will be to listen once again to the sacred mystery which gives itself up to be heard, through the traces of the god who fled, in language.

The interpretation of the symbol, the dis-covery of the mystery, urges on the new thinking. Each time that the symbol rings out in language, and that someone capable of hearing is there to receive it, it gives out a sudden light. It sends the hearer and the seer onto a path. The symbol is thus "historical," it is destined for us: "To bear along a path: this is the meaning in our language of the word *schicken*. We call *Geschick* the sending which gathers and which alone bears man along a path of unconcealment. It is from there that the essence of any history is determined."[36]

2. Language and Being

The symbol appeared to us as something tightly connected with the instantaneous surging-forth (*Ursprung*) of the meaning of language, in the event of understanding. The symbol is the region of speaking where the hiding-showing of mystery is thematized for itself, in words or objects. Then the origin of language is given to us to think. It manifests itself in the symbol without preliminaries, without any prior warning. Questioning the origin thus understood will allow for the ontological localization of the symbol.

When the Babylonian priest, in the chant of a cosmogony, solemnly proclaims the birth of the world from primordial waters, when the people purifies itself of its sins by immersing the statue of its goddess in the waters, or when men sanctify themselves by bathing in the sacred river, these rites count as so many words on the water which is the universal matrix; like the divinity that it symbolizes, it is creative, purifying, and sanctifying. Language does not

---

36 Heidegger, *Vorträge und Aufsätze*, 32: "Auf einen Weg bringen—dies heißt in unserer Sprache: schicken. Wir nennen jenes versammelnde Schicken, das den Menschen erst auf einen Weg des Entbergens bringt, das Geschick. Von hier aus bestimmt sich das Wesen aller Geschichte."

give itself otherwise than in the priest's invocation and the people's cheering. The symbol of water is lived in such a way, by means of its various immediate senses, as to lead us into the unique essence of language: the concealment-unconcealment which is the law of all speaking. The aquatic divinity is never more present to its faithful than the day of the celebration of its feast, when in a sudden flash the sacred meaning in its rites beckons, signals to us. Yet the divinity is only present in the symbol of water, and hence is itself absent. The law of the present-absent thus appears not to be restricted to the phonetic dimension of language. This is apparent in the case of ritual celebration: immersion, ablution, and lustration, even when they are without words, both manifest and mask the divinity, just as the words of the priest and the people's cheering manifest and mask it. The hiding-showing, the difference which rends into ambiguity the articulation of the origin in the symbol, cannot be reduced to the fissure between the first meaning and the second meaning in words: it is greater than the language which is proffered.

This difference itself must be an object of inquiry. Can the seeming multivocity of the word 'origin' be overcome? Under which condition will this word speak a single source which is communicated in diverse ways? In ritual doings, in the symbol's signifying, and in the speaking of language, is there one and the same origin which gives itself to be thought, in different figures?

Throughout the history of philosophy, the origin has in fact been thought, not only as necessary and real, but also as single. The fate of the origin in Greek, medieval, and modern thinking appears to be a gradual emptying-out (*exination*).[37] Our question will then be: does a philosophy of the symbol qua thinking of difference allow for a step backwards, where the memory of the origin becomes possible once again?

The Greeks used the term *phusis* to refer to all that is, insofar as it is. Today we translate this word as "nature," from the Latin *nasci*, to be born. The Greek word comes from *phuein*: hatching or opening out, which is also the root of the word *phainestai*, to enlighten,

---

37 [The author's term "exination" is apparently a neologism created from the Latin *exinanio*: to empty out, to exhaust, or *exinanitio*: to void, etc.; cf. Félix Gaffiot, *Dictionnaire illustré latin-français* (Paris: Hachette, 1934), 626.—Trans.]

to shed light on. In a rough distinction, Latin thinking attends to the generation of things, and Greek thinking attends to their appearance or emergence into light. Nature according to what the Greek word states is the whole of that which shows itself to us, it is showing itself. Whether we turn to the "still life" (*nature morte*) of a painter, or declare that art corrects or imitates "nature," whether we contemplate the objects analyzed by "physics" or the "physiognomy" of our fellow creatures—everything that is, can be shown. It has already shown itself to us, before something in particular occupied our consciousness. By showing itself, it renders itself present according to an "aspect": the *ad-spicere*, the human aim or intention, responds to the fundamental trait of that which is, that it appears naturally. The origin of all things, according to this vocabulary, lets itself be thought as the presence of that which is present: a presence which is prior to any human intention, and which makes it possible. The origin of all things is their appearing in presence.

In the eleventh century, an increasingly lively interest in Greek thought emerged in Northern Europe. Anselm of Canterbury put forth an argument which appears at first sight akin to the Greek understanding of nature. At the cost of simplifying to some extent, his way of proceeding may be summarized as follows.[38] Human thinking inquires into the origin of all things. That which appears in thinking must exist in order to appear. Since the mind has always represented something to itself which is the greatest of all beings, this greatest of beings exists. In other words: if God did not exist, thinking would not have found this reflection of God within itself, this disquieting "aspect." The minor part of this syllogism seems to be close to *phusis*: that which is, insofar as it is, can manifest itself to the mind. But what happened so that the argument could move from the understanding of the virtually knowable entity to a conclusion regarding the existence of God? Which path does this thinking take, in order to move from the presence which manifests itself in all things, to the affirmation of the God of the Christians? The major part of the argument extends appearing to the totality of entities. To say that God appears in thinking as the greatest entity which can be

38 Anselm of Canterbury, *Proslogion*, MPL vol. CLVIII, col. 223.

conceived is to understand God as an entity in the world. The ontology of manifesting presence retracts into an onto-theology of manifest presence. The supreme entity differs from other entities in its magnitude, it transcends and grounds them. The ontological proof of the existence of God illustrates a radical shift in the understanding of the origin: it is no longer thought as the manifesting presence of the entity, but as the cause and ground of the entities that it encompasses as a genus.

It was Kant who detected this dogmatic presupposition of the ontological argument.[39] Thereafter, the origin will only be a rule which guarantees the possibilities of *a priori* propositions: "*Ursprung a priori.*"[40] The understanding, as it works at unifying sensible intuitions and empirical concepts, needs a regulative principle which presides over this unification, but this function cannot allow one to conclude that a supreme being exists, the necessary first of a series of effects to be experimented with. The origin is an *Inbegriff*, an ideal prototype which contains in itself the sum of all possible predicates. But existence is not a predicate, and hence this primitive concept is only a transcendental ideal. From an understanding of being as a present entity, Kant thus arrives at the simple idea of a relation to concepts, and not of a first thing which enters into relation with other things.[41] Kant unmasked traditional ontology as the representation of something present, fully regulated in accordance with the sensible substance, and drew the requisite conclusion: we only have knowledge or cognition of phenomena, and the origin of this knowledge is only to be found in the interweaving of sensibility, understanding, and reason. The forgetting of *phusis* which allows the entity to appear to thinking, which gives the entity as appearing to thinking, historically inaugurates the proclamation we hear today of the death of God. In Heidegger's view, this forgetting is as old as Western metaphysics.

How was such forgetting possible? It is not a bad interpretation of a Greek word. Presence itself, in the present thing, hides. That

---

39 Immanuel Kant, *Critique of Pure Reason*, B 620-630: "On the Impossibility of an Ontological Proof of the Existence of God."

40 Ibid., B 17.

41 Ibid., B 607.

the entity is: it is this appearing which conceals itself and withdraws. Only the sun and the sea, the invocation of the priest, and the dance of the believers, manifest themselves to us ... The entity always presents itself to a certain "faculty" of man: its beauty exalts him, its usefulness stimulates his passion to transform the world. Yet before it solicits admiration or usage, the entity is. But the being of the entity evades us. Its place is usurped by a hypertrophied entity, and the universe appears as a heap of things disconnected from their emergence. The difference of hiding-showing is our lot. It is the law according to which being gives itself to us.

The forgetting of being as the manifesting presence of the present renders thinking unquiet, and drives it to go in search of proofs. Neglected by being, thinking wanders until it is held fast by the indubitable ground of things and of itself. This quest for a ground has provided our tradition with its noblest intuitions: Saint Augustine's "unquiet heart,"[42] but also Yeats' powerless center, which "cannot hold."[43] Heidegger views this neglect and the ensuing insecurity as the fatal destiny of the West.[44] Since Kant and Nietzsche, the thinking of the present, forgetful of presence, has shown that its essence is nothingness. The negation in nihilism properly targets and strikes presence itself. In this loss, something has disappeared whose appearing was previously self-evident. When reasons vanish, thinking inquires into its destiny: what is this loss which can shake the rest of the universe at its foundations? That which is lost is more than one reason among others: the sole reason or ground which posits the entity and has thinking at its disposal, has ceased to impose its order. The vanishing which fills our century with dread drives it to seek multiple assurances, i.e., forms of security: being itself has vanished, *das Sein selbst bleibt aus*.[45]

At the closing of this era of concealment (*cèlement*), the regions of entities become dislocated: "God" becomes the partner of the beautiful soul, the "world" becomes the kingdom of the man of action, and the "subject" becomes the last refuge of the philosopher, who is soon

42 Saint Augustine, *Confessions* I, 5.

43 W. B. Yeats, "The Second Coming": "Things fall apart, the center cannot hold."

44 Martin Heidegger, *Nietzsche* (Pfullingen: Neske, 1961), vol. 2, 355.

45 Ibid., 353.

expelled from there by the psychologists. The mystery of being fragments into the secret of God, the secret of the world, and the secret of man. Faced with this dislocation, the man of the new thinking will be the guardian of being. How will this man think symbols?[46]

In the ontological difference between being and entity, being is the origin of things as well as of thinking. It treats the entity with care, so that it will not be nothing, and this care or sparingness is the light of thinking. I said that the essence of language, unthought by metaphysics and the sciences, is the origin of understanding. Now I can add that being in its difference from the entity is the origin of the appearing of all things. It is therefore in language that being makes what is, appear. A thing "is" when language tears it from *léthé*, from concealment. Where language is lacking—but this is properly unthinkable—nothing may be. What about this third person singular, "is"? It is never encountered for itself. It seems to be nothing, is not a given, yet it gives: their presence, to things, and to thinking, its light. It gives language. As I said, the symbol thematizes the essence of language for itself, but it is also the privileged site where being unconceals its difference from the entity. The origin revealed by the symbol is being.

Actually, only that which gives appearing, which allows for appearing, appears in symbols. The symbols of water and wandering speak to us of the single origin, being, but this is neither the doing of these symbols, nor of man, nor the hermeneutician. Being appears nowhere else but in entities; the origin only allows itself to be invoked in symbols. The symbols are those entities which in saying merely refer to the origin in one of its shapes. Being allows the origin to be known more intimately in symbols than in any other region of entities.

---

46 Paul Ricœur, in *De l'interprétation. Essai sur Freud,* has come no closer to an ontological approach to the symbol than the structuralists whom he denounces for having forgotten "meaning" in language. His three determinations of the symbol prepare the way for this approach, but do not replace it: the symbol as the locus of double meaning (17); the symbol as the region where the fullness of language can be thought (79, and in other works), as well as our self-understanding (47); the symbol as a "concrete mixture" (476–77, 485).

Yet one must take note of a twofold movement of thinking. On the one hand, the symbol does not escape the forgetting of being, in and of itself. There are sacred tremors which are far from being a pure reference to the origin. On the other hand, the ontological interpretation tends to overtake or overcome a particular religious or poetic symbol in order to turn its gaze onto all that is, as a whole. This widening of perspective is necessary; it results from the ontological project itself. Everywhere being signals, it symbolizes itself in the entity. And the entity symbolizes being. It is the sole Symbol of being.

The entity realizes or manifests the being that it signifies. The "there" of being exhausts itself in its function of referring to the presence of which it is the present. There is no duplicity in the symbol. The referral it performs does not move from a close object to a distant object. Similarly, the being and the entity are not two things: there is only the entity, only the entity is. But all things are, and in them, being gives itself to thinking—this is the primordial symbolization which gives sustenance to thinking (*donne à penser*). The entity, Symbol of being: this does not mark a decision as to what being is. If, insofar as it is symbolized by the totality of the entity, it turns out to be nothingness, this nothingness is not nothing. Being gives something to be seen, even though it refuses to give itself to thinking. The ontological interpretation of the symbol is a certain gaze onto all that is. All things manifest themselves to this new gaze, not in their opacity, into which the man of action endeavors to cut as he sees fit, but in their originary purity. In the language of the mystics: the man who knows how to see is detached from the singular entity; all things give themselves to him in their primary limpidity, as they are in the unfathomable depths of the Deity.[47]

The ontological interpretation of the symbol, then, is nothing other than the thinking of the entity "aiming at," "with a view towards," being. Being allows the entity to be its symbol. Its symbolization makes one go backwards, taking the paths of hermeneutics in the opposite direction: it is not this particular symbol which refers to being, but the entity makes one discover that it symbolizes more than itself. The study of the symbol as the site in which dif-

47 See my *Maître Eckhart ou la joie errante* (Paris: Denoël, 1972), 207–27.

ference is thematized thus culminates in a hermeneutic reversal. The ontological interpretation of the symbol reverses itself into a symbolic interpretation of the entity.

The metaphysical search for foundations caused the question of being to become dislocated. The symbolic memory of presence makes God, man, and the world reintegrate their always-beginning game. Meister Eckhart says that the soul stripped of any attachment is the "there" of this playful identity.[48] Philosophy is but a preparation for this serene existence "without why." Philosophy is not that which restores the Three to their common emergence. Faced with the new thinking, philosophy is precarious. When the beckoning, the call of the symbols rings out, philosophy's work is done.

To understand the tight connection between the symbolic interpretation of the entity and the gathering of the Three in the thinking of the ontological difference, is to understand symbols. Then the symbol is no longer this or that, some object of celebration or element of a poem. All that is, symbolizes being. The entity evokes the presence in which all that is present is rooted, from whence it originates. It realizes the presence that it signifies. Such a thinking is a demand addressed to existence as the privileged bearer of the question of being, a demand that it renew itself.[49] The hermeneutics of the symbol naturally opens onto a calling to, onto a calling upon existence.

III. Hermeneutics and Existence

1. From Interpretation to Conversion

Once again, we will inquire into the hermeneutical experience which understanding gives rise to: what are its implications, no longer for the being of symbols, but for the existence of man himself, to whom understanding is given?

---

48 Angelus Silesius, *Der Cherubinische Wandersmann* (Jena: Diedrichs, 1905), chapter 2: "Dies alles ist ein Spiel, das sich die Gottheit macht, Sie hat die Kreatur um ihretwilln erdacht."

49 Martin Heidegger, *Sein und Zeit* (Halle: Niemeyer, 1941), §2, 5–8.

Our starting-point shall be the privileged experience of understanding we have in reading a text. What befalls someone who is compelled to enter into this hermeneutical relation, reading a document written in a language whose signifiers are understandable to them through their culture?—That which happens is inscribed between two limits: a surge of interest, bearing the potential reader towards the text s/he will read, and the result of this reading, the fulfillment of the hermeneutical relation which will mark its closure. Between the *terminus a quo* and the *terminus ad quem*, something happens: did becoming a reader change man in any way?

The most degraded case of such a hermeneutical experience manifests the intended result quite well. Consider the inexpensive novels available on racks in train stations. They provide their audience with an affordable sentimental fiction, an epic ready to be consumed. Their immediacy of understanding must render them captivating. The extreme simplification of the hermeneutical exercise facilitates the transport of the reader into the illusory beyond which s/he is seeking. They tend to assimilate us into their language. The illusion is enchanting because it develops a possibility of being in the world, or in language. This possibility is assimilable because we have always understood it: it is already ours. The beyond, here, is that which is the most understandable. It thus provides the most immediate reflection of our own familiarity with language. The traveler who leafs through these works on the train is thus neither in the vicinity of the hero of the novel, nor in a vehicle of public transportation: he is by himself,[50] in a new mode. The hermeneutical experience offers us a reality which is truer than our own, and which tends to abolish the latter in order to replace it. Harlequin novels, by accumulating words whose immediate meaning apparently makes the task of interpretation superfluous, prove to be quite efficient: they effortlessly establish a certain way of inhabiting language, that is, of existing in the world.

Fundamentally, a great literary work which leaves permanent marks on us, does nothing else. When we close such books, we are

50 [The expression "'by himself" should not be taken in the sense of solitude; "by" is the German *bei*, here, the French *auprès de*. It is used in the same way as in the expression "by their bedside."—Trans.]

no longer who we were when we opened them: there is a genuine transference of reality from the book to our existence. Put differently, following from the above: to read is to interpret, to interpret is to exist in a new way. The hermeneutical relation concerns our reality, for the text interprets us.

The interpreted word wishes to develop possibilities of being which were latent in me. It creates a reality: the repose to come, where the numerous words will signify an existence which is totally mine. The word "reality" thus designates much more than the totality of the objects which come into our hands, *res*. If it is understood from interpretive existence, the concept of reality becomes temporalized: the future as that which is possible, not yet in hand, determines us as much as "facts," present or past. The fact is mute, but reality tells me something about myself: it is a category of language. That which speaks to me is real. Language alone frees reality. It inaugurates a movement which bears us towards the arising of ourselves. In language, reality comes to pass.[51] Language indicates to me that there is a moment of repose in the assimilation of my existence to the saying of the interpreted historical reality. The reality of man is the fashion in which he himself accedes to, arrives at language, for himself.

The text thus performs a verification of the reader, and not the reverse. *Verum facere*, to render truthful, this is the trial of the reader who experiences speech as true inasmuch as it deploys its efficaciousness in the horizon of an existential project. Conversely, a part of speech is untrue when it cannot bear existence resting on it. False speech disappoints. Since speech is only true when it comes forth into the field of a living existence which it judges and verifies, the hermeneutical trial runs the risk of failing, and thereby creates the anxiety of our own future. Speech makes us take a step backwards: the verification of the given mode of existence, as well as a departure forwards: solicitation by an ordered mode of existence.

Now, this is precisely the efficaciousness of the symbol. It explicitly realizes the structure of language, the return-departure. Verification by means of the symbol, symbolic verification, opens us

51 [This could also read: "The advent of reality is in language."—Trans.]

up to the totality of possibilities ahead of us. The return to myself, capable of listening but deaf to interpretation, and the departure towards myself, who hears the summons or reprimand (*apostrophe*) and is free to obey, are a one-way trajectory towards the whereabouts of the origin. The symbol, the signifying concreation of this origin, effects a sharp verification of our reality, by conceding or granting to us an originary future. It casts off the nostalgia for a return to forgotten transparency. It fuels a great anticipatory dream: that the dislocation of things from their center is over, that the dislocation of words from their essence is overcome, that all is one, that in our own existence, "various facts," fuse into a sole signifying reality ... In the terminology of *Sein und Zeit,* the symbolic interpretation of the entity projects mortal existence towards the totality of what is qua reality of its possibility of 'being able to'.

The symbol demands that one exist, absolutely. This requirement of renewal appears as a pressing invitation to conversion. This word must here be understood in a phenomenological sense. Convert to what?, one asks. To oneself, to totality, or to death, to nothing... These answers are all equally valid, since we are trying to understand the ground of possibility from which the symbol interprets me towards a new existence. S/he who converts turns (*vertere*) towards something which s/he had hitherto turned away from. The reversal which is indicated in the prefix *cum-vertere* means an attention which is newly focused on something: that which I had turned my back to is now before me. Conversion is an about-face which reverses, turns me over. The reversal in attention is the rehabilitation of something forgotten, in such a way that the thing forgotten and rehabilitated henceforth occupies the broadest span in my field of attention. Conversion appears as a head-over-heels turnabout in intentionality. The law of *vertere* is the overturning of an order. The "convert," under the hold of a contestation, has "versed" himself out of his former existence. Conversion in an absolute sense means not only a new way of seeing, an added attention or intention; it tips all of existence over. In terms of purposiveness, it indicates that existence orients itself towards new goals; conversion is the transfinalization of existence. In terms of the analysis of symbols, it means that the new project is a rejection: the new end or goal is that from which we have always originated, it is the most ancient origin. The reversal of existence brought about by conversion is the return of the existent to its origin which beckons, or which signals in the symbol.

The sole Symbol, the entity, interpreted according to a sole project of being, the totality of reality, subjects existence to a sole "praxis": the return to the origin. In the sudden flash of understanding, where all that which is shows itself to be the symbol of being, existence renews itself in and towards its totality. Only the symbol effects such a totalization. God, man, and the world are reunited therein: the thinking which prepares for the Three and for conversion say the same thing; converted existence receives the gift of being signifying, and reuniting the Three in the future of being.

The interpretation of the symbol points towards conversion. Before I conclude these reflections with an outline of the "symbolic difference," allow me to make some remarks about Saint Francis of Assisi. "Lady Poverty" is a symbol which satisfies all the criteria enumerated earlier. Moreover, understanding (of the evangelic life) and conversion (to authentic existence) are intimately connected in Francis. In his "Testament," he writes that

> No one showed me what I had to do, but the Sovereign himself revealed to me what I had to live, according to the form of the Holy Gospel.[52]

This sentence, taken from the document which has been described as "the most solemn manifestation of his thought,"[53] contains the main elements of a conversion brought about by the symbol. Notice first of all that it must be understood with reference to a specific event in Francis' life. According to the early accounts, the scene to which it refers took place in the spring of the year 1207.[54] Francis had embraced the project of being engaged to "Lady Poverty" for

52 "Nissuno mi mostrava cio che fera, ma lo stesso Altissimo mi rivelo che dovessi vivere secondo la forma del Santo Vangelio" (Fra Francesco d'Assisi, *Scritti*, ed. V. Facchinetti [Milano: Casa editrice S. Lega eucaristica, 1921], 98). For Francis' conversion, see K. Esser & L. Hardick, *Die Schriften des hl. Franz von Assisi* (Werl i. W., 1956), Exkurs 3, *Busse*, 199–200.

53 P. Sabatier, *La vie de Saint François* (Paris: Fischbacher, 1894), 385.

54 Otto Karrer, *Franz von Assisi, Legenden und Laude* (Zürich: Conzett and Huber, 1945), 586.

almost two years, and for several months he had been living near the small church, Saint Damian, away from the city, and far from his family. We know that his father, after fruitless attempts to make him come back, decided to disown him. Prior to doing so, however, he wished to get back the money he had given to his unworthy son for the reconstruction of the old chapel where he had been spending his days.

It was in this context, before the court of law summoned by the bishop, that the decisive event took place. The father, Pietro Bernardone, demanded the sum which he considered to be his due. The bishop, in turn, reminded young Francis that if he wished to be wed to poverty, he had to return the donations intended for the "rebuilding of the house of God." Only then, free from the hindrances of the debtor, would he truly be poor.

The court ordinarily officiated on the steps of the cathedral. In front of the city notables, in front of the bishop and his own family, Francis declared: "Not only will I give him back the money belonging to him, but my clothes as well, with a joyous heart." Then he undressed, placed everything he had on him at his father's feet, and protested to all the citizens gathered there,

> Listen carefully! Until now I called Pietro Bernardone my Father. But since I now have the project of serving the Lord, I am returning this money which caused him so much grief, along with the clothes I had which belonged to him, and from now on I shall say: our Father who art in heaven, and no longer: my father Pietro Bernardone.[55]

The bishop then covered him with his cloak, understanding, as Ceprano's Vita adds, that he had just witnessed a great mystery.[56] Another Vita comments on the event in the manner of a midrash: "Naked, the man of God then conformed himself to He who was stripped on the Cross."[57] The trial of Assisi is the celebration of the wedding of Francis and "Lady Poverty."

---

55 Ibid., 47–48.

56 *Acta Sanctorum*, Oct. II (Antverpiae, 1788), 729, col. b.

57 Iulianus de Spira, Vita sancti Francisci, in *Analecta Franciscana*, vol. 10 (Florence, 1926–1941), 340: "iam se vir Dei nudus in cruce nudato conformat."—The

"Until now … from now on": Francis' conversion, even though it had been in preparation for two years, takes on the appearance of a sudden evidence. It is in the "now" of understanding that Pietro Bernardone is stripped of his paternal rights, and that the symbolic wedding is sealed. The revelation of the path is granted in the moment. The identification with the origin, in the symbol of the union with Poverty, occurs like a sudden event.

"The Sovereign himself revealed to me": one can only speak of the invitation heard, after the fact. When the origin signals, we can only say that the call rang out, that the revelation was given. He who speaks of his conversion speaks in identical fashion of the path which already, at the time of his testimony, is his own. The departure took place before the conversion reached language.

"I had to live, according to the form of the Holy Gospel": when the origin becomes a call, it opens a path. From now on you will live according to that which was shown to you in the symbol. It is characteristic of the phenomenon of conversion that in the experience of "from now on," speech manifests its efficaciousness over existence in the form of a praxis which urges one on. The symbol makes one do: "You will go and do…"; it urges the convert to leave his country.

2. *From the Ontological Difference to the Symbolic Difference*

The path opened up by the symbol—the conquest of the second meaning, the discovery of the essence of language—always speaks to the singular existence. What does this course mean for a singular existence?

To go along a path is first of all to leave a place in order to reach another. The pilgrim undergoes a succession of places and sites. Generally, when the curious consciousness asks the pilgrim about his road, it is only interested in two terms: from where is he coming, and where is he going? If the temporary guest answers with

---

editors comment that "Hic conformitatis cum Christo conceptus novus est in Iuliano." This seems to confirm the importance I grant to this episode.

the desired precision, the host agrees to his presence. He is offered shelter and maybe he receives advice on a short-cut or an *omnibus*, so that he may save his strength and reach his destination sooner. The curious consciousness has learned everything about the path, once it is informed about the starting-point, the traveler's homeland, and his point of arrival, his destination. What is proper to the road is the succession of places, and this is not considered in itself, but only in its usefulness, according to whether it assists or delays the march towards the goal to be reached. The ideal of the curious consciousness would be that the time taken to move from one point to the other, would be reduced to nothing. The path appears to it spontaneously as the shortest travel time between two geographic points.

This understanding of the path stems from a concern with the "why." Where does the path come from? Where does it lead? Both questions arise because of an uneasiness (an unquiet state), that of the why. Why the path? The spontaneous consciousness, anxious about causes and ends, a stranger to symbols, does not see the path in itself. It only worries, is only disquieted, over the reasons of the path.

Just as there are words for ordinary consumption—words considered as vehicles of a certain sum of information, and not as symbols of a call—similarly, I speak of a path for ordinary consumption: all paths, wherever they lead, inasmuch as the common consciousness asks about their why. If one asks the path to give reasons for its why, is this an adequate inquiry into the symbolic phenomenon? Only the "convert" can share with us what he learns along the way. We search for an expert in itinerant-wandering[58] who will have the authority to shed light on our understanding of the path. But shall we ask him a catalog of various questions on what he experienced along the way? His answers would be merely anecdotal. We ask, not that many words be spoken concerning the path, but that the

58 [When the word 'wandering' occurs alone in this text, it renders 'errance'; when the somewhat awkward 'itinerant-wandering' appears, it renders 'itinerance.' The author draws no distinction between the two, yet the former seems to express sheer wandering, whereas the latter visibly contains the notion of an itinerary, however undetermined.—Trans.]

sole word be spoken which gives seeing. Now, we have always already been launched onto a path.

From where do we come? Where are we going? We must unlearn this way of asking the question. If we wish to experience our essential itinerant-wandering, the concern with the why cannot be our business. To live without why, to let that which is be: the sycamores along the side of the road, its edges and sudden drops, the marsh further away where we dare not go, the noise of other travelers, and also solitude—this is the peregrination of s/he who has been touched by symbols. S/he follows another "method," his *hodos* makes him experience the true more deeply than the back-and-forth of reason does. Symbols effect the translation of discourse into a course, a path. The secret of serenity is *Gelassenheit*: to "let" symbols signify. Man converted to *Gelassenheit* lets that which is be, and he lets he who is on a path go his way.

One might say that this path is the slow acquisition of a convergence of the order of understanding and the order of existing. By yielding to the call of the origin which rings out in symbols, existence returns to its own reality. It leaves itself, gives itself over to the duplicity of the "already" and the "not-yet." It experiences this duplicity, the law of the present-absent, as the normal status of its new path. The symbol realizes the origin that it signifies, and similarly, existence is identical to its own origin. But the condition of this identity remains the path, the identity is peregrinal.

Letting-be on this path teaches this to us: it is not existence which converts itself to the origin, but the origin, in symbols, which converts itself to existence. The origin lets that which is be. Being lets the entity be. I term 'symbolic difference' the itinerant-wandering of *Gelassenheit*, in which existence experiences being as that which converts itself to existence in order to send it onto the path where the entity manifests itself, "let-be," given by being. The symbolic difference is the distance which reunites man and the origin, the entity and being, in an existence which has become peregrinal thanks to the conversion brought about by the symbol.

The ontological difference refers to an amphiboly of the word 'being': it means both that which makes the entity be and "being itself." The ontological difference is that which, between being as the ground of the entity and being as truth,[59] separates the available entity from that which no hand has at its disposal, but has us at its disposal. Heidegger calls that which makes the entity be, *Seiendheit*. This word states the ground of the entity in its difference with being itself. *Seiendheit* is being represented from the entity. The ambiguity of being lies in its letting itself be thought in this way. To think the ontological difference will on the contrary mean thinking this "letting" itself. It is being itself; ambiguity is being itself.[60] The difference, therefore, does not offer two things to our representation in order that we compare them according to their respective magnitudes, and conclude: being is the larger. The difference cannot be thought independently of the man who is the locus of its manifestation. Thinking is itself only in the unfolding of this difference. For Parmenides already, thinking belongs so tightly to the ontological difference that the *logos* and being come forth as if they were matched, brought together, by the light of truth alone.[61]

In *Identity and Difference*, Heidegger explicitly analyzes how thinking belongs to the ontological difference: the difference *qua* difference—"the site in which being reaches its repose"[62]—is properly the matter of thinking. But it is the unthought of the metaphysical tradition. On the evening of metaphysics, after the inquiry into being starting from man has turned into the localization of man, starting from being, the difference gives itself to be thought. Heidegger does not think the ontological difference, the better to think man, but in order to think being. Only that which gives itself is worthy of being thought: being. The ontological difference gives one to think: being.

The symbolic difference gives being to be thought, insofar as it calls man onto his originary path. The symbolic difference is not

---

59 "Unterschied zwischen 'Sein' als 'Sein von Seiendem' und 'Sein' als 'Sein' hinsichtlich des ihm eigenen Sinnes, d. h. hinsichtlich seiner Wahrheit (Lichtung)": Heidegger, *Unterwegs zur Sprache*, 110; *On the Way to Language*, 20.

60 "Das Wesen des Seins, genauer (die) Zwiefalt von Sein und Seiendem" (ibid., 118); translation, 26.

61 Heidegger, *Vorträge und Aufsätze*, 246–49.

62 Martin Heidegger, *Identität und Differenz* (Pfullingen: Neske, 1957), 63: "Die Differenz von Sein und Seiendem ist als der Unter-Schied von Überkommnis und Ankunft der entbergend-bergende Austrag beider."

thought in the service of man, any more than the ontological difference. But it says more than the ontological difference: it states the itinerant-wandering which being inflicts on existence awakened to symbols. It states the fate of the man whom the origin converts. Friedrich Hölderlin wrote that he received more from the gods than he could bear.[63] The words say this well: the experience (*Erfahrung*) of such a peregrination (*Fahren*) is perilous (*Gefahr*). When the origin signals, man must leave everything: the symbols "strike."[64]

From the ontological difference to the symbolic difference, the reflection on the essence of the word becomes a launching into the future this reflection opens up. The thinking of duplicity becomes a peregrinal existence. Its peregrination leads man nowhere, but it subjects him to the burning, overly close proximity of the origin. The symbol is the site where the difference manifests itself, between the claiming of the origin and the existence claimed. Then "one only inhabits the site one leaves, one only creates the work from which one detaches oneself, one only obtains duration by destroying time."[65]

Translated by Charles T. Wolfe

---

63 "Jezt fürcht' ich, dass es mir nicht geh' am Ende wie dem alten Tantalus, dem mehr von Göttern ward, als er verdauen konnte" (*Historisch-kritische Ausgabe* [Hellingrath, 1923], vol. 5, 327).

64 Ibid., "Wie man Helden nachspricht, kann ich wohl sagen, dass mich Apollo geschlagen."

65 René Char, *Sur la poésie* (Paris: GLM, 1967), new expanded edition, 45.

Symbolic Praxis

> The determinist, fatalist, and mechanist element was an immediate ideological "aroma" of the philosophy of praxis, which was necessitated and historically justified by the subaltern character of determined social strata. The futility of mechanistic determinism still has to be demonstrated; it is explainable as naïve mass philosophy, but once it becomes reflected philosophy, it is a source of passivity and imbecilic self-content.
>
> —Antonio Gramsci

In a prior article, "Symbolic Difference," I followed the indications provided by certain data (the symbolism of water, the symbolism of wandering) in order to focus on the ontological locus of the symbol. A difference then appeared in the origin, which revealed itself through gesture, sign, use, and trace. The symbol, distended by definition between man and his origin, is the privileged region of language where this difference is thematized for itself. The search for the concealment-manifestation at work in the symbol led to the difficult problems surrounding its interpretation, and it culminated with a summons or provocation towards existence. I mentioned some historical examples in which the symbol's efficacy with regard to a life was blatant: the symbol opens up a path whose course makes one experience the origin. The condition of this experience is to "live without why," to let that which is, be.

Symbols, by signaling to man, naturally give rise to a behavior. Symbols convert—to what end? This question opens the second, poietic wing which brings to a close the meditation on the being of the symbol. The phenomenology of the symbol gives one food for thought: it is speculative insofar as it reflects the origin which shows itself while it hides. The *poietics* of the symbol gives one something to do. Symbols create. The praxis which they invite us to is not inaugurated by man, but by symbols themselves. Thus, after the symbolic interpretation of all that is insofar as it is (the entity, the sole Symbol of being), which is the conclusion of phenomenology, *poietics* does not speak of *the* symbol, but of *symbols* (in the plural): objects, rites, works, etc. There is a rigorous reciprocity between these two directions of the inquiry, the apprenticeship of the symbolic interpretation of all things, and the carrying out of the call stemming from such symbols which create us, that is, from few things. The *poietics* of symbols is concerned with few things—it has to do with finite symbols, and it must be taken up in each of the realms towards which existence projects itself. Hence a *poietics* of "the Symbol" is not only impossible, *de jure*, but furthermore, the poietics "of symbols" would be a mad attempt, *de facto*, for the symbolic given is inexhaustible. The method forgoes universal discourse, it agrees to be multiple and without a conclusion. Its glory shall be that it attaches itself to certain symbols and brings their creative power to light.

To speak of efficacious signs is not necessarily Shamanism. Symbols do not fall into the game of magic or manipulation. One speaks of magic in order to describe an understanding of signs which invests them with an ineluctable physical efficacy over the course of things, and particularly over human life. Magic is a tool for the purpose of healing or for the loss of life, according to the wishes of the shaman. It invests one with a power of domination over others. Symbols, by contrast, exert no determinism, their efficacy is neither ineluctable nor, above all, destructive. They are signs which speak to our freedom. As origin-words (*paroles d'origine*), they anticipate the healing that they promise. By referring to them as efficacious or creative, I do not mean to speak of a mechanical causality but of a powerful solicitation they convey to whoever knows how to listen. The conversion of hearing, a free and decisive act, is the condition of the efficaciousness of symbols. This also excludes all of the myths and symbols our civilization generates for the manipulation of the masses: one does not create symbols, one does not calculate their influence. To celebrate human ingeniousness in them is, strictly speaking, to pervert them. This would be a slippage from a *poietics* to a cybernetics of symbols. Even the symbol that the poet brings into the world is never a newborn: it escapes the poet, but the artist has no parental rights over it. Literary creation is the condescension of symbols that make themselves into language for a race with converted hearing.

Kant's Theory of the Symbol

The symbolic praxis that I have described is also irreducible to a practical or moral philosophy. In Kant, the symbolic function of the imagination reconciles the theoretical and practical discourses of transcendental philosophy. I shall briefly expound the contents of the section of the *Critique of Judgment* entitled "On Beauty as the Symbol of Morality,"[1] in order to assess the scope of this approach.

The three Critiques must be read together as the Kantian system. The analysis of the speculative use of reason, in the *Critique of Pure Reason*, culminated in the unsurpassable measuring of cognition by sensible intuitions. Anything that does not stem from the empirical schemata is condemned to uncertainty and thus cannot be said to be real. The realms of the true and the real are constricted, shrunken in relation to certainty; the *Critique of Practical Reason* analyzes the consequences of this shrinking for moral conduct. How is the moral imperative, a synthetic *a priori* practical proposition, possible? The answer is provided by the concept of freedom, the keystone of the entire critical system. That man is free can be proven, for if the will were determined by the laws of nature, if it were subjected to the necessity of physical processes, there would not be a practical subject, but only the merciless play of causes and effects. Now, the subject experiencing sensible intuitions experiences itself exercising a causal activity on these objects. The condition of such an activity, by means of which the agent experiences itself as a being endowed with reason and will, can only be the principle of freedom. In the guise of an *ad absurdum* argument, this is the transcendental positing of freedom. A subject can only be thought of as acting if it is placed under this regime, and this necessity of thought, in turn, grounds the possibility of an imperative which offers this freedom, recognized as necessary, the right use of its moral power. Speculative transcendental philosophy opens the way for practical transcendental philosophy. Whereas the former asserted the determinism of phenomena, the latter accedes to freedom, the *a priori* ground of possibility of moral

---

1 Immanuel Kant, *Critique of Judgment*, trans. Werner Pluhar (Indianapolis: Hackett, 1987), §59, 225–30; The original German can be found in Immanuel Kant, *Kritik der Urteilskraft* (B. Cassirer: Berlin, 1922), 428–31.

acting. The two *Critiques* differ merely on the point of view they bring to bear on man. The one is the search for the *a priori* principles of the theoretical faculty of knowing; the other is the search for the *a priori* principles of the practical faculty of moral acting.

Section 59 of the *Critique of Judgment*, in which Kant discusses the symbol, brings these two points of view together into one. The symbol, in Kant's eyes, delineates the trajectory where the speculative and practical faculties of man meet. The symbol is an intuition of imagination. It contains the "indirect presentations" which expound the non-sensible reality of a concept of reason:

> Hence all intuitions supplied for *a priori* concepts are either *schemata* or *symbols*. Schemata contain direct, symbols indirect, presentations of the concept. Schematic presentation is demonstrative. Symbolic presentation uses an analogy.[2]

The symbol is thus put into a parallel with the schemata of the understanding. These connect the rational to the sensible by means of imagination; from the sensible, the schema derives the matter of a concept, which it provides to the understanding. The symbolism, on the contrary, wholly creates an "indirect presentation" or free intuition. It intervenes in the cases of concepts of reason where such an intuition is lacking. Kant gives the example of a despotic State: one cannot form a schema of it, since such a State does not allow itself to be apprehended by a direct sensible intuition. One can nevertheless compare it with something sensible, one can establish what he calls, in a rather imprecise fashion, an analogy - for example, by presenting it indirectly as a hand mill. In this way one creates a replacement intuition. Schemata and symbolism are the two activities of the imagination: the one provides the representation of empirical realities, and the other, that of non-empirical realities. The concepts of a despotic State, of morality, and of God[3] are Kant's three examples of that which we can only cognize symbolically.

---

2 Kant, *Critique of Judgment*, 227. [I have replaced the translator's "exhibition" (for *Darstellung*) with the usual "presentation," which is used by Schürmann.—Trans.]

3 "[A]ll our cognition of God is merely symbolic. Whoever regards it as schematic—while including in it the properties of understanding, will, etc., whose objec-

The symbolic function is a general mediation which allows concepts of the supra-sensible to be formed; moreover, it brings together the speculative and practical points of view on man. The faculty of judgment, when it presents a symbol to itself, does the work of reconciliation: necessity, the requirement that the symbol conform to the concept that is symbolized, is reconciled with the free creation of the imagination, since intuition has broken loose from the moorings of empirical determinisms.

> In this ability [of cognizing the intelligible or the supra-sensible], judgment does not find itself subjected to a heteronomy from empirical laws, as it does elsewhere in empirical judging—concerning objects of such a pure liking it legislates to itself.

By doing so, it is tied to something

> that is neither nature nor freedom and yet is linked with the basis of freedom, the supersensible, in which the theoretical and the practical power are … combined in a unity.[4]

In other words, the symbolic cognition of the supersensible manifests the unity of the theoretical and practical faculties, in the spontaneity of reason giving laws to itself. The symbol, the free intuition of a necessary concept, opens the way to the foundation of the theoretical and the practical, by the cooperative agreement of freedom and necessity in the imagination. The ground of the theoretical and the practical, the primitive trunk of which they are the two ramifications, is provided by imagination. As is shown by the case of the apprehension of the beautiful, the imagination is at work "immediately, but only in reflective intuition, not in the concept," "without any interest," freely, "in accordance with the lawfulness of the imagination," and as "universal, i.e., as valid for

---

tive reality is proved only in worldly being—falls into anthropomorphism, just as anyone who omits everything intuitive falls into deism, which allows us to cognize nothing whatsoever, not even from a practical point of view" (ibid., 228).

4 Ibid., 229.

everyone, but as unknowable through any universal concept."[5] The aim of this passage is to prove in an intuitive fashion, by analogy with beauty, that the nucleus of the emergence of necessity and freedom—or, which amounts to the same thing, the emergence of the speculative and practical faculties—is in the imagination. To say that the beautiful is pleasing without a concept, as Kant asserts here, is to locate aesthetic experience on the side of "symbolic," rather than "schematic" intuition. Beauty is a free creation of the imagination; this is why it can be considered as the symbol of the categorical imperative, the moral law which reason gives to itself, necessarily and freely.

Kant provides us with a path where the speculative and the practical meet. But on the one hand, the "practical" means the symbolic creativity of the imagination, and thus the imagination in the act of giving itself laws. This conception of the "practical" is quite narrow. On the other hand, Kant grants the symbolic realm a breadth which is equal to that of all non-empirical concepts. For this reason, Paul Ricœur deemed Kant's understanding of the symbol to be "too broad."[6] Kant's critical *a priori* prevents one from receiving the symbol as a given. This is why a phenomenological method must part ways with him: starting from the inventory of symbolisms, and following their interpretation in view of the question of being, I inquired into the manner in which symbols unfold themselves with regard to human existence. The latter method witnesses the appearance of the non-empirical in the empirical, where the transcendental method witnesses the empirical presentation of a non-empirical concept which never appears. The two methods are opposed: the former is the recognition of the essential mystery in the sensible present, and the latter is the sensible presentation of an essentially mysterious concept. For the phenomenologist, what is irreducible is the symbol; for Kant, it is the empirical irreducibility of the concept, whose intellection demands that it be illustrated by the symbol. Kant's symbol is just a "speaking otherwise" (an allegory) under the authority of something absent; it provides didactic support for the concept which

---

5 Ibid. (translation modified).

6 Paul Ricœur, *De l'interprétation* (Paris: Seuil, 1965), 19–20.

falters, faced with the trial of empirical verification, the concept which in itself has too strenuous a presentation. Imagination finds itself freed, but on parole. The transcendental project suffers from an overly narrow practical understanding - it only knows a *mental* "doing" - and an overly broad understanding of the symbol.

The task that then presents itself is to examine, in a selective and exemplary manner, the consequences of a narrower understanding of symbols, as the summons of the origin that they signify, and to examine a broader understanding of praxis—as the way of being of an existence converted to the symbol. These consequences will affect the imaginative layer of man, where freedom mingles with necessity, yet they will overcome the servitude of Kant's "thinking otherwise." The issue will no longer be a practical discourse on the *a priori* conditions of moral acting, but existence insofar as, prior to any moral commitment, it is beckoned to by the empirical reality of symbols. The multiplicity of the pathways of existence reflects the multiplicity of symbols. A general *poietics* or discourse on praxis is as impossible as a theory of the "symbol as such." I shall show how the feast, song, dwelling, and labor generate their own ways of being beneath the hidden and manifest origin, by means of the symbols that they convey.

1. The Feast

To celebrate a feast is to acquire a practical knowledge of the Origin. The feast, all feasts, provide a body of transparency for the sole Origin, they are archeophanic. An athletic victory, a fashion parade, a commemoration of war victims, the birth or the death of the god who once visited humans, new moons, marriages, investitures—something summons us which is more than the fact of victory, birth, or marriage; it is the hidden meaning of manifest events. The hidden meaning is closer to the heart of the participants in the feast than the object which is brought forward: those whom the feast brings together, through the symbols towards which they flock, are attracted by a second meaning—which the invitation cards do not announce.

Becoming festive, entering into festivities, requires remarkable know-how, ease and self-mastery. The atmosphere of luxury, games, and conversation, the sudden inflections of laughter, all of this must be perfectly mastered, must be self-evident, if the feast is not to fall into its opposite, uneasiness and sadness. It is difficult to celebrate a celebration, a feast, properly: it is the moment of truth, when it is revealed whether man carries his life with grace, or whether he endures it with boredom, stiffly. The day of the feast, the wrinkles must disappear. At the entrance of the festivity hall, one's occupation should no longer be discerned from one's hands. Each participant conveys to himself and the others that it is a day of benediction, that the hard weeks have ceased, that a sacred time has come, and that one must rid oneself of the old man of working days. At the start of the feast, a signal rings out: the ringing of bells, three blows struck backstage—profane time has given way to sacred time, to the Great Time. By going to the feast, men first feel this transmutation of familiar time, which is also the time of boredom, into another time. The threshold is marked by the adjournment of daily chores, and by the beginning of a life-style marked by facility and abundance. It is a formidable task to celebrate a feast, for the move from the careful, worrying era to the carefree era must occur in a difficult equality of souls.

Which are the symbols exalted by the feast? The first is doubtless the contagion of joy among the participants. The crowd gathered around a great cause is happy, due to its very collectivity. The joy that is both in common and wholly external, is propagated by the signs which make the crossing of the threshold popular. A solitary feast is a sad feast; it is not a feast at all. Man in feasting needs others, all the others. On Simhas Torah, certain orthodox communities in Israel even invite the former persecutors into their ring. A feast-breaker is a trouble-maker (*un hors-la-fête est un trouble-fête*). There are no "intimate" feasts. Every feast requires the abolition of segregations, and the participation of all citizens in a single, great collective rejoicing. The participants signal their intense communion to one another; the result being the visible separation of existences. Everyone does the same thing, drinking and eating, even though each one literally does it for himself. The first symbol which is celebrated is the intimate union between men. They discover themselves as belonging to one another. The conviction is born that destinies are a common matter; the solidarity resulting from this discovery overwhelms one with exhilaration.

The feast is difficult for yet another reason: without any restraint, it would be war. The host and the guests must conform to rules. The feast is the enemy of tumult and debauchery. This is even true when the senses, on the eve of the great day, reach the paroxysm of their drunkenness. Each one of the foodstuffs has its hour; the more this orderly disposition of the banquet is respected and carried out with grace, the freer the participants will feel. The respect of rules and rites tames the feast and makes it into a *latent* war. War is the grimace of the feast, the feast upset, disturbed by the instincts of conquest. Harmony is thus continuously won from, over and against a rumbling, savage force which accompanies and threatens the feast, but from whence it also derives its majesty. Beneath the gleam of the holiday there is a sleeping beast.

It happens that all barriers fall and animality seems to have the upper hand: the entire society approves and encourages practices which are directly opposed to the laws of the city. But this effervescence may only be the culmination of the very order of the feast. There are feasts in which all the gestures of everyday life must be made backwards, the lowest member of the community must take the place of the chief-in a word, common sense is systematically contradicted. The carnival is to be classified among these feasts. Everything seems permitted—as long as one remains within the spirit of the carnival, that is, within its rule of jests and games, as well as within the strict limits of the time imparted. At the close of Mardi Gras, seriousness reassumes its rights and reasserts the rule of common sense. The feast thus conceals an immense outburst of laughter in the face of the established order. However, even in proper licentious excesses, the feast is not a disturbance, or an upset.

What is this rule which is proper to the feast? In any case, it is certain that a "history of the feast" such as the one constructed by Roger Caillois remains insufficient if it is merely based on the rites of transgression of the law.[7] The submission demanded by the feast

7 Roger Caillois, *L'homme et le sacré* (Paris: Gallimard, 1939), 88–89.

translates the claiming power of symbols. To transgress the law is then only a passage under the legislation of symbols; it is the abolition of a universe whose institutions are calculated according to profitability, and the explosion of an intermittent age in which life is "without why." In this regard, mystical experience alone is comparable to the feast.[8] Freed from the servitude of subsistence, men in the feast eat and drink, make merry, but not principally in order to nourish themselves; they light fires in the countryside, but not in order to warm themselves or roast the game; couples come together, but not with an eye toward a marriage contract, or procreation, or even a testimony of love. Life bathes in a freedom and gratuity which appear to stem from a lost age and announce a future age, at the same time. Symbolic praxis extends, broadens Kant's free synthesis of the imagination to the dimensions of existence in its entirety. All of life then obeys the two categories of "purposiveness without purpose" and "lawfulness without law."[9] For Friedrich Schiller, this is the possibility of a reconciliation of the senses with reason; for Herbert Marcuse, it is that of a non-repressive society, beyond the reality principle.[10]

The signs that are exchanged serve no other purpose than recognition among companions in the feast. In the playful exploration of the hidden meaning of the world, everyone is an actor and everyone is a spectator. The painter Jean Dubuffet describes his "chimaera-city" as being characterized by the self-presencing of the crowd: "a city in which there will no longer be any onlookers, only actors, and no more audience, only actors." Such an exchange under a non-productive law is called play. "In a genuinely humane civilization, the human existence will be play rather than toil."[11] The symbol of play, with its rules defying the common sense of productivity, is the second symbol which contributes to the *poiet-*

---

8 Angelus Silesius, *Der Cherubinische Wandersmann* (Basel: n. p., 1955), 35: "Die Ros' ist ohn' warum: sie blühet weil sie blühet, Sie acht' nicht ihrer selbst, fragt nicht, ob man sie siehet."

9 Immanuel Kant, *Critique of Judgment*, §§ 15–17, 22. The original terms are "Zweckmäßigkeit ohne Zweck" and "Gesetzmäßigkeit ohne Gesetz."

10 Herbert Marcuse, *Eros and Civilization* (Boston: Beacon Press, 1955), 115–79.

11 Ibid, 171.

ics of the feast. The rule of the feast, which institutes a body of actors, is nothing other than an introduction to the concreteness ("cum-crescere") of symbols: the aim is to grow under their hold and go forward along the path towards which they point. The false disorder of the feast, that which abolishes its spirit, wanders out of the concreteness of a humanity reconciled by play.

This dialectic of the two legalities in the feast grants it a cosmic dimension. The repressive laws of ordinary life are abolished, exuberance establishes a liberating ritual: this passage is a genesis. The most ancient meanings of the word "cosmos" suggest a canon of rules of conduct ("head-dress" in Homer's time, the ranks of a troop in classical Greece: in each case, a norm of ordered arrangement). The feast, the ephemeral victory of the pleasure principle over the reality principle, brings about a chaos. The order of the world gives itself once again to be conquered. The ordering of the feast is peregrinal; by means of the gradual birth of the new order, it makes the community relive the victory of the beautiful order over the demons of the fray and dissolution. Men witness the emergence, once again, of the cosmos from primordial disorder. They participate in it as actors, their behavior mimics the arrangement of the elements into a liveable earth. The Great Time of Genesis is taken up again in each celebration from where the previous season had left it. The time of the feast is when disorder is no longer, for everything is not permitted, and the ordered universe is not yet; it is the time of the hatching of the world. The cosmic dimension of the feast is present in each sabbath. The day of rest is itself "an aesthetic composition which satisfies the mind without explainable reason," according to Alain's markedly Kantian definition of the feast.[12]

A feast is not interrupted on a whim, it is more than a pastime. It sketches out and announces the properly illegal reconciliation of the individual with totality. The one whispers: speak, Master, your servant is listening; the other feasts. The latter is graver. In him, the origin celebrates itself. Seized by symbols, he knows that the root or ground of things can only be consoling.

---

12 Alain, *Vingt leçons sur les Beaux-Arts* (Paris: Gallimard, 1931), 109–20; see also his *Système des Beaux-Arts* (Paris: Gallimard, 1926), 47–76.

The glow of symbols is resplendent on bodies. Their reflection is the mark of the costume and the procedure, which together make up the third element of the feast. The costume is not an ordinary item of clothing. It may be less comfortable, with its precious trappings, flowers, belts, garlands, luxurious cloths. It means that one casts off the old skin. Psychoanalysts inform us that clothing represents the fetal membrane; a change of clothing is thus literally a new birth. In its material qualities, the party gown dictates a behavior, including taking care not to dirty oneself, and holding oneself in such a way that others may admire one's elegance. The costume of the feast imparts a more measured procedure; it prevents one from leaving the household. Lastly, it enhances one's bearing, one's presence: so many hints of a man at rest. Not everyone can wear a festive costume. It requires that one be natural. A costume is a custom, a second nature, and rather than hiding one's lack of self-control, it projects that lack in broad daylight. The bearing one has as one wears an outfit—either self-assured and proud, or on the contrary worried by the glances one gets, and therefore stiff, formal, blunt—all of this says a great deal about the disposition of one's heart to feast.

Costume and bearing come together in the procession, when they become so charged with meaning that they serve as the carriers of the individual, by putting all ceremonial weight behind him. Without the assistance of ceremonial garb or fashion, it would be quite difficult for him to withhold the glances. The costume erases any excessively personal bearing of the person in sight. A naked man cannot lie, and every costume is a lie. The procession that one comments on or that one follows, is the moment of truth of the costume and of the equanimity of the soul of its wearer. The secret of the enthusiasm generated in the seventeenth century by the invention of the powdered wig resides in its capacity to conceal the traits of one's personality.[13] The raised, artificial hairpiece both complements the face with its curls, and turns gazes away from the face. It completes the process of disguise (*travestissement*). It

---

13 Richard Alewyn and Karl Sälzle, *Das große Welttheater* (Hamburg: Rowohlt, 1959), 38–39.

would be a shame for the apparel of one character to be in dissonance with that of the others: as a source of confusion for himself, and a source of discomfort or irony for the audience, this lapse would be a painful hindrance to the festive spirit. Success requires a great deal of *savoir-faire*, disguised as nonchalance. The feast is the human resonance of symbols. It is stamped with the seal of man, and followed by a joy to which intelligence gives its consent. From the feast, we learn the opposite of what Pope Pius XI taught about man: we learn that man is not "made to work as the bird is made to fly." Man is made to recognize the symbols of his essential freedom, and to comply with their invitation by entering into the feast. In order to be authentic, knowledge and freedom must be rooted where the reality principle can be overcome by the pleasure principle, namely, in imagination. "To reduce the imagination to slavery, even if what one crudely calls happiness might be at stake, is to draw back from any element of the higher justice that one finds in oneself. Imagination alone tells me what *can be.*"[14]

Symbols lead us into 'doing': they attract us to gatherings, recruit us into processions, draw us into roundabouts where all severity is lost; they awaken us to laughter and dance, and wipe wrinkles off of faces. They retrieve ancient gestures lost in the busy-ness of reason and bring them back to the surface. Forgotten words are heard once again. The feast is delectation[15] in the unheard-of. Its symbols—the fusion of many, the rule of freedom as the rival of institutions, the costume—make one enter into a dynamics of emancipation (*affranchissement*). They draw man out of the isolation and servitude for which he was no more made than he was made to be naked. They intimate the origin without oppression to him, and by summoning him to the feast, they fulfill what they intimate. The feast contests anything that is not a word from the origin spoken to us, and therefore it is the fundamental way of being of converted existence.

---

14 André Breton, *Premier Manifeste du Surréalisme* (1924) (Paris: Gallimard, 1946), 15.

15 [*Délassement*, usually rendered as 'relaxation'; one may hear in this word an echo or rather a harbinger of *délaissement*, 'releasement'.—Trans.]

2. The Song

Whoever wishes to experience the symbolic force of the song must cease to sing alone. Like the feast, the song's essential statement is: Come! The song, born of the scream, retains a power of enlistment which makes it ring out like a call. But as it emerges from immediate terrors, and is neither a tale nor an alarm, it becomes an acclamation, a sound of praise. It no longer transmits any information nor is it mono-directional; it does not restrict itself to the reciprocity of a duet. In all of these, language is still merely an exchange of signals. What is proper to the song is to make language culminate in an ephemeral embodiment to the primitive conversation between all men. Who or what is acclaimed? Nothing other than the song's power to gather itself. One does not sing in order to communicate a content; rather, one searches for a content, the better to be able to sing together. One word alone is sung: "We." The song expresses the union that it creates. It realizes this union so perfectly that there is no place for the singers to reflect upon the union. The union only becomes conscious in the negative experience of disharmony, which not only stops incentive short but shatters agreement. Differences appear. Consonance, as it takes flight, fills us with regret. In regretfulness, the desire for harmony becomes conscious. Cacophony marks the return to discursive thinking. The now of the perfect chord, on the contrary, suspends discourse, and thereby, desire. The art critic within us who appreciates the intermingling of voices, is the functionary of an intimate regret; he brings reflection, and thus already brings ugliness and discord.

Here, beneath the seeming grace, a two-headed monster lies dormant. It threatens immediacy with its dissonance and reflection. Dissonance is the return of noise into composition; reflection is the return of the individual. If, moreover, the feast naturally demands the support, the participation of music, it is because song is the oldest of the arts; it is praxis *par excellence*. Greek sensibility appears to have been defenseless faced with music. The ancients attributed a certain power over the human soul and feelings to each of the three sonorous modes, Dorian, Phrygian, and Lydian. Grace itself is threatening. Thus the first of these modes, according to Aristotle,[16] has good humor at its disposal, and augments the virtues. The second brings one to laughter and enthusiasm; it inflames the passions. The third moves one to tears, causes fear and pity, and teaches one the feeling of the beautiful. Flute playing affected the Greeks like a stimulant, whereas lyre-playing calmed one's fancies and evoked the idyll. Music was always viewed as a bewitching power, to such an extent that Plato, in his severe utopia of the perfect republic, allowed only "these two modes—a violent one and a voluntary one, which will produce the finest imitation of the sounds of unfortunate and fortunate, moderate and courageous men."[17] One can glimpse remainders of this conception in the eighteenth century, in certain vocal compositions. In Mozart's opera, the magic flute that the queen of the night grants to Tamino, invests him with power: "With it you shall act as all-powerful, and transform the passions of humans."[18] Already in the Bible, the young David cured King Saul of his madness with his zither.[19]

The category of "healing" (the German *heilen*) must not be understood here only in the strictly physical or psychic sense. The song has the power to bring about within us, in a fleeting moment, the state of an intact, whole (*heil*) humanity. If music is so dear to us, it is because it makes us experience a beyond, a not-yet which beckons to us through its harmony. For a short moment, it allows the body to sense healing and integrity, the rudimentary forms of salvation (*das Heil*). Singing together recalls the forgotten identity of man and totality; whence its poignant strength. That which, in the space of a breath, is communicated to the nerves in the praxis of the song, is the possibility of totality. The passion for music is the passion of the possible. It conjures the infinity of the possible that makes one dizzy. In the music of the Middle Ages, the "devil's chants" and the Gregorian hallelujahs are two forms of the same sonorous anticipation of the possibility of totality.

---

16 Aristotle, *Politics*, Book VIII, 7, 34b.

17 Plato, *Republic*, trans. A. Bloom (New York: Basic Books, 1968), Book III, 398c–399e.

18 "Hiermit kannst du allmächtig handeln, der Menschen Leidenschaften wandeln" ("The Magic Flute," I, 5).

19 Samuel I: 16, 14-23.

The price to be paid for this anticipation is a merciless submission to the rules of composition. The perfect song is the fruit of a laborious conquest, the outcome of which is that the unheard becomes attuned to hearing.[20] Even today, music generates hardly avowable nostalgias, even if this power is perceived in different ways, depending on the culture. The song, which is the perfect musical form, is a symbol, it fulfills the evanescent promise of a total deliverance. The now of the beautiful harmony is, is not yet, and is no longer. It makes the healing of time palpable to us during a short sensation. To other artworks, one may respond: music, in order to ravish us, requires succession. It is the art which takes place in time, par excellence. This character trait makes it the pinprick of the elsewhere and the not-yet in the here and now. A sentence attributed to Stravinsky runs as follows: "Music, powerless to express anything whatsoever, establishes an order between man and time." It organizes duration by means of elements of sound. Thus it humanizes duration and confers upon the moment a dimension of "the final moment." Music inaugurates plenary time, properly human time.

In opposition to the wilted time of chores, it brings to bear its promise of an eternal flowering. To sing is to forget the year in which one lives. Here, in movement and mobility (*la mouvance et le mobile*), that which is by nature absent makes itself present. The listener falls silent, not only in order to hear the sounds better: the coming of the origin, present-absent in the song, reduces one to silence. Heidegger calls the song "the celebration of the coming of the gods."[21] The many words grow silent, each individual's intimate speech fuses in a single common word. Solitude is abolished. The Same is given up by all to the recognition of all. The *Same* in each person sings. The song says "Yes," fundamentally. The acceptance of what is, which is ordinarily silent, is announced by the song loudly: it is good to sing. The Yes of assent to that which is, is proclaimed from the outset by the song. The song tears the origin from forgetting, it is memory, absolutely.[22]

---

20 ["L'inouï s'accorde l'ouïe"—Trans.]

21 Martin Heidegger, *Unterwegs zur Sprache* (Pfullingen: Neske, 1959), 182.

22 Franz Rosenzweig, *Der Stern der Erlösung*, 3 vols. (Heidelberg: Schneider, 1954), I, 37–38, 43–44; II, 50ff.; III, 165. 'Yes' is the fundamental word, the *Urwort*.

The song gathers up the "has-been" in the imminence of a promise. As memory, it tears one away from forgetting; as promise, it involves one in hope. For the Marxist Ernst Bloch, music is entirely a utopia, a war-concept in the hermeneutics of nostalgia, of expectation, of hope.[23] Music can only be understood in reference to something that is not yet closed, which never ceases to overcome itself and to take on new forms. The song essentially refers to a growth. The historical tendencies of human society, Ernst Bloch writes, are most purely reflected in the mirror of sound; no art is determined by the dialectics of classes as much as music. It is a way of existing, much more than a mere pleasure of the senses. This starting-point allows Bloch to draw up a chart of the parallels between various musical forms and the societies that they express: plain-chant reflects feudal society, the fugue reflects corporations, and the sonata, with its conflict between two themes, reflects emergent capitalism. In Brahms's music, the era of the great industrial bourgeoisie is perpetuated, just as in contemporary music, society as objectified and alienated by relations of production is perpetuated. Music confirms historical materialism, that is, man's gradual coming-to-himself. It will only reveal its essence at the end of the process, when life will be identical with consciousness, and man will be identical with his species-being. "The expression of music is still in ferment, it has not yet seen the light of day as something constituted and definable ... *cantus essentiam fontis vocat*."[24] Music plays the role of a seismograph for society, it reflects the ruptures beneath the surface, and lends an organ to the demands for change. Music enjoins us to hope.

At the outcome of human history, music will have wholly become language, or language, music. For Bloch, a thread of efficaciousness runs through history, whose movement translates into the bringing of the sociological conditionings of music to light: men sing the way they sing, due to the material conditions of production. In the cotton fields and on urban work-sites, one does not hear the same songs. The capitalist living off his private income does not go to

---

23 Ernst Bloch, *Das Prinzip Hoffnung* (Frankfurt: Suhrkamp, 1959), 1243–90.
24 Ibid., 1258.

the same concerts as the owner of a grocery shop. As long as this conditioning is not abolished, music will remain fragmentary, and in a process of completion. The song anticipates and sketches out the society without classes. It thus responds to the definition of utopia as the resolved anticipation of totality in the fragmentary, by means of the power of the imagination. Bloch quotes the composer Schoenberg whose *Handbook* bears the paradoxical formula, "Harmony concludes with the new, the infinite, the unfinished."

The limit of such a philosophy is its theory itself—"science," as Marx said. Phenomenological *poietics* does not construct any theory, it affirms the essence of a praxis. With praxis, observation ceases. Expectation, like memory, only comes to the song within the limits reached when music ceases. Bloch includes music in man's "expressions": the expression of the composer who communicates himself, or of the musician who reproduces this communication, the expression of an epoch, a society, a country. But once music is reduced to expression and perception, it reverts back to information. It informs us about the juncture of its birth. This is an ideological understanding of music, not a phenomenological one. The dichotomy of performer and listener, or of soloist (a word which says a lot about specialization in an art that has become a market value) and critic, is precisely what I have tried to overcome by speaking of the song "where there are only actors," and not musical representation. The metaphysical desire for representation, in the listener, is translated into a perception of sounds, if it does not fall into imagery (The Lovely Month of May, The River Rhine, Requiem, etc.). The metaphysics of representation is opposed to *poietics*, as Kant's symbol is opposed to the sonata of Vinteuil: there is no passageway, save the conversion of hearing (which is an abyss), leading from one to the other.

The song, if it is understood according to its essence, never leads from an 'I' to a 'you'. It is never the vehicle of anything, it transports no emotion. It contains no message for a crowd of ticket-holders. But the symbol constitutes a homogeneous body for itself, a singing body. It is for this body that Bloch's construction of a utopia of deliverance is alive, as long as the beautiful harmony lasts. A theory of the symbol that begins with historical materialism destroys the phenomenon of the song *qua* event of the word of the origin, which is spoken to us.

Aesthetic sensibility, as it wishes to forget the merciless world for as long as the symphony lasts, is ahistorical; Marxist ideology is historical and nothing else; *poietics*, on its part, grants access to a new historicity of the song. I have said that movement is essential for a full understanding of the song. Now this movement, each time and in as much as we enter into its cadence, effects the gathering (*sym-ballein*) which defines the song, and through which it is opposed to hearing. The song gathers in the event of perfect consonance, and opens up a path for men, of common exploration of their common cause. Truth, approached symbolically, draws closer to us. It makes use of those who are brought together by its coming. Its use is celebrated by the song.

In symbolic praxis, utopia is granted a different meaning than in Marxist ideology. It speaks of the truth of man, not at the close of "music's career to come,"[25] but here and now, while we are singing. Utopia utters the no-place (*ou-topos*) and the good place (*eu-tpos*) inseparably, it utters the essence of the song, inasmuch as utopia is the unknowable restorer of originary existence. The song carries out the unveiling of our essential wandering, in which the origin lets us experience its comings.

The symbols conveyed by the song are the given collectivity and the anticipated totality. A third element must be added: the cosmic dimension. It is less important, due to the fact that it casts the two previous elements in a mythological light. From the Pythagorean school to Goethe, there has been talk of the harmony of the spheres, an audible effect for privileged beings of the beautiful ordering of heavenly bodies and planets.[26] In a universe understood as a perfect objectification of intelligible laws in the sensible, music was like the trace which revealed the spiritual lost in the material. Singing then

---

25 Ibid., 1257.

26 According to Ptolemy (*Harmony*, Book III, especially § xvi), the various intervals stem from the varying astrological constellations: the constellation of the Moon, Venus, and Mars gives the chord 'E-A-D', the constellation of the Sun, Jupiter, and Saturn gives 'B-E-A', etc. Boethius' teaching was that there was a triple emanation of music: musica mundana, the motion of the cosmos according to mathematical laws, musica humana, the conjunction of soul and body, and musica instrumentalis, the organization of matter. Goethe, lastly, begins the second part of Faust with the angel's cheer, "Die Sonne tönt nach alter Weise in Brudersphären Wettgesang..."

became a kind of propaedeutic to the contemplation of God, similar to gazing upon the starry sky or studying logic.

The belief in the harmony of the spheres is the cosmic, *hierarchized* representation of the totalization of the sensible and the intelligible. It is a myth—and hence the cooperation of various symbols—insofar as man, after his death, is supposed to enter into his rank in this glorious choral. Saint Cecilia, as the legend tells us, even had this experience of music in her life on this earth, since she could hear the chorus of angels in song.[27] Whether one accepts or rejects eschatological myths, the transformation of social relations into a musical interaction between men will always remain one of the waking dreams which feed action. That which is not yet but will be, some day: the transmutation of the world into an immense song is inaugurated when two or three people sing together. They are not all of humanity, not yet; they are still surrounded with spectators and indifferent individuals, but their song will extend to all of humankind, will reach the stars and the angels, and then there will be universal reconciliation. As Roger Garaudy says, "It is characteristic of the ideology of a rotting class to be incapable of imagining harmony between men and the universe." She who sings, not only imagines it in his or her very activity, but fulfills it as if in passing. The song is the most powerful symbol of deliverance: those that it brings together 'are' already humanity delivered.

3. Dwelling

Man feasts, sings, and lives in communities. Architecture, the ancestor of all spatial arts, organizes the volumes of the collectivity itself. It is the art of tracing limits through which social existence articulates itself. A construction plan effects the divide between inhabited space and all other spaces. Fortress walls, gates, doors, windows mark the threshold between nature, public places, and the private house. Like the latter, public places constitute a fab-

---

27 Augustine, in *De Musica*, is probably the first to replace the ancient harmony of the spheres with the song of the joyful and the angels. For instance, he refers to music as "praeludium vitae aeternae, ut a corporeis ad incorporea transeamus" (VI, 2).

ricated space. Both are thus opposed to natural space. They are social spaces proper, organized in the one case for money, in the other case for the rewards of money, such as rest, leisure, creation, and even feelings. The architect puts these three types of space—nature, business, and dwelling—into relation. Le Corbusier said of contemporary town planning, "The twentieth century did not build for men, it built for money." One of the three spaces won out over the others.

However, none of the three are absent from one another. At the heart of business districts, there are parks. From the buildings of Wall Street, one sees the bay of the Hudson river. Fabricated spaces receive their various characteristics, production, exchange, defense, or warehouse, as they emerge from non-fabricated spaces. A contract is not signed on a garden bench. But thanks to gardens, nature pushes its boundaries into the heart of urban existence. For Le Corbusier, "architecture is the masterful, concrete and magnificent play of forms of light": natural space is not only present in privileged places (parks, bays, etc.). It is above all light, and hence is omnipresent. Dwelling opens onto natural space: great glass panes reaching to the ground, children's parks on the roofs of buildings, balconies, patios, all of that which adorns rest sites and family sites also sets them into relation with a dimension not created by man.

Public space is the most complex: a school requires a greater permeability to nature than an administration building or a factory. A toll booth on the side of the highway is a commercial space isolated in the midst of unbuilt expanses. A town hall, a station, a stock exchange, in contrast, are normally far from open spaces. Interaction with volumes is not part of their being. As to the edges of business districts and residential zones, their *de facto* tendency towards disintegration indicates the *de jure* autonomy which is proper to both spaces. When the city becomes mainly a place for capital transactions, commercial space is hypertrophied at the expense of the two other spaces. Then men become "standardized termites."[28]

---

28 Ernst Bloch, *Das Prinzip Hoffnung*, 861.

Dwelling must be understood from this interaction between volumes. In order to create it, the architect must transmute nature and displace business; the former co-penetrates the dwelling, but due to needs for respite and beauty, the latter are excluded therefrom, even as they juxtapose to the dwelling another world, also man-made. The limits of natural space integrated into a dwelling may coincide with the horizon, as in Versailles. In cities, ordinarily planned out in two dimensions, natural space ends at the neighbor's wall or in the street. The vertical city, the skyscraper, opens up a third dimension which has remained absent from our sensibility until quite recently. Thanks to this new, infinite dimension, Le Corbusier's "machine for living," despite the way in which it is expressed, has the effect of locating man in relation to a space which is not industrial, but natural. The modern dwelling tends to include an infinite volume of nature and to exclude anything pertaining to public volume. The center of town is less and less likely to be a residential neighborhood. The country house is literally detached from the comings and goings of the city: its ground no longer matters, and it no longer has any. "Today houses often look as if they are about to leave for a trip … Like boats, they have a flat roof, portholes, gang-ways, beams."[29]

The architect effects the dividing-up of spaces. Thereby, he allows symbols to speak. The first symbolism is the agreement between volumes itself: in the dwelling, inner and outer are reconciled, the human world and the natural world. The dwelling makes visible the tendency towards unity by which the young Marx had defined society: "thus society is the consummated oneness in substance of man and nature—the true resurrection of nature—the naturalism of man and the humanism of nature both brought to fulfillment."[30]

To speak of dwelling merely in terms of a refuge from the cataclysms threatening private life is to increase the disunity. Along with the relations of hostility between man and nature which characterize industrial capitalism, one finds the forgetting of symbols. A more originary thinking recalls the interaction between

---

29 Ibid., 858.

30 Karl Marx, *Economic and Philosophic Manuscripts*, trans. Martin Milligan (Moscow: Foreign Language Publishing House, 1959), 104.

spaces in which the essence of dwelling appears, and it understands the latter as the already real manifestation of a possible unity. Memory discovers that a 'humanism' of nature and a 'naturalism' of humanity have always already been at work, whenever humans build dwellings. The interaction between spaces points to a totality that has not yet been acquired, but which lets itself be thought through a symbolic interpretation of dwelling. The agreement between the three realms—nature, business, and dwelling—remains essentially incomplete. But the incomplete provides a starting-point: dwelling as the play of spaces shows the way towards "societal conditions which create a basis for the transformation of work into play."[31] In other words, at the end of the path opened up by symbols, the space of business will have undergone a transformation, in such a way that it will be rehabilitated as a dimension of dwelling. The concept of 'play' applied to social relations flows directly from the interaction by which I defined dwelling. Housing constructions will no longer be placed at a distance from the site of production and business, and become games. The three spaces will be reconciled.

Dwelling *qua* symbol makes one 'do': by means of the regression towards unity as it is outlined architecturally, it makes one progress towards a unity to be conquered. Dwelling brings the different spaces together. Thereby, it fulfills the totality that it signifies.

In the enclosure of the house, one is "at home." Man lives neither alone nor with all of his brethren at once. A house is the intermediate step between the hermit's retreat and the city. The roof under which a group of men gathers assigns a parcel of earth to them; ground, walls and roofing enclose and indicate the harmonious accord of the house-hold. "At home" means: with one's own. The allotted terrain on which one establishes oneself with one's own constitutes the link with the homeland. Architecture, Bloch says, is the "lineament of a country."[32] In its geographical aspect, dwelling sketches out a second type of unity; it not only signifies the perfect

---

31 Herbert Marcuse, *Eros and Civilization*, 197.

32 Ernst Bloch, *Das Prinzip Hoffnung*, 871.

play between spaces, but also perfect accord among humans. It is the place in which one is rooted in a community, on a given parcel of land. Dwelling enables the essential activities of public life: elections, speaking out, government service, education of children, defense, etc. The stateless individual is excluded from all of this, lives nowhere. His or her speech is merely tolerated, and can be silenced with impunity. Dwelling is the miniature anticipation of a state without stateless individuals: it means the reconciliation of the individual with all, of the individual with his or her functions in the midst of everyone else.

Finally, dwelling reveals a third symbolism, which is tied to the two others. Not only does it give us the accord between spaces and the agreement between humans to think; it also essentially gives a measure which gathers the human and divine in a self-identical event. I have spoken of buildings, volumes, and the dimensions gathered together by the architect, as well as the ground on which humans settle. But have we found the essence of what is called 'to dwell'? What is it that makes an understanding of dwelling as the play of spaces and as a homeland possible? Do the two aspects mentioned have something in common which is even more fundamental than accord and agreement?

They have a *measure* in common. The interaction between spaces measures the private life of man, the homeland measures his public life. Prior to inhabiting a building or a social rank, the human inhabits measure. This belonging precedes man, before his existence traces the limits of its unfolding for itself.

How does man *qua* inhabitant belong to measure? Which measure is this? The house keeps, guards man by protecting him. But the man also guards the house, he is its keeper, who brings spaces together. Habitat and inhabitant guard one another. Similarly, would measure be the guardian of man, and man the guardian of measure? In this kind of reciprocity, what are we to understand? An objection presents itself: how can that which man has made be the guardian of his essence? This objection raises a prior question: is measure manmade? Measure, both private and public, is unthinkable without man and his constructions. But without measure, is man thinkable?

In one of his last poems, Friedrich Hölderlin suggests an answer.[33] The poem has been handed down to us without a title. It begins with the following words:

> In lovely blueness with its metal roof the steeple blossoms. Around it the crying of swallows hovers, most moving blueness surrounds it. The sun hangs high above it and colors the sheets of tin, but up above in the wind silently crows the weathercock.

The steeple bathes in the space of nature. But a man inhabits it: the bell ringer. He is separated from the infinite blueness, he lives in silence. His space is the stairwell. The windows establish an interchange between inside and outside. They allow the vast expanse of space to enter; the sun, the cries of swallows. The windows allow the sound of the bells to escape and ring out across the countryside. These openings are actually gates, through which the interchange of volumes happens. They are manmade, yet they resemble the trees of the forest: the gates do not belong to either of the two species totally.

> If now someone comes down beneath the bell, comes down those steps, it is a still life, because, when the figure is so detached, the man's plasticity is brought out. The windows from which the bells are ringing are like gates in beauty. That is, because gates still conform to nature, these have a likeness to trees of the wood. But purity too is beauty.
>
> Within, out of diversity, a serious mind is formed.

The last line sums up this part of the poem. The interchange of inside and outside makes the mind "serious"; it is made "out of diversity," that is, out of the two spaces. "Seriousness," in Hölderlin, expresses the being of a thing. Man's being is "formed" with the beauty of the windows, the pure windows which make up the site of interchange between the two spaces. The purity of these bor-

---

33 Friedrich Hölderlin, "In lovely blueness," trans. Michael Hamburger, in *Poems and Fragments* (Cambridge: Cambridge University Press, 1980), 602 and 604.

ders, windows, and the seriousness of man, all say the same thing. Man's being is the image:

> Is God unknown? Is He manifest as the sky? This rather I believe. It is the measure of man. Full of acquirements, but poetically, man dwells on this earth.

The harmonious understanding of this poem will be achieved when its two parts suggest one and the same utterance. Dwelling as interchange between spaces, and man as image of God: the possibility of these two thoughts stems from a single ground. The ground is an event, a crossing. The space of dwelling is experienced by the bell ringer when he climbs the stairwell to ring the bells. The being of man is experienced when he raises his eyes from earth to sky. God is "manifest as the sky." Man "dwells on this earth." But God is "the measure of man." Man becomes himself when he crosses the space between earth and sky. Man is only man in such a crossing. His essence is to be guarded by this measure. To cross and to measure evoke a gathering, here: the being of man is to bring together the divine and the earthly by letting himself be measured by them. Man alone "dwells," he alone is the site where the two come together in a common measure. This reciprocity between guard and guardian remains mysterious, however; unknown and manifest at once, like God himself and the sky.

Perhaps man is only properly at home within measure understood as a crossing between human earth and divine sky, and also as their gathering. Perhaps this measure presides over every construction and every initiative of speech (*prise de la parole*). When one inquires into the essence of dwelling, one is allowed to think the being of man as the intermediate region between the terrestrial and the divine, the region which defines symbols. They are of the earth, taken from our world, but they are more than the earth. Dwelling manifests the divine even as it conceals it; it fulfills the image-being of the man it signifies; lastly, it shows that measure, the mystery of God who appears as he withdraws, is received and not made. Hölderlin sums up these features of the symbol in the expression "poetically man dwells." The properly human poiesis is to bring together—in "acquirements"—the dimensions which are already reconciled when the ringing of the bell moves from the man-made tower towards the infinite horizon. To speak of symbols is to speak of this reconciliation. It denies that the earth is the real meaning of things. Hölderlin asserts the radical insufficiency of any measure established by man: "Is there a measure on earth? There is none."

4. Work

Symbols lead to 'doing': clapping hands on the day of the feast, combining voices in songs and hymns, reconciling citizens with the stateless; lastly, they make us work. In each case, the sole origin calls on us to return, to a life freed from necessity, in the feast; to a universe in harmony, in the song; to a separation under the same roof, in the dwelling; through work, the origin beckons s/he who knows how to hear towards the absence of oppression in the relations between man and the powers of the soil. The origin takes on the figure of restored unity between man and earth.

The technological universe does not reconcile man with the natural forces surrounding him; rather, it aggravates the rift separating them. The technician, seen from the Marxist angle as the dichotomy between man and nature, professes furor and ruse. He boasts of developing the globe, but he merely increases its divisions: so much for furor. Under the heading of the construction of the world, he proceeds to methodically destroy its unity: so much for ruse.

The verb "to work," *travailler* (in French), derives from the popular Latin "tripaliare," to torture with the "tripalium." This torture consisted in distending the body of the condemned person between three poles or reeds ("triplais" means "three poles"). The idea of exhaustion is maintained in the English verb "to travel"; its French equivalent, voyager, merely suggests the path to be traveled, not the effects of the path on the traveler. Giving birth is the woman's "labor" (*travail*), namely, her most painful servitude.

In the relation between the worker and the work produced, work is a constraint imposed on the object, which gives it the desired form, and makes it usable. The worker appropriates matter for human needs. The use that will be made of the object itself belongs to the realm of labor. This time, the object will no longer be tortured, rather it will be a torture instrument. It will have become a tool, "useful" for torture. Work appears as a process of brutalization which always wins out. It reaches men as well as things. Work alienates men and things equally: all that remains of their being is utility.

The logic of work is to reduce nature to the state of a corpse. The relation of utility converts the living organism into inorganic matter which can be maneuvered to suit one's needs. Indeed, the synthetic products provided to us by automatized industry bear this cadaverous aspect, characteristic of the civilization of work, on their smooth surface. These soulless objects, which are washable but cannot even rot, illustrate the ambiguity of the project of exploitation, domination, and usage of the earth—an ambiguity reflected in the term "to exploit" itself, since it means both 'to cultivate' or 'to maximize',[34] and 'to abuse for one's own profit', 'to defraud'.

The systematic reduction of the earth to a corpse brings a history which began long ago to an end. The earth was first the object of a gaze, then of a doing, and finally of a murder: it has borne the brunt of all the progress of civilization. That which is living demands respect. Hence, before the technological extinction of the earth, there is its death notice. The entrepreneurial spirit knows how, casually, to turn the cultural fact that the earth has given up its ghost, to its own advantage. The technological death sentence of the earth is its second death; the first took place amidst general agreement, when it was declared to be a reservoir of energies open to any exploitation. It is no coincidence that capitalist industrialism is contemporary with Nietzsche and his proclamation of the dead God.

Here is a text from a Wintu Indian of California, on the "white man" and nature:

> The White people never cared for land or deer or bear. When we Indians kill meat, we eat it all up. When we dig roots we make little holes... We shake down acorns and pine nuts. We don't chop down trees. We only

---

34 [*Faire valoir*, to get the most out of something, e.g., in the case of a property.—Trans.]

> use dead wood. But the White people plow up the ground, pull up the trees, kill everything. The tree says, 'Don't. I am sore. Don't hurt me'. But they chop it down and cut it up. The spirit of the land hates them... The Indians never hurt anything, but the White people destroy all. They blast rocks and scatter them on the ground. The rock says 'Don't! You are hurting me'. But the White people pay no attention. When the Indians use rocks, they take little round ones for their cooking ... How can the spirit of the earth like the White man? [...] Everywhere the White man has touched it, it is sore.[35]

Death has already taken place when the elements of an organism fall into pieces. "Things fall apart, the center cannot hold," Yeats wrote. The dislocation of nature into an aggregate of materials available for technical maneuvers is thus not only the loss of a unity, but of a life. The life of the earth is precisely that in things which resists the reduction to primary matter. Not only living beings, but also the energies in the ground, institutions and communities, all the regions towards which existence unfolds itself, let themselves be treated, either as an organic unity, or as objects to be handled and manipulated. When 'handling' or manipulation takes over, forgetfulness makes its way into man's relations with nature. The appearance of a victory hides a loss: the vast quarry of raw materials given into the hands of man points to the end of any homogeneous, internal growth of the universe. But we need to inquire into the conditions of possibility of such a death sentence.

I suspect the workings of a perverted symbolism in the workings of the process which I have described. One does not work without a reason. That an entire civilization may identify with the "performance principle" (Marcuse) cannot come to pass without a powerful appeal to symbols. But which symbols are they, and how could their call lead to destruction? Until now, we have witnessed symbols of reconciliation: the feast, the song, and dwelling anticipate a totality through play, whereas work, in its present forms of exploitation, is opposed to play by definition. Work is always

---

35 Dorothy Lee, *Freedom and Culture* (Englewood Cliffs, NJ: Prentice-Hall, 1959), 163–64.

subject to a Why: one works for a salary, for comfort, for food ... The why opens onto a not-yet, a far-off state of things that praxis strives to bring closer. This is the genuinely symbolic part of work: the internal coherence of the universe has not yet been achieved, and existence itself has not yet become alive in all of its fractions. Human needs still need to be met. The ancient harmony between man and nature is no longer, and the new one is not yet. "The bourgeois world of the machine lies in the middle, between that which is lost and that which is not yet settled."[36]

Work is thus not-yet what it must be: it still exists under the sign of the 'No' to nature either as a living configuration or as a subject. The not yet of work is the 'Yes' of assent to things; they too are still alienated. Ernst Bloch detects a hidden utopia even in an accident at the workplace and in an economic crisis—both pierce holes in the technical network. Such failures manifest "the abstract, poorly mediated relation of men to the material substrate of their action."[37] Work thus suffers from the typically modern ailment of not-yet concretely mediating the material subject and the human subject in production. Work has not yet fulfilled its own essence, and this not-yet is the pinprick inciting us to work. The symbol which makes one work is the following: that nature shall be the subject, the partner of man. The symbol is perverted when man no longer encounters anything else but himself in what he does. As long as the relationship between life and labor remains inauthentic, reconciliation remains utopian.

The essence of work in technical activities is present in the mode of concealment; it remains mysterious. It withdraws behind the relations of domination, exploitation, use, and exchange. But the reverse is also true: technical activity is the perversion of the essence of work, the trace of its flight. The disarray in which we find ourselves when faced with our own civilization results from the concealment of this mystery as mystery: as our civilization has been stamped with a practical understanding of work which is false, it remains the most opaque mystery for us today. The essence

---

36 Ernst Bloch, *Das Prinzip Hoffnung*, 809.

37 Ibid., 811.

of work is thus more obscured than the essence of the feast, the song, or the dwelling. Work demands interpretation and meditation to an even greater extent than the other symbolisms. A word is necessary which unveils the second sense of work and shows the way towards the rehabilitation of nature as a subject. The conversion of work that it elevates us to would only abolish confrontation, merely altering the modes of work, not its essence. But the latter reconciles ingenious artifice with the natural tendencies of growth. The not yet of this symbolism is hence the abolition of man's exploitation of the earth. Therefore,

> the Marxism of technology, once it is meditated to the end, is not a philanthropy for mistreated metals, but rather the end of the naïve transposition which applies the point of view of the exploiter and the tamer to nature.[38]

In the terminology of the young Marx, what I have referred to as the conversion of work and the memory of its essence is termed '*omnilateral*' activity, as opposed to unilateral or alienated labor. "With this division of labor...the worker becomes ever more exclusively dependent on labor, and on a particular, very one-sided, machine-like labor."[39] In the Marxist vocabulary, "alienated" and "divided" express the same state of affairs, the non-essentiality of nature as well as of man. "Division of labor" thus means much more than the monotony of a stereotyped gesture; this expression in fact refers to the hostility between man and nature which results from non-symbolic thinking.

Every symbol makes one 'do'; that of work makes one work. But if one acknowledges this symbolic dimension which is present in relations of production, one radically alters them. This is why symbolic thinking is precisely not a demobilization, even if it is a hermeneutics which, due to the 'reception' of the second meaning, seems to be close to a religious attitude. It remembers that symbols alone, understood within an appropriate hearing, mobilize praxis.

---

38 Ibid., 313.

39 Marx, *Economic and Philosophic Manuscripts,* 25.

Symbolic praxis is without conclusion: the acting provoked by symbols is as varied in its forms as symbols are inexhaustible in their meanings. A man at a feast behaves differently than a worker, a crowd striking up the Marseillaise experiences something other than an inhabitant of the radiant city. Yet a constant theme has appeared throughout our investigation: in the form of a utopia, as in the case of work entirely oriented towards society without divisions and reconciled with nature, which has become a subject; in the form of an ephemeral already-there, as in the three other symbolisms, where the symbol communicates the intuition of a possible. It suggests that life can be intact, without oppositions. Certain contemporary wars have become symbols today: to those of us in Western civilization who know how to hear, they serve as eye-openers to the fractures in the midst of which we live. We hear and we move into action.

A second constant theme is the material, sensible structure of symbols. They are never signs of the mind which speak purely to the mind. On the contrary, the intuition arising from contact with them is born from the bottom up. The concrete symbol addresses itself to visual, auditory, even olfactory emotion. Intuition moves from expression to idea, or to meaning. It looks for words which the immediate call does not yet know. It is the execution of dance, song, labor, and thus the body's work or doing which gives us something to understand. Symbols are something sensible, which speaks to the mind and incites to action. Through the senses, they allow us to hear the possible wholeness of existence, and by means of the praxis which is inseparable from it, they lead us to inaugurate this existence.

Lastly, a third constant theme has to do with what I have called the 'path'. I described symbolic difference as a peregrination bringing existence close to the origin, which becomes manifest in the symbol. This peregrination, in our perspective, appears as the gradual extension of the totality sketched out by praxis; the 'path' is that of the slow conquest which moves from the multiple to the one. At the outcome, the origin gathers all things into the identity of play. Symbolic praxis provides a knowledge of the origin which is not just peregrinal, but carnal. A symbol is always a source of happiness; it is a reunion. The circle in which the origin preserves and cares for us is closed. Symbolic thinking thus provides access to what the moderns have often unlearned to think; namely, the origin as a lost, yet immanent totality.

Translated by Charles T. Wolfe

Situating René Char: Hölderlin, Heidegger, Char and the "There Is"

> To *situate* means here first of all to point out the proper place or site of something. Secondly it means, to heed that place or site. These two methods, placing and heeding, are both preliminaries to a topology. And yet it will require all our daring to take no more than these preliminary steps in what follows. The topology, as befits a path of thought, ends in a question. That question asks for the location of the site.
>
> —Martin Heidegger

We want to situate Char's poetry. Neither the poet himself nor the literary critic raises the question of the site. To situate a script, that is, a way of writing determined by an understanding of being, one has to give some thought to the locus out of which the poet speaks and writes. Where do poets like René Char and Saint John Perse or, also, novelists like Peter Handke stand if their script and speech hint at an experience with language that seems already somehow familiar to us and yet still foreign, strange, too "avant-garde"? To situate a work of prose or poetry is to raise the question of its beginning: where is the place from which the script originates? Although such an elucidation cannot be the explicit preoccupation of the poet himself, this does not deny him any reflective knowledge of his own undertakings; he is not the dumb mouth of destiny. Rather his experience with language is probably more immediate than the philosopher's—so immediate that the question of the origin of the poetic script will finally throw us back upon the humble, historically conditioned, always over-determined experience with our mother-tongue.

To situate René Char's poetry, to question the place or site from which it arises, requires a historical framework. Even within contemporary literature, a post-war poet cannot write any longer as did Rimbaud, or a post-war novelist as did Musil: in half a century our experience with language has mutated. In poetry René Char is among those today whose script manifests the threshold between a former ("modern" and therefore still metaphysical or representational) experience of language and a present or perhaps imminent ("postmodern," beyond metaphysical, non-representational) experience of language and being. The historical framework of this topology of René Char's poetry will remain somehow implicit; it is that of the history of metaphysics. Char's script is localized in relation to this history and to its end.

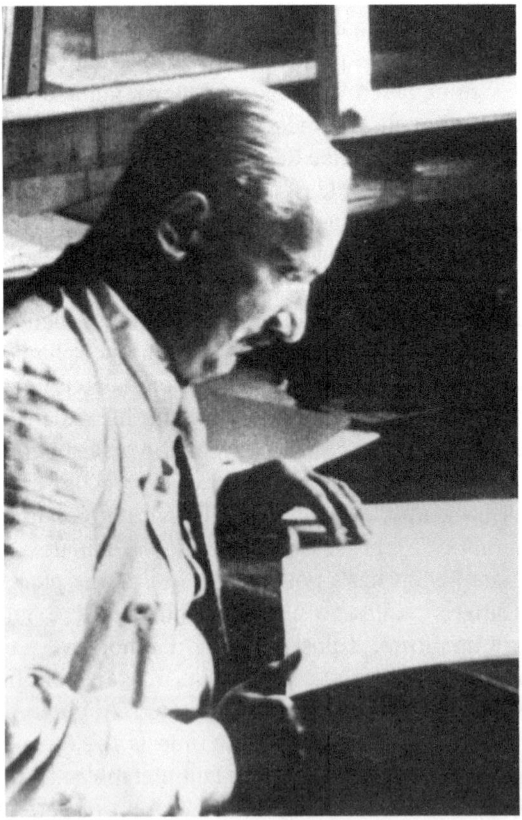

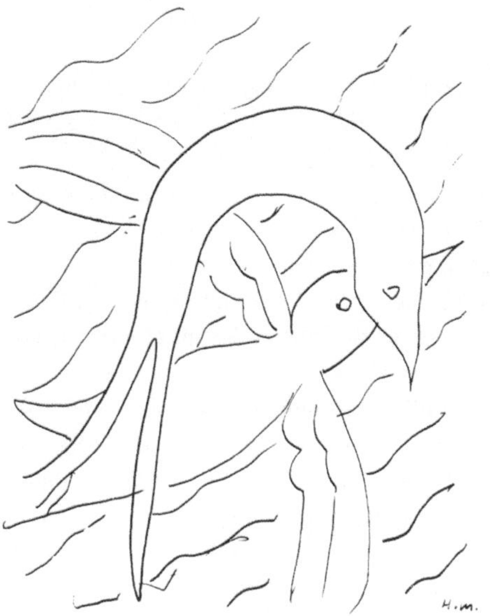

"In May 1946 I sent the manuscript of the poem 'The Shark and the Gull' to Henri Matisse at Vence. During the visit that I had paid to the great painter we had not spoken of any poem in particular. I had convinced myself that Matisse was well and that his treasures continued being executed with the same sumptuous regularity as usual. Back at L'Isle-sur-Sorgue I sent him the manuscript of my poem (I love Matisse and his discrete goodness: this poem to thank him for a precise act). He answered me that in a recent series of drawings he had *discovered* the same theme. Here is one of these drawings."—René Char[1]

---

1 "J'adressais, au mois de mai 1946, à Henri Matisse, à Vence, le manuscrit du poème 'Le requin et la mouette' composé quelques semaines auparavant au Trayas. Au cours de la visite que j'avais faite au grand peintre, il n'avait pas été question d'un poème plutôt que d'un autre. Je m'étais persuadé que Matisse allait bien, que ses trésors continuaient à s'élaborer avec la même somptueuse régularité qu'à l'ordinaire. De retour à L'Isle-sur-Sorgue je lui adressais donc le manuscrit de mon poème (J'aime Matisse et sa bonté discrète: ce poème pour le remercier d'un acte précis). Il me répondit qu'il avait dans une série de dessins récents découvert le même thème. Voici l'un de ces dessins." The drawing and the accompanying lines are reproduced from: *Cahiers d'Art*, Paris 1945/46, 77. By permission of the editors of the *Cahiers d'Art*.

"The Shark and the Gull"

Here is one of Char's best known poems, "Le requin et la mouette" ("The Shark and the Gull"), not previously translated into English:[2]

> Je vois enfin la mer dans sa triple harmonie, la mer qui tranche de son croissant la dynastie des douleurs absurdes, la grande volière sauvage, la mer crédule comme un liseron.
> Quand je dis: *j'ai levé la loi, j'ai franchi la morale, j'ai maillé le cœur,* ce n'est pas pour me donner raison devant ce pèse-néant dont la rumeur étend sa palme au delà de ma persuasion. Mais rien de ce qui m'a vu vivre et agir jusqu'ici n'est témoin alentour. Mon épaule peut bien sommeiller, ma jeunesse accourir. C'est de cela seul qu'il faut tirer richesse immédiate et opérante. Ainsi, il y a un jour de pur dans l'année, un jour qui creuse sa galerie merveilleuse dans l'écume de la mer, un jour qui monte aux yeux pour couronner midi. Hier la noblesse était déserte, le rameau était distant de ses bourgeons. Le requin et la mouette ne communiquaient pas.
> O Vous, arc-en-ciel de ce rivage polisseur, approchez le navire de son espérance. Faites que toute fin supposée soit une neuve innocence, un fiévreux en avant pour ceux qui trébuchent dans la matinale lourdeur. (FM, 197)[3]

> (At last I see the triple harmony of the sea, whose crescent cuts the dynasty of absurd sufferings, the great wild aviary, the sea, credulous as a bindweed.
> When I say: *I overcame the law, I transgressed morality, / unfurled the heart*, it is not to justify myself before this weigher of nothingness whose murmur extends its victory palm beyond my persuasion. But nothing

---

2 All translations which follow the original texts in parentheses are mine.

3 In the references to René Char's works, the following abbreviations are used:

PP *Poèmes et Prose choisis*. Paris: Gallimard, NRF, 1957.

FM *Fureur et Mystère*. Paris: Gallimard, NRF, 1962.

PA *La Parole en archipel*. Paris: Gallimard, NRF, 1962.

NP *Le Nu perdu*. Paris: Gallimard, NRF, 1971.

A-H *Arrière-Histoire du Poème pulvérisé*. Paris: Jean Hugues, 1972.

NT *La Nuit talismanique*. Genève: A. Skira, 1972.

> that has seen me live and act hitherto is witness here. My shoulder may well sleep, my youth come running. From these alone immediate and operative riches must be drawn. Thus there is one day of purity in the year, a day that hollows its marvelous gallery into the sea-foam, a day that mounts into the eyes to crown the noon. Yesterday nobility was desert, the branch was distant from its swelling buds. The shark and the gull did not communicate.
> Oh You, rainbow of this polishing shore, bring the ship closer to its hope. Make every supposed end be a new innocence, a feverish advance for those who stumble in the morning heaviness.)

A first group of images speaks of the sea which appears triply immense: by the thickness of its water, the width of its front, and the depth of the horizon. The "crescent" of the sea cuts suffering: it traces a bulging line like a woman before childbirth. The sea is the "great wild aviary," it encloses life. Here everything is heavy. The water attracts the stroller and invites him to plunge. Gravitation makes his sufferings fall. At the same time the water is soft. It offers no resistance. It is "credulous as a bindweed." These little winding lilies with slender, twining stems bend and yield to the wind, and when the breeze is strong they even roll themselves up. Thus the sea. Its waves follow the impulses of the atmosphere. The sea is straight horizontality, the continuous shelter, the volume of one piece whose docility welcomes living beings as a refuge. This insistence on the weightiness in which life originates and is regenerated does not go beyond traditional figures of aquatic symbolism. In Char it is inspired by the sight of the Mediterranean.[4] We shall see that the entire oceanic symbolism is here a pre-text before the real text.

This first type of imagery is opposed by another. "*I overcame the law* ..." This sentence is printed in italics. To overcome, to transgress, to unfurl: these verbs break the oceanic horizontality. They

---

4 Char writes about this poem: "It was at Trayas on the border of the Mediterranean in the winter of 1946 that the theme of "The Shark and the Gull" imposed itself on me. I went to see Henri Matisse at Vence, and we spoke of it. That perfect wedding haunted him.—This poem has fulfilled itself by the foaming charm that it has procured me long after its flight, like a cock's crowing: brutal to the soul, and master of the silence that follows" (A-H, 40).

indicate a rebellion. The law overcome, morality transgressed: thus the maternal order represented by the sea is broken. Aquatic symbols are ambiguous, since the water gives life and purifies but also drowns and kills. Char calls the sea the "weigher of nothingness." No shelter resembles the matrix more than the tomb. "I unfurled the heart": against the seductive rumor the "I" stands up as if about to leap. In René Char the "heart" represents precisely this sudden rise and affirmation. Another poem, "The Swift," begins thus: "Martinet aux ailes trop larges, qui vire et crie sa joie autour de la maison. Tel est le cœur" (FM, 223). (Swift with wings too wide, who turns and cries his joy around the house. Such is the heart.) The bird that turns and cries is opposed to stability, to the established order of the house. The heart bears the impulse to destroy all cycles. Impromptu, it becomes infatuated. As such, Char praises a woman: "Seins pourris par ton cœur" (NP, 40) (breasts rotten by your heart). Any repose, anything that rests and stays put, every familiarity, threatens the heart. "Qui a creusé le puits et hisse l'eau gisante/ Risque son cœur dans l'écart de ses mains" (NP, 30). (Whoever has dug a well and raises the resting waters/ Risks his heart in the spread of his hands.) When fingers spread and imitate the formless waters, the danger of drowsiness becomes most alarming. The timeless protection that the water recalls and offers must be broken by a mutinous heart. Into all systems of security, the poem seems to say, man introduces discontinuity.

These are the two dimensions within which Char's poetry speaks: gravity and transgression. The arrival at the seashore is one of those moments in which they may unite. "Nothing that has seen me live and act hitherto is witness here." Yesterday's dullness is forgotten. No one is there to recall torpidities. The past is no longer. The extended time, the time that lingers, is the last fabric to be torn. Duration is the most captivating of all dwellings, the narrowest of all prisons. Its dismissal is forcefully urged. Char cherishes the dawns. The early morning, the moment without precedent, makes the world rise anew, immaculate. The moment of waking is much more than the rediscovery of things familiar. It makes the world begin, absolutely. "Nous sommes une fois encore sans expérience antérieure, nouveaux venus, épris" (PA, 48). (We are once again without previous experience, newcomers, infatuated.) The arrival upon the seashore has something of the morning insurrection: once again we begin. It is fatal to settle down, any establishment sacrifices the instant to duration. "La sagesse est de ne pas s'agglomérer" (PP, 237). (Wisdom is not to agglomerate.) Erosion and degradation threaten the freshness of the heart. Even the reverie on the waterfront is perilous if it lasts. In "The Word in Archipelago," Char says, "Ne regardez qu'une fois la vague jeter l'ancre dans la mer" (PA, 152). (Give but a quick look on the wave casting its anchor in the sea.) Everything that stabilizes itself diminishes.

The symbols of the shoulder and of youth, curiously associated in the poem, signify the same departure. "My shoulder may well sleep, my youth come running." They belong together. The shoulder, the angle of the torso, points upwards as a volcano does, says the "Pulverized Poem": "Violente l'épaule s'entr'ouvre;/ Muet apparaît le volcan" (FM, 178). (With violence the shoulder opens partway;/ the volcano appears, mute.) To be a child, to be constantly on the edge of a departure, is Char's "privilege." In a commentary on the "Pulverized Poem" he writes: "Moi qui jouis du privilège de sentir tout ensemble accablement et confiance, défection et courage, je n'ai retenu personne sinon l'angle fusant d'une Rencontre" (A-H, 20). (I enjoy the privilege of feeling all together dejection and confidence, defection and courage; still I have never retained anyone except *the spurting angle of an Encounter* [italics added].) Rare are the lives that resemble an eruption, new at each moment; rare is the resolution of duration into the instant. "There is one day of purity in the year."

The key to this poem is the opposition between duration and instant, massive horizontality and vertical takeoff. Actually it is a poem about poetry. The one pure day "hollows its marvelous gallery into the sea-foam, a day that mounts into the eyes to crown the noon." This rare day, this instant, *reconciles* weight and lightness, submission and transgression, the dive and the flight, or again the oceanic spread and man's freedom. The docile sea and man in revolt belong to each other in the poem. The entire poem hastens the union of the two dimensions. It is a call to fuse sedentary life and departure, to establish oneself on the road. "Épouse et n'épouse pas ta maison" (FM, 99). (Espouse and do not espouse your home.)

The Now of the poem abolishes yesterday's dispersions and separations. "Yesterday... the shark and the gull did not communicate." In the now of the poem the shark and the gull do communicate at last. The gull is constant leaving, vertical flight, whereas the shark settles in the depth, gravity is its shelter. The gull has no refuge. When both communicate, the rainbow appears, offspring of the light and water drops. The sky and the ocean mingle. The poem aspires to the union of the two opposite dimensions down to the prayer that concludes it: "Make every supposed end be a new innocence, a feverish advance for those who stumble in the morning heaviness." The morning heaviness—this is the supreme paradox which translates Char's dream of unity. The morning is the hour of rising, of innocent beginning, of the gull. Heaviness is of the impenetrable sea, of the house, of the shark. As if a lightning flash, the poem makes me a unifier. Reality is antinomic, but the heart, man, or the poet unites. The language of the poem is the multiple matter in which things diverse and opposite enter into relation.

Not One Origin, Two

We now possess a first element for a topology of Char's poetry. We asked: where is the place from which it speaks? Where is its origin? The answer is clearer now: the origin lies somehow within the poem itself. Only when and insofar as the poem is spoken or understood do the dimensions of the shark and the gull communicate. The realm of the poem begins with its utterance. For a brief moment a world is opened in which the opposite is one—even more: in which the world is "world," that is, *there* for man. In Char's poetry an experience comes to language which is properly an experience of the origin. However, this origin is not distinct from the script of the poem itself. In or with the poem the world begins. Char's language is originary in the sense that it is itself the origin of what the poem achieves. We take the word "origin" literally: *oriri*, to rise, to appear, to come forth. Thus we say that language here gives rise to poetry which in turn gives rise to a world unified. Yet to claim that Char's script is originary implies no reference to anything mythical; the origin is not the inception of some process or history. Rather, when the poem is said and understood, the world just begins. But its world lasts as briefly as the poem itself. "La vitalité du poète n'est pas une vitalité de l'au-delà mais un point diamanté *actuel* de présences transcendantes et d'orages pèlerins" (FM, 78). (The vitality of the poet is not a vitality of the beyond, but an actual diamond point of transcending presences and migrating storms.) Thus this poetry is entirely of the earth; it has no other ground, no mythical foundation: it refers to language alone as its provenance; it founds a world which is inseparable from its speech. To understand Char is to see that this passionate celebration of the pure "there is" and this violent exclusion of any "it was" constitute the very structure of his script. If poetry still remains mysterious, if the presence is still called "transcending," this points solely towards the unspeakable subject-matter of poems such as "The Shark and the Gull," namely the mere presence of what is present. The subject-matter here is the visibility of the visible. "Quoique affaire terrestre, comme la vie dont elle est l'endroit victorieux du temps, claire ou opaque, la poésie reste un mystère en acte" (A-H, 11). (Although it is a matter of the earth, just as life whose right side, victorious over time, it is, poetry, whether clear or opaque, remains a mystery in act.)

Two notions of the origin appear to be phenomenologically defensible: the origin as the presence of what is present, and the origin as cause. The first may be described as nuptial: Char's poem announces the nuptials of the shark and the gull. The second may be called natal: cosmogonies speak of the cause or nascency of the world. Both notions imply an event, but nuptials occur in the present whereas nascency is a happening of the past, of the beginning of an era. It should be understood that Char's situation—the origin is not remote but is the presence of the present—disrupts the epistemological continuity that, in the eyes of theoreticians of symbolic forms, links poetic to mythological language. This kind of epistemological continuity may still characterize modern poetry, but it becomes undone already with Rimbaud. A myth relates events that occurred *in illo tempore*. The ritual by which the myth is celebrated revives these events for today so that history begins again: *incipit vita nova*. The important point is that in the innumerable manifestations of the sacred, the origin addresses man according to either temporal mode: the myth recalls and thus calls upon its believer.

This double temporality belongs to the essence of any myth, at least to its basic forms, which are cosmogonic and soteriological. On the one hand such a myth remembers: "In the beginning there was…"; on the other hand it exhorts: "This is the day…" The myth's double temporality, recalling and calling, is due to its essentially etiological intent. Recollection instates a duration, namely the time since those early days when the gods made or visited or saved the earth. Exhortation yields a presence, a renewed existence. Birth and rebirth, the origin as nascency and as nuptials, constitute properly the mythological time-structure. The word "religion," whether understood as *re-legere* or as *re-ligare*, suggests this link between present and past. All forms of the sacred draw their energy from the conjunction of these two modes in which the origin shows itself: the preservation of a message from the past and the exigency of a new hearing and a new existence in the present.

Thus, phenomenologically, "origin" designates two events. Char is so important to us because his poetry excludes violently any such amphibology. He rejects mythical or religious etiologies and turns deliberately to the actual happening in language of the presence of things present. His script reflects a particular understanding of time. The divine is no more; duration, which tied man back to his beginnings, is expunged from time. "Quand s'ébranla le barrage de l'homme, aspiré par la faille géante de l'abandon du divin, des mots dans le lointain, des mots qui ne voulaient pas se perdre, tentèrent de résister à l'exorbitante poussée" (A-H, 29). (When man's dam was shaken, sucked in by the giant rift of the desertion of the divine, words afar, words that did not want to get lost, tried to resist the exorbitant thrust.) The words of poetry have thus come to be simple words of the earth, words of today. Cut off from their numinous roots they have no glorious history to extol but only that glory which human eyes can see. The poet fulfills his task of manifesting the visible with "l'effort, le courage et l'amour" (A-H, 29) (with effort, courage and love). However, he is not the only one to bring the visible to speech. The fullness of language is not entrusted to him alone. He is only one of "les rescapés en si petit nombre" (A-H, 29) (the rescued in so small a number). Who are the others, his companions? Those who know how to converse. Language is primarily dialogue. In an era deprived of the divine, language manifests its essence in the discourse between humans. The rescued ones (from the collapse of religious creed into technological dogma) experience the unique sense of "mystery" or "transcendence" that remains in Char's poetry: the simple presence of one dialogue partner to the other. This presence, as that of the shark to the gull, although it occurs in language, is irreducible to the words exchanged in dialogue.

The difference between the presence and what is present does not construct a new afterworld, a new beyond; and yet, the unity that language establishes between the shark and the gull or between two speakers is not simply the sum of the beings that it brings together. Char's language is mundane, it is deprived of otherworldly roots, but it is not one-dimensional. It operates a communication that is not limited to man. A poem is a "mystère qui intronise" (FM, 83) (a mystery that enthrones). Perhaps we are to understand poetry in a very large sense here: "Tu es dans ton essence constamment poète" (A-H, 47). (You are in your essence constantly a poet.) In the collection *Formal Divide*, many sentences begin with "In poetry ...," as if poetry were some separate domain of language. But elsewhere Char simply says, "Man ... ." "Il y a un homme à présent debout, un homme dans un champ de seigle, un champ pareil à un chœur mitraillé, un champs sauvé" (FM, 40). (There is man now, standing, a man in a field of rye, a field similar to a choir peppered with gunfire, a field that is saved.) The man who saves the field here is evidently the poet. But not necessarily the professional versemaker: any word that gathers together (in German *dichten*, to poetize, suggests *dicht*, intense, together, concentrated) is poetic. Language is at home in the now that gathers together. In "The Shark and the Gull," this gathering is symbolized by the "marvelous gallery" hollowed in sea-foam. Other texts suggest that here again the symbol is meant to evoke the poem itself: Char calls the poem "le tunnel dérobé," "la chambre d'harmonie," "la piste captieuse" (the hidden tunnel, the chamber of harmony, the captious track) and the poet "dans la chambre devenue légère, le donneur de liberté" (FM, 37) (the giver of freedom in the chamber now turned light). In that sense any human whose speech is responsible deserves the epitaph written for a poet: "Enlevé par l'oiseau à l'éparse douleur,/ Et laissé aux forêts pour un travail d'amour" (PA, 92). (Taken away by the bird from the scattered suffering/ And left to the forests for a work of love.)

The poem thus realizes the unity of the world that it signifies. It does not only press for a new existence. If man constantly poetizes, his speech brings together the dimensions of the world, the lightness of the bird and the gravity of the forest. But the poem realizes the unity that it signifies only for the moment of its articulation. Its world springs up and founders immediately. Success here does not abolish desire: "le poème est l'amour réalisé du désir demeuré désir" (FM, 76). (The poem is the realized love of desire remaining desire.) By its nature the poem is an ephemeral victory over dispersion and dislocation.

In the poem all things just begin. "Le poète, grand Commenceur" (FM, 83) (the poet, great Beginner), says Char. Again, this beginning is neither mythical nor religious. The presence that it inaugurates neither founds anything nor even lasts. The poem only lends a voice to the presence of things, it is the elocution of their pure presence. It opens for them a space where they belong to each other. The poem lets them be. It lets be whatever is. Thus it operates the identity of the non-identical. "Le poète peut alors voir les contraires ... aboutir, poésie et vérité, comme nous savons, étant synonymes" (FM, 72). (The poet can then see things contrary come to their end ... poetry and truth, as we know, being synonymous.)

The truth of things, their instantaneous blooming, does not last in a poetry whose origin is nothing divine but only language itself. Truth realizes itself "sometimes": "L'homme n'est qu'une fleur de l'air tenue par la terre...; le souffle et l'ombre de cette coalition, certaines fois, le surélèvent" (PA, 81). (Man is only a flower of the air held by the earth...; the breath and the shadow of this coalition sometimes elevate him.) Hardly achieved, this presence is already regretted: "Oiseaux qui confiez votre gracilité, votre sommeil périlleux à un ramas de roseaux, le froid venu, comme nous nous ressemblons!" (NT, 43). (You, bird, who entrust your frailty, your perilous sleep to a heap of reeds, when the cold has come how we resemble one another!)

The Hymn to the Rhine

With René Char the origin of poetic script lies in the mere present: the poet, "great Beginner," discloses a meaning which is always new. The origin appears as nuptials. Char spells "Beginner" with a capital letter: the poet's ministry is to establish an order. In the poem, the shark and the gull are present, belong at last to each other. When silence comes back, chaos rules again: "Le poète ne retient pas ce qu'il découvre; l'ayant transcrit, il le perd aussitôt. En cela réside sa nouveauté" (PA, 73). (The poet does not retain what he discloses; as soon as he has transcribed it he loses it. In that lies his novelty.) The Beginning is to be understood as instantaneous novelty. It is to this sudden nakedness of the world that Char dedicates his effort. "Great Beginner" is a polemic title: Char's battle is delivered against mythological origins, against any reference to ancestral incipiencies. It is on this decisive understanding of the origin that Char differs radically from another poet, Hölderlin, whom he otherwise resembles in many respects. Char and Hölderlin know of only one subject-matter of poetry, poetry itself. They share the same predilection for rivers. But running waters as a symbol of the poem do not mean the same thing in one and the other. The situation of Hölderlin is not the same as Char's.

"Quand on a mission d'éveiller, on commence par faire sa toilette dans la rivière" (PP, 237). (When one has the mission to rouse, one begins with washing in the river.) The rouser begins, and so does the river. No one enters twice the same river, Heraclitus is reported to have said. The running water is at every moment young. Each dive is like a dive into a fountain of youth: the coolness *begins*, as violent as a child. The same is true for the poet. The communion that he institutes appears suddenly and immediately dissolves. "La poésie est de toutes les eaux claires celle qui s'attarde le moins aux reflets de ses ponts" (PP, 94). (Poetry is of all clear waters the one that lingers the least with the reflections of its bridges.) The poet dwells in white waters, as the trout. He settles in unhabitable elements. "L'éclair me dure" (PA, 72). (Lightning makes me last.) Char calls the Sorgue River of his native Vaucluse "rivière où l'éclair finit et où commence ma maison" (FM, 218) (the river where lightning ends and where my house begins). He wants all humans to dare to choose the unstable. "Donne aux enfants de mon pays le visage de ta passion" (FM, 218). (Give the children of my country the face of your passion.) The Sorgue River operates a departure, everything it touches becomes effulgence. Even the earth splinters into thousands of particles and movements: "Rivière, en toi terre est frisson" (FM, 218). (River, in you the earth is shiver.) The praise of the Sorgue ends with this request: "Rivière au cœur jamais détruit dans ce monde fou de prisons,/ Garde-nous violent et ami des abeilles de l'horizon" (FM, 219). (You, river, whose heart is never destroyed in this world mad with prisons, keep us violent and friends of the bees on the horizon.) Only an indestructible heart can will the anti-compact, the explosive fever of a swarm of bees. And such a heart alone can ally a pulverized systole with a sedentary, earthy diastole. Such a heart is made to the image of the river: violent in the fragmentations that it operates and nevertheless constant in its run. Such is also the paradox of poetic language: "obscurité prénatale et lumière" (PA, 73) (prenatal obscurity as well as light). Let us now listen to Hölderlin. In 1801 he finished the hymn entitled "The Rhine." Here are its first lines:

> Im dunkeln Efeu sass ich, an der Pforte
> Des Waldes, eben, da der goldene Mittag,
> Den Quell besuchend, herunterkam
> Von Treppen des Alpengebirges,
> Das mir die göttlichgebaute,
> Die Burg der Himmlischen heisst
> Nach alter Meinung, wo aber
> Geheim noch manches entschieden
> Zu Menschen gelanget; von da
> Vernahm ich ohne Vermuten
> Ein Schicksal. ...
> Jetzt aber, drin im Gebirg,
> Tief unter den silbernen Gipfeln
> Und unter fröhlichem Grün,
> Wo die Wälder schauernd zu ihm
> Und der Felsen Häupter übereinander
> Hinabschaun, taglang, dort
> Im kaltesten Abgrund hört'

Ich um Erlösung jammern
Den Jüngling, es hörten ihn, wie er tobt',
Und die Mutter Erd 'anklagt'
Und den Donnerer, der ihn gezeuget,
Erbarmend die Eltern, doch
Die Sterblichen flohn von dem Ort,
Denn furchtbar war, da lichtlos er
In den Fesseln sich wälzte,
Das Rasen des Halbgotts.
Die Stimme wars des edelsten der Ströme,
Des freigeborenen Rheins. ...[5]

(I sat among dark ivy at the forest's gate just as golden noon, to visit the source, descended from the steps of the Alpine ranges, for me the divinely-built, the castle of the Heavenly, following old opinion, whence even yet many a secret decree reaches men; and thus I unsuspectingly received a destiny ... Amidst the mountains, deep down below the snowy summits and under the jubilant green, where the shuddering forests and, craning over each other, the crags look down upon him all day long, I now heard in the coldest abyss the youth wail for release; there, as he raged, accusing Mother Earth and the Thunderer who begot him, his pitying parents heard him, too; but the mortals fled from the place,

5 Friedrich Hölderlin, *Sämtliche Werke*, ed. Paul Stapf (Berlin und Darmstadt: Tempel, 1958), 314–15, hereafter referred to as *Werke*. Franz Mayer, "René Char et Hölderlin," *Cahiers de l'Herne* 15 (1971), 81–88, has attempted a comparison between the two poets. He sees the function of modern and postmodern poetry in the anticipation of a historical reality to come: "L'avenir est ainsi, pour Char comme pour Hölderlin ... une réalité historique" (p. 88). It seems to me that the kinship between the two poets lies, on the contrary, in the attention that both give to an origin that arises within the poem, neither before nor after. For both Hölderlin and Char the future is *advenir*, a present event, rather than à *venir*, to come. Virginia La Charite, *The Poetics and the Poetry of René Char* (Chapel Hill: University of North Carolina Press, 1968), sees the time-structure of Char's poetry also as derived from an attitude of hope, turned towards the future; according to her interpretation "the great Beginner" would mean hope "for a better future" (p. 93). This line of interpretation was first that of Maurice Blanchot, "René Char," *La part du feu* (Paris: Gallimard, 1949), 17. Read in such a way, poetry would again found some kind of duration, a new era, whereas for Char and Hölderlin no inception occurs in the poem, but only its own rise and death in the present now.

> for as he writhed without light in his fetters, terrible was the demi-god's raving. It was the voice of the noblest of rivers, the free-born Rhine.)

The hymn begins with a description of the Alps. According to the myth, they are the fortress of the gods, of heavenly architecture. From these heights the gods still send decrees whose destiny or "mittance" (*Schicksal*, from *schicken*, to send) the poet, "I," receives and grasps (*So vernahm ich ohne Vermuthen ein Schicksal*). These decrees are rough; within the desolate scenery of rocks a youth, son of the Earth and the Thunderer, writhes in his chains. It is the Rhine who fights furiously his way through the rocky masses. Hölderlin calls him the "noblest of rivers," a demi-god. In Hölderlin as in Char, the river symbolizes the poem; in both cases also it unites duration and instant, the solid and the light or the lightning. The son of the gods is "saxifragous," the rock breaker. Char dedicated a poem to Hölderlin entitled "Pour un Prométhée saxifrage. En touchant la main éolienne de Hölderlin" (PA, 125) ("For a Saxifragous Prometheus. Touching the Eolian Hand of Hölderlin"). It begins thus: "La realité sans l'énergie disloquante de la poésie, qu'est-ce?" (Reality without the dislocating energy of poetry, what would that be?) The violence of the young and raving Rhine symbolizes the violent rise of the poetic word. Char probably also has Hölderlin in mind when he writes in *Formal Divide*: "Fureur et mystère tour à le séduisirent et le consumèrent. Puis vint l'année qui acheva son agonie de saxifrage" (FM, 70). (Furor and mystery seduced and consumed him by turns. Then came the year that concluded his saxifragous agony.) It was fatal for Hölderlin to unite lightning and the earth, furor and mystery. Five years after he had finished "The Rhine" he fell into madness. One has even the impression that Char paraphrases the first lines of the hymn: "Nous regardions couler devant nous l'eau grandissante. Elle effaçait d'un coup la montagne, se chassant de ses flancs maternels. Ce n'était pas un torrent qui s'offrait à son destin mais une bête ineffable dont nous devenions la parole et la substance" (FM, 222). (We watched the growing water flow before us. It wiped out the mountain in a single blow, breaking forth from its motherly womb. It was not a torrent that offered itself to its destiny, but an ineffable beast whose word and substance we became.)

If examined more closely, however, the difference between Char's and Hölderlin's use of the river symbol, and therefore the difference between their ways to understand the poem, is radical. All along its current the Rhine is seen by Hölderlin *close to its source.* The poet's mediation remains near the origin of the divine decrees: "Ein Rätsel ist Reinentsprungenes. Auch/ Der Gesang kaum darf es enthüllen" (*Werke,* 315). (A riddle is what is of pure origin, song itself may hardly disclose it.) Wherever the Rhine passes, it is "pure origin." The poet's utterances remain thoroughly faithful to the "heavenly" messages which, "beyond question," reach mankind by his mediation. "Ein Rätsel ist Reinentsprungenes"—this means something different now from "poète, grand Commenceur," the poet, great Beginner. If Char's ministry consists merely in lending a voice to what is present in as much as present, Hölderlin's hermeneutic function is one of translating and transmitting. The origin that addresses man in Hölderlin's poetry is sacred, arises from elsewhere. Whereas Char announces the nuptials of what is visible, Hölderlin turns back towards the invisible nascency of which he is the servant and the herald. The entire hymn exalts this presence of the natal, not yet nuptial origin; it is a hymn to man's wandering identity with his birth.

> Und schön ists, wie er drauf,
> Nachdem er die Berge verlassen,
> Stillwandelnd sich im deutschen Lande
> Begnügt ...
> Doch nimmer, nimmer vergisst ers.
> Denn eher muss die Wohnung vergehn,
> Und die Satzung und zum Unbild werden
> Der Tag der Menschen, ehe vergessen
> Ein solcher dürfte den Ursprung
> Und die reine Stimme der Jugend. (*Werke,* 316–317)

(How fair is the way he now, after leaving the mountains, glides onward in calm content ... But he never, never forgets. For sooner the dwelling shall perish, and the laws, and the day of men become a calamity, than such as he forget the origin and the pure voice of youth.)

These lines express Hölderlin's human ideal: the nearness of the past inception and the memory of the pure voice of our early years. The poem speaks of the ideal itself as much as of its loss. Hölderlin's time, our time, is the one where the gods seem to be no more. Rivers have become factors of calculus in the navigation business and cheap means of industrial evacuation and refrigeration. This is the age of the night to which Hölderlin opposes the age of the day, that is, early Greece.

> Aber weh! es wandelt in Nacht, es wohnt, wie im Orkus,
> Ohne Göttliches unser Geschlecht. Ans eigene Treiben
> Sind sie geschmiedet allein, und sich in der tosenden Werkstatt
> Höret jeglicher nur ... (*Werke*, 290)

> (But alas! today's mankind errs through the night, it dwells as though in hades, deprived of the divine. They all are solely enchained to their own agitation, and in the middle of the boisterous workshop everyone hears only himself.)

An age such as ours must again learn how to listen. Hence the sanctity of Hölderlin's mediations. A human being close to the source, the poet, does what the river does. He transmits the life-giving decrees of the gods to the mortal inhabitants of the valleys. At each step he remembers his early beginnings. He remains impetuous. He is the mediator who consumes himself in his task. When Hölderlin feels madness imminent, he compares himself to the demi-god Tantalus "who received from the gods more than he could digest." To be a poet is not a matter of talent. The poem succeeds when the natal origin, the mystery of birth, becomes language. The saying of the poem *is* the arrival of the gods. As a demi-god, the poet experiences the lasting nearness of the *archē*. Only when the gods grant their presence do his stammerings become a poem. The hymn "Patmos" says: "Nah ist/ Und schwer zu fassen der Gott" (*Werke*, 328). (Near, and yet hard to grasp, is the god.) In fact, the poet does not seize. Rather he is seized, "struck by Apollo."

Hölderlin's poems thus preserve a certain past; they enunciate both the ancientness and the nearness of our provenance: the ancient glory of language as incantation is the terrible privilege of those who dare remember. The origin is here understood as proximity of the divine, forgotten though it is in needy times. The man of this proximity is necessarily a stranger. Only in that condition can he, "like the god of wine, render intelligible to the heart the language of the purest ones," that is, of the gods (*Werke*, 318). The poem is divine speech, the only one that we still possess. By such an elevation of everyday words into hymnic song, language comes into its own.

Hölderlin's situation is that of the end of metaphysics: the divine ground holds no more, the foundations appear shaken. What used to be the most powerful presence, the divine, has fallen into oblivion. Only the poet remembers. What, then, is Char's situation? In his poetry there is no regretfulness of sacred decrees, no recollection. The site from which he speaks is nothing mythical, not "a stronghold of the Heavenly," no "sacred Alps," but man's own language in its humble event. Char's situation is properly postmodern, perhaps beyond metaphysics altogether. It may be that Char says less than Hölderlin: no holy injunctions are transmitted. It may be that he says also less than Nietzsche: no madman cries after God. But in saying apparently less, does he not speak from another locus, still too novel to think of, a place beyond representations and beyond that threshold where the overcoming of metaphysics is still the dominant problem? In that case Hölderlin would have experienced the decline of the truth of being, and particularly the decline of the truth of the supreme being. Since the very quest for certainty, security, and salvation has become meaningless in his situation, Char points more decidedly towards a new beginning. Yet Char's project has nothing to do with the simplifying label "atheism," but very much with a new thought of being. The truth of being lies no more in the principle of reason and in logic, but in the *princeps*, the beginning, which the logos as poetic speech is itself.

Both Hölderlin and Char poetize the origin. But in Char the dimensions of the visible communicate due to his script; his poem exists when the visibility of the visible alone becomes language. In Hölderlin a restoration occurs; the natal origin—in the mythical sense, as he states explicitly—addresses a mortal race that has forgotten its own essence. The task of Hölderlin's hymn is to recall the divine as one calls back a fugitive. "The Rhine" ends precisely with the wedding between the mortals and the immortals:

> Dann feiern das Brautfest Menschen und Götter,
> Es feiern die Lebenden all,
> Und ausgeglichen ist eine Weile das Schicksal. (*Werke*, 319)

> (Then gods and men celebrate their nuptials, all the
> living celebrate, and Destiny becomes equal for a while.)

For the time of the poem the difference between mortal and immortal is abolished. It is not by chance that Hölderlin composes "hymns," whereas Char renounces any kind of praise or acclamation. *Hymnos*, in Greek, designates primitively the "hymen" songs that were accompanied by flutes and lyres. The songs are started off by the friends that guide the young couple to the bridegroom's house. Hölderlin's hymns are hymeneals of the mortal and the immortal. In contrast, the only wedding Char admits of is that of the dimensions of the earth, of the shark and the gull, but never of heaven and earth. Char's ontological situation lies above—or underneath—whatever might resemble "une vitalité de l'au-delà" (FM, 78) (a vitality of the beyond).

In Hölderlin's view a double giving takes place in poetry. On the one hand the poet assists the mortals, to whom he points out the originary road to follow:

> Nachdem er lächelnd auch
> Der Menschen geschäftiges Leben
> Das odemarme, wie Segel
> Mit seinen Lüften gelenkt hat. … (*Werke*, 319)

> (He steers the busy life of men, short-breathed as it is, like sails, with his own inexhaustible breezes.)

But on the other hand, as a mediator, the poet also gives to the gods. The wedding that he calls for also profits the immortals: to the "most-blessed" he offers his fragility. This fulfills their only need:

> Bedürfen die Himmlischen eines Dings,
> So sind's... Sterbliche. Dann
> Muss wohl, wenn solches zu sagen
> Erlaubt ist, in der Götter Namen
> Teilnehmend fühlen ein andrer,
> Den brauchen sie. ... (*Werke*, 317)

"If one need remains to the Celestials, that need is for mortals." Gods are impassible, suffering is unknown to them. Therefore, "if to say such a thing is permitted, another must be compassionate and feel on their behalf." In need of mortals, the gods use, *brauchen*, the poet. To bear such usage and such usury he has only his endurance to count upon. His happiness is of the weightiest kind.

> Nur hat ein jeder sein Mass.
> Denn schwer ist zu tragen
> Das Unglück, aber schwerer das Glück. (*Werke*, 319)

> (Each has his measure. For hard though to bear is unhappiness, still harder is happiness.)

Around him men breathlessly render the night more comfortable. But the poet "knows God." He has been measured with the double gauge of divine and human needs. He remains the wailing youth, guardian of the source and guarded by it. As the hermeneuts, the priests at Delphi, he goes back and forth between the oracle and the people's square. His sayings are essentially interpretative.

> Denn schonend rührt des Masses allzeit kundig
> Nur einen Augenblick die Wohnungen der Menschen
> Ein Gott an. ... (*Werke*, 308)

> (A god, always heedful of measure, touches as a guard in a single moment upon the dwellings of man.)

Man's dwelling, language, which is thus "touched" by the divine, is the poem. Hölderlin's concept of origin is both mythical (mainly in the hymns) and historical (in his translations and aesthetic writings). In either case, though, what he recalls is early Greece. The contrast with Char is evident. There is no sacred dimension of existence or of history that speaks through Char's poems and whose recollection would be entrusted to the poet. What does speak in Char's verse is the ephemeral harmony of mortal speech which for an unsettled existence builds and unbuilds instantaneous dwellings.

"There Is" in the Poem

It is not enough to say that in Hölderlin's poetry the origin appears as mythical and remote, and in Char's as actual and present. Nor have we understood the situation of Char once his script has been labeled post-metaphysical. The event of language by which the origin manifests itself in his poetry needs to be questioned for its own sake. Hölderlin thinks the era of Western history and tries to renew its early vitality, its divine infancy. In this sense his poetry is a memorial. As a recollection and as a revival it opens the space of a second beginning. Char seems to retain only the contemporaneous part of the essentially ambivalent language of the origin, smothering its romantic overtones. Only the present instant remains: "La lumière a un âge. La nuit n'en a pas. Mais quel fut l'instant de cette source entière?» (NT, 34). (Light has an age. The night has none. But which was the instant of that integral source?)

In the poem there is the sea; there are the Sorgue River and the Rhine; there is the shark communicating with the gull. But prior to all this there is in the poem the "there is" itself. Since Rimbaud, the poem has said: whatever is, is. Sometimes it takes a more pressing tone, when it says: whatever is, may that be. But this wish that it formulates is fulfilled right away. What is at stake in the poem is the presence of everything to everything. Only the presence. Not an intention, but the intonation alone. Rimbaud is the poet of poetry when he writes in his *Illuminations*:

> There is a clock that does not ring.
> There is a quagmire with a nest of white birds.

There is a cathedral …
There is a small car …[6]

The same celebration of what is purely present is found in Apollinaire's *Calligraphies*:

There is a vessel that has taken away my beloved.
There are six sausages in the sky …
There is an enemy submarine …

and so on, for twenty-four "there is's."[7]

Is all this to say that poems such as these and Char's eliminate any *difference* from language? Is their verse content with the beautiful sequences of auditory and visual elements? Against theories of structural linguists, it is clear that the "there is" introduces by itself a difference, a mystery, if that is the word, which neither turns our eyes away (as it does in Hölderlin) from the purely visible and audible nor keeps them riveted to the order of words and things that make up the poem (as, for instance, in Roman Jakobson's theory). Thus the question of the situation of René Char's poetry, the question of how the origin has to be understood in his script, becomes the question of identity and difference in the "there is." We may even be entitled to go a step beyond Char, to risk the defoliation of our anthologies, and to concentrate our attention not upon the things shown, but upon the showing itself. When the poem is said,

---

6 Arthur Rimbaud, *Œuvres* (Paris: Garnier, 1960), 256–257:
Au bois il y a un oiseau, son chant vous arrête et vous fait rougir.
Il y a une horloge qui ne sonne pas.
Il y a une fondrière avec un nid de bêtes blanches.
Il y a une cathédrale qui descend et un lac qui monte.
Il y a une petite voiture abandonnée dans le taillis,
ou qui descend le sentier en courant, enrubannée.
Il y a une troupe de petits comédiens en costumes,
aperçus sur la route à travers la lisière du bois.
Il y a enfin, quand l'on a faim et soif, quelqu'un qui vous chasse.

7 Guillaume Apollinaire, *Œuvres poétiques complètes* (Paris: Pléiade, 1969), 817:
Il y a un vaisseau qui a emporté ma bien-aimée.
Il y a dans le ciel six saucisses. …
Il y a un sous-marin ennemi. …

things are present, reconciled, called together by its speech. This recognition of their being-there is probably common to all poetry we know of. But being-there *is not* the being that is there. The present is different from the thing present, as the visibility of the thing shown is different from the shark and the gull that the poem makes visible.

The poem is the burning articulation of a desire: may all things be there. May pure presence be. Even more, it announces and already realizes what it desires. The dimensions of the earth communicate, but this communication *is not* the water and the sky, or gravity and transgression. The poem is the tangible sign, offered to our eyes, our ears, our lips, that all is one, that mere presence *is*. The poem is the color of hereness, its fulgor and its splendor. The difference that the "there is" introduces into the poem is the difference between the presence and the things present or the visibility and what is rendered visible.

The German idiomatic expression *es gibt*, "there is," means literally "it gives." "Among dark ivy at the forest's gate" there is the river. Hölderlin thinks the *es gibt* literally when he continues: "A riddle is what is of pure origin." One may ask: what is it that gives? The Alps give the Rhine. The gods give destiny. However, that which gives cannot be properly named. But out of that region, we are told, "secretly much, beyond question, still reaches man." That which gives is the origin of presence. It gives presence. When the poem calls all things together, they are mysteriously granted to us, bestowed by That which gives. In order to understand the essence of poetry, solely the provenance of this giving deserves to be questioned. Heidegger sees in this idiomatic turn *es gibt* the possibility of a new examination of ontology: "the memorable is what gives food for thought. ... The memorable grants."[8] The source of a river is memorable, it remains so down to the estuary. "As you began you remain" ("The Rhine"). Heidegger comments: "We try to carry our sight towards that which gives and towards its giving, and we spell the 'It' with a capital letter."[9] That which gives is different from what it gives.

---

8 "Das Bedenkliche ist das, was zu denken gibt... Das Bedenkliche gibt." Martin Heidegger, *Vorträge und Aufsätze* (Pfullingen: Neske, 1954), 132.

9 "Wir versuchen, das Es und sein Geben in die Sicht zu bringen und schreiben das 'Es' groß." Martin Heidegger, *Zur Sache des Denkens* (Tübingen: Niemeyer, 1969), 5.

There are thus three semantic layers that we have to distinguish carefully: the things present (the shark and the gull), their presence (the poetic speech or script), and the event of the presencing (the essence of poetic language). In the vocabulary of Heidegger's writings of the 1930s: beings, beingness, and Being. Or in the vocabulary of *On Time and Being*: *das Anwesende*, *das* Anwesen*lassen*, *das Anwesen*lassen. Based upon the difference that the German expression "there is" suggests, this threefold layer gives an answer to any inquiry into the way things and words are present in a poem. Both Hölderlin and Heidegger give witness to this Germanic way of speaking and therefore of thinking.

Superficially the "*es gibt*" of Heidegger (commenting on Hölderlin) resembles Rimbaud's "*il y a*" and the English "there is." But the similarity is deceptive, as the kinship between Hölderlin and Char is deceptive. "*Es gibt*" and "there is" belong to two different worlds. Both the English "there is" and the French "*il y a*" eliminate any mythical reminiscence from the poem. This is not so with "*es gibt*," particularly when spelled with a capital letter. Hence the danger of misunderstanding some of Heidegger's latest writings. The invitation to silence before the mystery of That which gives, as well as Heidegger's reference to Hölderlin, may easily mislead the reader. Even in his texts about the event of presencing, it is still the visibility of the visible that is thought of. Thus he is closer to the way of thinking that says "there is" or "*il y a*" than to Hölderlin's hymn "The Rhine" and the recollection into divine mittances as implied by "*es gibt*." If Heidegger still speaks of the sacred and of the mystery, this must be understood in Char's way: the communication of the dimensions of the earth is sacred; the presencing of the essence of language that renders things present is mysterious. "There is" and "*il y a*" tell more humbly the proximity of being than Heidegger's own mother-language.

Char's poetry is far from any celebration of non-human grantings, from any grace or giving. It expresses nothing more than the spectacle of what is. Hölderlin's poetry, or the "*Es gibt*," implies a stretched-out temporality, a return to the beginnings. Char's poetry, or the "*il y a*" and the "there is," in the purely vertical temporality of the instant, consumes horizontal history as the lightning consumes the day. On this point some of Char's titles may lead to confusion: "Retour amont," or "Le nu perdu" ("Return Upstream," "Nudity Lost"). But in no way does Char display the nostalgia for a lost paradisiac nudity, and the return upstream is not an ascent to the causes. Rather, "amont éclate" (NP, 48) (upstream bursts). The only path that Char traces for us leads to the being-there of what is there.

Char's situation is beyond metaphysics insofar as the pure "there is" to which he gives voice destroys causal scaffoldings. Thus the armistices concluded both by Hölderlin and by Char are of opposite terms. Hölderlin's hymns are the script of an Absent. They are the presence of this Absent qua absent. That which grants Hölderlin's poems to be the locus of reconciliation between man and his origin arises from elsewhere. Hölderlin's poetry settles a momentary armistice between man and the sacred. In Char the armistice is between a carnivorous beast, the shark, and the light-feathered gull, both of which *are there* in his poetry, belonging to each other and appropriating each other. In Hölderlin the cities founded by the legislating stream are *from elsewhere*, from the gods. "Then man and gods celebrate their nuptials." Heidegger's interpretation of this line refers again to the Absent which, through the text, becomes present. These weddings, he writes, celebrate "the encounter of those among men and gods who give birth to the mediators between men and gods and who endure this intermediacy."[10] In other words, out of this wedlock the poet is born. The offspring carries the mark of what is absent into the present.

Poetry is that section of language in which being lets itself be explicitly experienced as event and as appropriation. But each native tongue prepares for this event and this appropriation a dwelling which is particular to it. The German "*es gibt*" comprises a difference between what is shown and its origin; this language lives from such a reference to what is absent, or from the manifestation of the non-manifest. It is a metaphysical language. The German language experiences the appropriating event as the intrusion of

---

10 "*Das Brautfest* ist das Begegnen jener Menschen und Götter, dem die Geburt derjenigen entstammt, die zwischen den Menschen und den Göttern stehen und dieses 'Zwischen' ausstehen." Martin Heidegger, *Erläuterungen zu Hölderlins Dichtung* (Frankfurt: Klostermann, 1963), 98.

a distinct and forgotten origin into the customary proximity. The poet's saying is here understood as a translation: he translates to our ears the anonymous gift by which the poem lets whatever is be present. The poet is the guard of this gift, and inversely this gift guards (*schont*, *hütet*) him.

The French and English languages stay among what they show—but radically. "*Il y a*" and "there is" open a difference between what is and its presence. The poem makes the purity of the there be seen. It is as mysterious as the sun at noon, which is the sun "and" which is there. Without involving any double, any invisible afterworld, Char's poetry and the tongue in which it is written live within this difference, between things of the Earth and their being-there. Char is the poet of the visible mystery for whom and by whom presence is different from things present but not other than they, hence also identical with them.

As for the English language, one nuance is striking in this context: "there is" applies in English both to human existence (*Dasein*, être-là) and to the more general presence of beings (*Es gibt*, *il y a*). The lack of this distinction in English reveals perhaps another kind of ontology which would have to be worked out from contemporary poetry in that language.

Political Thinking in Heidegger

> It is a decisive question for me today how a political system, and or what kind, can at all be coordinated with the technological age. I do not know an answer to this question. I am not convinced that it is democracy.
>
> —Martin Heidegger (1966)

Until his death Heidegger remained deliberately—and embarrassingly—discreet, to say the least, as to the political dimension of his project to phenomenologically "destroy" metaphysics. As is well known, he committed an error of political judgment in 1933 when he thought he knew "how a political system, and of what kind, can at all be coordinated with the technological age." Indeed, under National Socialism he praised "the inner truth and greatness of this movement (namely the encounter between global technology and modern man)."[1] Later, having acknowledged his error, he would

---

1 Martin Heidegger, *Einführung in die Metaphysik* (Tübingen: Niemeyer, 1953), 152; *An Introduction to Metaphysics*, trans. Ralph Manheim (New Haven: Yale University Press, 1959), 199. The lecture course was held in 1935. When compared to a later commentary on it (interview with *Der Spiegel*, May 31, 1976, 206), the parenthesis raises some questions:
Why was it not delivered orally although it stood in the manuscript in 1935? Because of "the stupid, the informers, and the snoopers" in the audience, Heidegger says. Does Heidegger want to give this parenthesis, thirty years later, an anti-Nazi ring which would have provoked an informer? Does the line contain a protest against National Socialism ?
In the context, the parenthesis hardly sounds like a criticism: in 1935 Heidegger still trusts that if modern man can come to grips with technology it will be through National Socialism. Then how far did his disillusionment really go, when he resigned from the rectorate a year earlier? Does the line contain some form of allegiance to National Socialism?
In 1935 technology is not yet seen in the context of Western metaphysics. The later notion *Gestell*, then, depoliticizes technology, since man's encounter with it is no longer thematized in the context of political forces. So does the line perhaps hint at a relationship between technology and fascism which Heidegger would never take up again?

evade questions about the practical implications of his thought like a burnt child. When asked about his political stand he would simply reply: "I do not know an answer to this question."[2] It is not established that we should believe him on this point. In a hardly refutable study, Karsten Harries[3] has recently shown how deeply the themes of Heidegger's inaugural address "On the Self-Determination of the German University" (May 1933) are rooted in *Being and Time* and how they reappear in the praise of the great statesman (likened to other "creators," the poet, the artist, the thinker) in later writings of the 1930s. The evidence produced by Harries that the call for a leader ready to use violence and able to "walk alone" is neither an accidental nor an isolated theme in the *Rek-*

Protest, allegiance, and an implicit charge that technology is the hand of fascism cannot be meant at the same time. The basic ambiguity in Heidegger's comment on his earlier remarks lies in the understanding of technology. His attempt to read later developments of his thinking into the line from *An Introduction to Metaphysics* is somewhat self-contradictory: one cannot praise National Socialism for allowing control of technology and at the same time equate National Socialism with "Americanism" and "the Communist movement" as being determined by "planetary technology." In 1935 National Socialism is said to possess an inner truth and greatness because of a potentiality that neither Americanism nor Communism could offer. The same line which in 1935 opposes National Socialism to planetary technology is used in 1966 to claim a fundamental identity between National Socialism and global technology.

2 The lines of the epigraph are taken from "Nur noch ein Gott kann uns retten. Spiegel-Gespräch mit Martin Heidegger am 23. September 1966," *Der Spiegel* 23 (May 31, 1976): 206; "Only a God Can Save Us Now," *Graduate Faculty Philosophy Journal* 6 (Winter 1977): 5–27.

3 Karsten Harries, "Heidegger as a Political Thinker," *Review of Metaphysics* 29 (June 1976): 642–69. Whether or not the structure of "resolve" implies a need for authority—and this seems questionable—Harries's remarks on *Being and Time* show once again how inconsistent was Karl Löwith's attempt to draw political implications out of a supposedly nihilistic concept of existence in *Sein und Zeit*; see Karl Löwith, "Les implications politiques de la philosophie de l'existence chez Heidegger," *Les Temps modernes*, no. 14 (1946): 343–60 and his *Heidegger: Denker in dürftiger Zeit* (Frankfurt: Fischer, 1953). Harries, on the other hand, fails to acknowledge what in 1953 Habermas called the shift in the "quality of appeal" from *Being and Time* to *An Introduction to Metaphysics*. In *Being and Time*, Habermas wrote, "Heidegger still praised the quasi-religious resolve of the private, single existence as finite autonomy," whereas the praise of power and violence was the momentary "fascist coloration" of the later discovery of the "history of Being" (Jürgen Habermas, *Philosophisch-politische Profile* [Frankfurt: Suhrkamp, 1971], 67–75).

toratsrede provides a safe platform for further reflection. In fact, it makes further reflection inescapable: If before and after the "turn" in his thinking Heidegger was, to be sure, a political thinker, and if his political standpoint does shine through several of his writings, what was that standpoint? Or, in the vocabulary of *Being and Time:* If authentic existence has no higher authority but only its own resolute actions to justify itself, what kind of action is adumbrated by that ontological inquiry? The link between an ontic way of living and the ontological description of existence is indeed said to be a "positive necessity." Also, once the political tendency in some of Heidegger's texts prior to the lectures on Nietzsche (1936–40) has been established, it will come as no surprise to some of his readers thirty years later to hear him say about the most appropriate political system for today: "I am not sure that it is democracy." But where do we go from there?

One line of argument suggests a pure and simple identity between the enduring political standpoint behind Heidegger's thinking in general and his misled commitments in the early years of Nazism. The literature that argues such a direct continuity between Heidegger's fundamental convictions and those events is abundant. Theodor Adorno set the tone for much of it by polemicizing against Heidegger's language as an ideological expression of fascism.[4] Several documentations were published, followed by accusations and rectifications.[5]

---

4 Theodor Adorno, *Jargon der Eigentlichkeit* (Frankfurt: Suhrkamp, 1965), esp. 8–9; *The Jargon of Authenticity*, trans. Knut Tarnowski and Frederic Will (Evanston: Northwestern University Press, 1973). A similar course is followed by Georg Lukács, *Die Zerstörung der Vernunft* (Berlin: Aufbau-Verlag, 1954). Lukács elaborates on "a climate of despair" in so-called existentialist writings, a climate which would have helped to prepare and enforce Nazism.

5 Guido Schneeberger, *Nachlese zu Heidegger: Dokumente zu seinem Leben und Denken* (Bern, 1962) and Paul Hühnerfeld, *In Sachen Heidegger* (Munich: List, 1961). Schneeberger's and Hühnerfeld's positions, together with that of Adorno, have been carefully analyzed and criticized by François Fédier in *Critique*, nos. 234, 242, 251 (1966–67). See the review of these debates in Beda Allemann, "Martin Heidegger und die Politik," in Otto Pöggeler, ed., *Heidegger: Perspektiven zur Deutung seines Werks* (Cologne: Kiepenheuer & Witsch, 1969), 246–60.

Heidegger himself remained aloof from these debates. His remark, "I am not sure that it is democracy," taken together with this aloofness (as well as the decision, after the war, to repeat in print the praise of the inner truth and greatness of National Socialism) may seem to provide a hint for a lifelong nostalgia for the integration under one leader of the "service of knowledge" (*Wissensdienst*), the "service of labor" (*Arbeitsdienst*), and the "service of weapons" (*Wehrdienst*). Such was indeed the project for a "community of combat between teachers and students" as outlined in the *Rektoratsrede*.[6]

A second line of argument insists on the development of Heidegger's thinking. Like other intellectuals of his generation, he would have discovered the necessity of political thought only after an initial shock or catastrophe. His disciples considered him hardly familiar with political questions and, initially, without a definite opinion in this domain. It is true that the lectures on Nietzsche, spread over five years before and after the beginning of the war, contain some more or less open criticism of the National Socialist ideology. In his seminars and courses during the war his criticism was actually so plain (*deutlich*), Walter Biemel writes, that his students clearly understood it, although such clarity could have meant a death sentence.[7] But articulating a coherent political thinking is quite different from courageously aiming occasional criticisms. Heidegger obviously has not developed a "political theory," if under that title one expects to find a doctrine of law, or of representation and participation, etc.

Thus a third line of argument has to be attempted. My own starting point is threefold: Heidegger's thinking is by no means deprived of a political dimension; the political implications must be interpreted out of his fundamental philosophical project, and not the

---

6 Jean-Michel Palmier, *Les écrits politiques de Heidegger* (Paris: L'Herne, 1968), by far the most congenial of all these studies, takes off from this threefold "service" (114–45) in order to develop "the figure of the workingman as the epochal [*historiale*] figure of the modern world" (169–293). He compares Heidegger's writings on technology with Ernst Jünger's *Der Arbeiter* (1932): "We suggest as an hypothesis that the origin of Heidegger's meditation on the essence of technology remains unintelligible without the encounter with Ernst Jünger's writings and the Germany of 1933" (215).

7 Quoted in Palmier, *Les écrits politiques de Heidegger*, 283.

other way around; a middle term between Heidegger's thought of Being and a political thinking that might agree with it was never developed by Heidegger himself. Hence the groping in the dark in trying to discover even the elementary contours of his political thinking. If further reflection is inescapable, then its primary task is to work out the missing link between what has traditionally been called ontology and practical philosophy. Traditional philosophies of action have consistently been supported by some philosophy of being. Likewise Heidegger's nonmetaphysical way of raising the question of Being affects, and must be carried over into, the domain of political thinking. This paper should be read as an attempt to contribute to the elaboration of such a middle term. The five titles developed below result from an inquiry into the ontology of symbols undertaken earlier.[8] This inquiry led to a reformulation of the ontological difference as "symbolic difference." What is meant by this title? Furthermore, if the symbolic difference is to exhibit political thinking in Heidegger, how is the symbol related to the ontological difference, and what kind of political thinking results from such a reformulation of the ontological difference? It may be unfortunate that with Heidegger we never escape speaking of Being and its difference from beings, but there is no other access to his thought.

The Symbolic Difference and the Destruction of Metaphysics

The ontological difference can be thought of metaphysically as well as phenomenologically. In metaphysics "the Being of beings is thought of in advance as the grounding ground."[9] Phenomenologically, on the other hand, the difference between Being and beings appears as the preservation of both "in a process of unconcealment

---

8 Reiner Schürmann, "The Ontological Difference and Political Philosophy," *Philosophy and Phenomenological Research* (forthcoming). In this article the symbolic difference is derived from the referential essence of both Being and language. [See this volume, 135–162.—Eds.]

9 Martin Heidegger, *Identität und Differenz* (Pfullingen: Neske, 1957), 55; *Identity and Difference*, trans. Joan Stambaugh (New York: Harper & Row, 1969), 58.

that keeps in concealment."[10] To think of the ontological difference in a metaphysical context precludes any historical perspective: the metaphysical First is a conquest over becoming, time, history. To step back from metaphysical constructions to their phenomenological destruction[11] allows us to think of the ontological difference in its historical process (*Austrag*). Phenomenologically the "is" of beings is one mode, ever new, in which Being appears in, or gives itself over to, beings. The step backward from the metaphysical to the phenomenological version of the difference not only allows us to think the possibility of history but also to think Being otherwise than as the most universal ground of beings. Even more, phenomenologically it is "impossible to represent 'Being' as the general characteristic of particular beings." Being has a thoroughly historic character: "Physis, Logos, Hen, Idea, Energeia, Substantiality, Objectivity, Subjectivity, the Will, the Will to Power, the Will to Will"[12] as well as Technology are names for a mode of self-disclosure of Being by which it shows and hides itself at the same time. Thus the question arises whether instead of a representable universality something all-pervading (*etwas Durchgängiges*) comes to light "which pervades Being's destiny from its beginning to its completion."[13] This all-pervading aspect is the duplicity of concealment and unconcealment throughout the figures in which Being has historically been represented.

There is one domain among beings that thematizes explicitly this simultaneity of concealment and unconcealment, namely, the symbol. In a symbol a manifest sense points toward a hidden sense, and this reference requires interpretation. The symbolic realm is defined by this "double sense." It is the realm in which the question of Being shows itself to be inseparable from the hermeneutics of veiling and unveiling. This trait proper to the symbol is pre-

---

10 Ibid., 63; 65 (translation slightly modified).

11 The title of the unpublished section of *Being and Time* was to be: "Basic Features of a Phenomenological Destruction of the History of Ontology According to the Guiding Thread of the Problem of Temporality" (Martin Heidegger, *Being and Time*, trans. John Macquarrie and Edward Robinson [New York: Harper, 1962], 39).

12 Heidegger, *Identität und Differenz*, 64; *Identity and Difference*, 66.

13 Ibid., 66; 67.

served in the etymology of the word itself: *symballein* designates the movement by which two elements (the two shards of a *tessera hospitalis*) are "joined together," literally "thrown together." Without rehearsing here analyses which have been carried out elsewhere,[14] let it suffice that it is in this literal sense in which the adjective "symbolic" comes to be coextensive semantically with the Aristotelian "energetic" that the title "symbolic difference" has to be understood. To the metaphysical understanding of the difference the symbol is paradigmatic of *what* it manifests and occultates at the same time; to the phenomenological understanding of the difference it is paradigmatic of *how* it signifies. In a metaphysics of *analogia entis* and participation, it is the first cause that is both revealed and hidden by its effects; in a phenomenology which has taken the step backward from onto-theological constructions, it is symbolization as such, that in-between the first sense (present) and the second sense (absent) which is both revealed and hidden in the historic constellations of truth. The phenomenological difference does not eliminate, or disprove, or reject metaphysics, it surmounts or surpasses (*verwinden*) it. In his latest writings Heidegger points clearly to a way in which the phenomenological difference preserves, while still overcoming, the metaphysical difference.[15] Ontol-

---

14 Besides the article mentioned in n. 7, see a series of four articles in *Cahiers internationaux de symbolisme* 21 (1972): 51–77; 25 (1974): 99–118; 27 (1975): 103–20; 29/30 (1976): 145–69. [For the first, second, and fourth of these texts, see this volume, 7–42, 43–76, 77–104, respectively.—Eds.]

15 Schematically, the metaphysical difference is that between beings and beingness (*das Seiende-Seiendheit*), and the phenomenological difference is that between beingness and Being (*Seiendheit-Sein*). The two are preserved by "the difference between 'being' as the being of beings, and 'being' in respect of its proper sense, that is, in respect of its truth (the clearing)" (Martin Heidegger, *Unterwegs zur Sprache* [Pfullingen: Neske, 1965], 110; *On the Way to Language*, trans. Peter D. Hertz [New York: Harper & Row, 1971], 20). In *Zur Sache des Denkens*, the metaphysical difference appears between what is given and "givenness," whereas the phenomenological difference appears between presence and presencing, or again between "givenness" and *Es gibt* (Martin Heidegger, *Zur Sache des Denkens* [Tübingen: Niemeyer, 1969]; *On Time and Being*, trans. Joan Stambaugh [New York: Harper & Row, 1972], 5). Thus Heidegger speaks of the "enduring truth" of metaphysics (Martin Heidegger, *Zur Seinsfrage* [Frankfurt: Klostermann, 1956], 35; *The Question of Being*, trans. William Kluback and Jean T. Wilde [New York: Twayne, 1958], 91).

ogy can be both ousiology and phenomenology. The latter does not abolish the former, although it destroys its constructions by asking how Being has come to be understood as constant presence. The symbol is paradigmatic for the phenomenological understanding of the ontological difference because of its referential nature and the interpretive effort that it requires to be comprehended. This is the first element of the symbolic difference.

It is the second element that brings us into the realm of human practice. A symbol requires some kind of action in order to be understood; unless one actually joins the maenads in their frenzied Bacchanalia one will never understand the symbolic reality of Dionysiac dissection and regeneration. A symbol, to be understood, requires a type of doing as its practical *a priori*. In Heidegger's vocabulary: In order to understand the essence of Being as releasement, one has to exist as released oneself. Releasement is the properly phenomenological attitude which lets things be so that in their being "Being itself" may show itself. In a phenomenon which is left to itself Being appears as letting-be. To recognize an attitude of existence as the condition for the understanding of Being is to recognize that it is neither Being nor beings that make man act, but a certain way in which Being appears as different from beings. In a symbol what is symbolized calls upon the hearer. Likewise, in a symbolic understanding of the difference, Being incites existence to "rejoin," *symballein*, its origin. The symbolic difference is that way to be of Being itself by which it appears as calling upon existence to let itself be in order to understand Being as letting-be. The phenomenological difference says how Being shows itself to thought; the symbolic difference says how it calls upon existence as upon its own. This calling, or this advent and address, pertains to the very structure of symbols: their second sense calls upon the interpreter and lets itself be explored by way of renewed existence. The symbolic difference thus says more than the ontological difference in either its metaphysical or its phenomenological version: it speaks of Being insofar as Being itself urges our existence upon a more originary road.

The third element locates the symbolic difference within phenomenology as practiced by Heidegger;[16] it also indicates that the practice required by the symbolic difference is irreducibly polymorphous. Indeed, the ontological difference when thought of within phenomenology reveals Being not as a selfsame universal but as multifarious. The preservation of the "metaphysical difference in the phenomenological difference" already indicates this severalness: Being appears as "beings," as "beingness," and as "Being itself." But "Being itself" is not a subsisting One. Heidegger is not an ontological monist. This is the point that makes the translation of his thinking into the political realm so difficult and, as we shall argue, subversive. The severalness of Being has been thematized first under the title of "History of Being," then as the *Geviert* (quite appropriately translated by Richardson as "fourfold polyvalence"). Being as symbolization, as concealment-unconcealment, must be thought of as an ever new event rather than as a subsisting origin in a sequence of causation. The symbolic difference carries the destruction of a representable First to its practical consequence, that is, to an existence without *archē* or *telos*, "without why," but one appropriated by ever new constellations of truth.

The active sense of *symballein*, the practical *a priori* in the understanding of the symbolized, and the severalness of the event of symbolization are the three characteristics of the symbolic difference as a phenomenological reformulation of the ontological difference.

The Symbolic Difference as Subversion

The symbolic difference so understood can be used as the missing link between a phenomenological ontology and a practical philosophy. It is totally correct to say, as one commentator does,

16 Until his latest writing, Heidegger maintains that it is "Being of beings in its unconcealedness and concealedness" which is "the thing itself" in accordance with the principle of phenomenology (Heidegger, *Zur Sache des Denkens*, 87; *On Time and Being*, 79). That Heidegger always considered his thinking to be phenomenological is underlined for instance in *Unterwegs zur Sprache*, 121–22 (*On the Way to Language*, 38–39).

that Merleau-Ponty and Heidegger have "undercut all of what Heidegger would call the metaphysical theories concerning the relation between what is to be thought and what is to be done or achieved politically."[17] The same author also rightly states that "the realm of politics is a derivative realm, and the legitimacy of conduct in this realm is determined by principles which do not, in the final analysis, belong to it." Political philosophy is derivative of ontology. Yet I doubt that the enduring political preoccupation behind Heidegger's thinking is with establishing the "essential characteristic of legitimate, effective political conduct."[18] The phenomenological destruction has concrete consequences that invalidate, and finally reverse, the grounding of political conduct: legitimation cannot mean, for Heidegger, referring action to some primordial ground or ultimate reason. The reversal of the essence of reason, or of foundation, results directly from the way in which the symbolic difference has appeared to us: it is not beings that call for a ground, but Being as the "groundless ground" which calls upon existence. Such reversal is literally a subversion, an overthrow (*vertere*) from the foundations (*sub-*). The symbolic difference, as the middle term that carries the phenomenological destruction into practical subversion, translates the "turn" in thinking into an "overturn" in action. The categories for understanding such action, as I see them, are at least five: (1) the abolition of the primacy of teleology in action; (2) the abolition of the primacy of responsibility in the legitimation of action; (3) action as a protest against the administered world; (4) a certain disinterest in the future of mankind, due to a shift in the understanding of destiny; (5) anarchy as the essence of the "memorable" requiring thought as well as of the "do-able" requiring action.

(1) *Teleology*. The symbolic difference would fail as an operational concept if it did not help us to think the *abolition of teleology in practice*. But phenomenologists of religions tell us that conduct induced by symbols has indeed no goal; the "great time," *magnum tempus*, which recurs with every festivity contains its own goal,

---

17 Bernard P. Dauenhauer, "Renovating the Problem of Politics," *Review of Metaphysics* 29 (June 1976): 629.
18 Ibid., 628, 639.

namely, having a great time. Heidegger borrows from Meister Eckhart the expression "living without why" in order to suggest this practical abolition of teleology. He also borrows from Nietzsche, whose thought of the eternal recurrence, he writes, "eternalizes the lack of a final goal."[19] Goalless action thus is not only the condition for thinking the symbolic difference, it is also its consequence. Being shows itself as releasement only to an existence that is itself perfectly released; and to think Being as releasement renders existence released. If there is political thinking in Heidegger, its elaboration has to take into account this release from purpose in action. The strict reciprocity between the thought of Being and existential letting-be provides the critical—both crucial and discriminating—access to the political dimension implied in the phenomenological version of the ontological difference and made explicit by its symbolic reformulation. Besides the scarce allusions to Eckhart or Nietzsche, some better known phrases in Heidegger point to the same abolition of teleology in practice, for instance "woodpaths." These are paths of peregrination toward originary Being, he says, but they lead nowhere:

> "Wood" is an old name for forest. In the wood are paths which mostly wind along until they end quite suddenly in an impenetrable thicket. They are called "woodpaths." Each goes its peculiar way, but in the same forest. Often it seems as though one were like another. Yet it only seems so. Woodcutters and forest rangers are familiar with these paths. They know what it means to be on a woodpath.[20]

Being and language call existence upon a road, but this road has no other goal than the origin of Being and language, which is manifold and which is so close to us that it is not a goal at all. Heidegger's

---

19 Martin Heidegger, *Nietzsche*, 2 vols. (Pfullingen: Neske, 1961), 1: 437.

20 Martin Heidegger, *Holzwege* (Frankfurt: Klostermann, 1950), 3; *Early Greek Thinking*, trans. David F. Krell and Frank A. Capuzzi (New York: Harper & Row, 1975), 3–4 (with one change in the translation). Hannah Arendt, "Martin Heidegger at Eighty," *The New York Review of Books*, Oct. 21, 1971, 51, says of the thinking so described: "One cannot say that it has a goal"; it is not conducive to "reaching a goal sighted beforehand and guided thereto. … The metaphor of 'woodpaths' hits upon something essential."

thinking about human action is no more a "practical philosophy" than his thought of Being is an "ontology." The most prominent treatise of "practical philosophy" in the Western tradition begins with a declaration of faith in teleology: "Every art and every investigation, every action and pursuit, is thought to aim at some good," Aristotle writes in the *Nicomachean Ethics*. But in "thinking" about human action practice will no longer be defined exclusively as purposive activity. The paths upon which existence finds itself engaged when it thinks Being out of symbols and as *symballein* "end in an impenetrable thicket." They lack an assignable end.

In other words, such an existence is already misunderstood when it is pressed to produce reasons for its behavior. If it were possible to dismantle the entire machinery of behavior, of goal-directed actions and their evaluation of inner motivations and outer determinations, if action could be thought of otherwise than as strategy, then thinking would introduce into practical philosophy what it has already become accustomed since Heidegger to discover in ontology: that each path "goes its particular way, but in the same forest. Often it seems as though one were like another. Yet it only seems so."

Traditionally the normative concept of teleology serves to regulate and eventually legitimize human conduct. It makes acceptable conduct depend on the rational establishment of an end that is thought to be good or desirable if achieved. But if conduct induced by symbols has no goal, then there are indeed moments when we dare renounce the dominance of meaning and purpose. Those are the moments in which we adhere to symbols and in which Being manifests itself as symbolization. Striving and performing are basic characteristics of existence only if, prior to any practical theory, Being is fixed into causal schemes. Only upon the condition of such a calculative ontological *a priori* does human action exhibit a natural proclivity toward ends, toward final causes. One may wonder whether the description of "care" in *Being and Time*[21] and the insis-

---

21 "Care" is "being ahead of oneself—being already in...—being alongside with..." (Heidegger, *Sein und Zeit* [Halle: Niemeyer, 1941], 196; *Being and Time*, 241).

tence on projection[22] have entirely left this teleological perspective behind. In later writings, though, the "without why" is precisely introduced to restrict the domain of the *a priori* principle that nothing is without reason, that is, without a cause:

> We see ourselves brought before a remarkable state of affairs: something, the rose, is, to be sure, not without reason, and it is nevertheless without why. Something falls within the range of validity of the commonly conceived Principle of Sufficient Reason. The same something falls out of the range of the strictly conceived Principle of Sufficient Reason.[23]

This principle commonly states that nothing is without reason, but "strictly conceived" it states that nothing is without why. All things certainly have their causes, they have a "because"; but there are phenomena that have no "why." Even the abolition of teleology in action seems to be clearly seen by Heidegger as a result of this critique of the principle of reason: "Man, in the most hidden ground of his Being, truly is only when in his own way he is like the rose—without why. We cannot pursue this thought any further here, however."[24] This last sentence reveals a remarkable shyness of a thinker before the practical consequences—subversion by goalless action—of his own thought.

(2) *Responsibility*. The thought of the symbolic difference also displaces responsibility. However complex the problems connected with the concept of responsibility may be (its role in legal and moral philosophy, the frequent identification of responsibility and liability to punishment, the understanding of freedom which thoroughly commands this concept, etc.), it seems to always imply a personal commitment (the Latin *spondere* means "to promise"; the Greek *sponde* is a "libation" or a vow) which one can be summoned to

---

22 "Understanding projects the being of existence upon its 'for-the-sake-of-which' [*Worumwillen*]"; however, "projecting has nothing to do with comporting oneself towards a plan that has been thought out" (Heidegger, *Sein und Zeit*, 145; *Being and Time*, 185).

23 Martin Heidegger, *Der Satz vom Grund* (Pfullingen: Neske, 1957), 73.

24 Ibid.

account for. A responsible person is able and ready to respond to such a summons and thereby to legitimize his doings. He is answerable to others for his dealings. Now, the acknowledgment of a summons is also at the very heart of the symbolic difference. What is "symbolic" about the difference is precisely the call by which Being claims a certain mode of existence from man and thus calls him upon another road. On this other road we shall not be surprised if we experience a transvaluation of responsibility. Is the counting of duties and rights and the accounting for performances and wrongs not thoroughly calculative in nature? If the origin of the summons appears to be Being itself, must responsibility not be thought of otherwise than in terms of accountability? But what would be a nonmetaphysical understanding of responsibility?

> Unexpectedly it may happen that thinking finds itself called upon to ask: ...what do you make of the Difference if Being as well as beings appear by virtue of the Difference, each in its own way? To do justice to this question we must first assume a proper position face to face with the Difference. Such a confrontation becomes manifest to us once we accomplish the step back.[25]

The step backward that brings us into the proper position for the thought of Being displaces responsibility so that it no longer means accountability but respondence. It no longer refers to contents and actions "for" which one may be held accountable, but it designates a way of life. The "for" disappears from sight altogether. This does not mean that no one is ever responsible for any decision, action, or outcome. The displacement locates the question of responsibility on another level; it puts man into another position. The proper position out of which the Difference can be thought is that of response

---

25 Heidegger, *Identität und Differenz*, 61; *Identity and Difference*, 63–64. The step back is a step out of the problematic of legitimation: the question of metaphysical ontology is "a question of the legitimation of the Being of beings" (Heidegger, *Zur Seinsfrage*, 17; *The Question of Being*, 55). One does not surmount metaphysics, Heidegger adds, by constructing other forms of legitimation, that is, by turning to some other figure (*Gestalt*) than the "human essence as the previously unique form of the legitimation of the real" (*Zur Seinsfrage*, 24; *The Question of Being*, 69).

and correspondence. To what? To "the calling of the Difference."[26] Thus in the phenomenological difference, response and correspondence are attitudes of thinking: Being as the Difference calls upon thought so that in response it may think the Difference as it appears in historical events or in speech events.

In the symbolic difference, response and correspondence are attitudes not only of thinking but of *doing*. The practical transformation of responsibility is rooted in Heidegger's notion of the address. What happens to responsibility when response and correspondence are mediated by the symbolic difference and are understood practically? What kind of doing results from the displacement of responsibility? Heidegger comes amazingly close to describing such practical consequences when he comments on Nietzsche's doctrine of the Eternal Recurrence. He quotes the following lines from *The Will to Power:* "Let us think this thought in its most terrible form: existence as it is, without meaning or aim, yet recurring inevitably without any finale into nothingness; the Eternal Recurrence."[27] Then Heidegger writes: "This thought [of the Eternal Recurrence] thinks beings in such a way that out of the whole of beings a constant call reaches us." This call, he says, not only "eternalizes the lack of a final goal," as already stated, but it also requires a decision from man, an active response.[28] In regard to the thought of the symbolic difference this active response is easy to describe: it consists in nothing other than *introducing into practice the eternal lack of a final goal*; it consists in the existential "yes" to the abolition of teleology. This displacement of responsibility—sheer response to the constant call out of the whole of beings—can only be labeled as irresponsible by calculative thinking. In Nietzsche's vocabulary, it gives birth to the Dionysian child.

In Meister Eckhart's vocabulary, responsibility as it is ordinarily understood is utter servitude: "Those who seek something with their

---

26 Martin Heidegger, *Unterwegs zur Sprache*, 30; *Poetry, Language, Thought*, trans. Albert Hofstadter (New York: Harper & Row, 1971), 207.

27 Friedrich Nietzsche, *The Will to Power*, trans. Walter Kaufmann and R. J. Hollingdale (New York: Random House, 1967), 35 (with one minor change in the translation).

28 Heidegger, *Nietzsche*, 1: 437.

actions, those who act for a why, are bondsmen and hirelings."[29] "If you ask a genuine man who acts out of his own ground: 'Why are you doing what you do?' he will reply, if his answer is as it should be: 'I do it because I do it.'"[30] The thought of the phenomenological difference takes the concept of responsibility altogether out of the context of action and interprets it as a response in thought to the advent of Being in beings. The symbolic difference, on the other hand, reintroduces responsibility into action, but as a respondence to the practical summons to exist originarily. In this reappropriation responsibility is freed from the metaphysical preoccupation with legitimation of action. Whatever I do, "I do it because I do it."

(3) *Protest.* Such action is assuredly the most powerful protest against the technologically organized universe. Pierre Klossowki, commenting on Nietzsche's *circulus vitiosus deus,* calls such abolition of sense and goal "the blossoming of a delirium," *l'épanouissement d'un délire.*"[31] Indeed, the abolition of teleology and the displacement of responsibility are harmful. How could society *function* if Eckhart's "without why," Nietzsche's "eternal recurrence," and Heidegger's ontological difference understood as *symballein* were to be taken seriously? What happens to the commonwealth "when the most powerful thought occurs to one, then to many, then to all?"[32] Now that, in one form or another, it *has* occurred to *some* (at least Eckhart, Nietzsche, and a few Heideggerians), it launches a literally subversive attack against the Aristotelian question, "What is the *function* of man?" as well as against the universally shared interest in the orderly functioning of collectivities.

Heidegger's protest against the technologically organized world is the aspect of his thought most frequently solicited by those of his

---

29 Meister Eckhart, *Die Deutschen Werke,* ed. Josef Quint, 5 vols. (Stuttgart: Kohlhammer, 1936–76), 2: 253.

30 Ibid., 1: 92.

31 Pierre Klossowski, "Circulus vitiosus," in *Nietzsche aujourd'hui?,* 2 vols. (Paris, Union Générale d'Éditions, 1973), 1: 101; see also his *Nietzsche et le cercle vicieux* (Paris: Mercure de France, 1969), *passim.*

32 Friedrich Nietzsche, *Werke: Kritische Gesamtausgabe,* ed. Giorgio Colli and Mazzino Montinari, 8 vols. (Berlin: De Gruyter, 1967–77), 2: 306, n. 11; cf. Heidegger, *Nietzsche,* 1: 345.

followers who want to elaborate a political philosophy on the basis of his phenomenological destruction.[33] Here again the discovery of the symbolic difference only makes explicit the practical implications of this destruction which remain hidden in Heidegger. It tries to think of individuals as linked by the origin symbolized by Being and language; such originary existence, if it is lived concretely, upsets technological functioning.

Technology has never been an object of condemnation for Heidegger. In the interview already quoted he says that technology indeed "tears man more and more away from the earth and uproots him," and yet Heidegger does not see the situation of man in a technological world as "a fate, inescapable and impossible to disentangle."[34] This stand is in agreement with the essay "The Question of Technology," in which he says that "there is no demonry about technology, but only the mystery of its essence."[35] The essence of technology, "provocation and challenge to nature," is not itself technological, rather it is the mode in which the truth of Being is preserved for our times. Technology is one mode of unconcealment. Heidegger calls a mystery whatever conceals itself while at the same time it shows itself. Technology conceals and discloses the truth of Being in this fashion. As a constellation of truth, technology is both dangerous (it is the supreme provocation) and salutary (we have no other access to the truth of Being than through technology). It is probably not by chance that Hei-

---

33 Otto Pöggeler, *Philosophie und Politik bei Heidegger* (Freiburg: Alber, 1972), 43–67. According to Pöggeler, Heidegger agrees with the reform Marxists on at least four points: the critique of totalitarianism, the opposition between reason and nature, science as an ideology, and the claim to theory as protest (40–41). See also the more elaborate treatment of the political implications of Heidegger's critique of technology in Palmier, *Les écrits politiques de Heidegger,* 213–93.

34 Heidegger, "Nur noch ein Gott kann uns retten," 206, 214. Such disentanglement is precisely the task of "the other thinking" (*das andere Denken*), of which Heidegger says: "I do not know how this thinking may become efficacious. It may well be that the path of a thought today leads to silence, in order to preserve thinking from becoming sold out [*verramscht*] within a year" (ibid., 212). Nevertheless, Heidegger anticipates such an efficacy, "perhaps in 300 years." The repeated and deliberate "I do not know" thus does not exclude a practical dimension of his thought; Heidegger only wants to avoid that terrain.

35 Martin Heidegger, *Vorträge und Aufsätze* (Pfullingen: Neske, 1954), 20.

degger first developed this ambiguous character of technology in the lecture course already mentioned, *An Introduction to Metaphysics*, given only one year after his resignation from the university rectorate. In these lectures technology ceases to be thought of as a masterable tool, although the notion of *Gestell* (frame or constellation) is not yet reached.

Heidegger is one among contemporary philosophers who shows that asking questions is no small matter; his protest against the technologically administered world precisely consists in questioning the essence of that world. As in the life of Socrates the questioning is the protest (except that the Athenian senate perceived this subversion through inquiry better than the German chancelleries after 1935). Yet one can go further ahead in actual protest without falling back into idealist constructions. The step ahead becomes thinkable with the symbolic difference. Protest then becomes an imperative for openness to new constellations of truth: Exist in such a way that new epochs of disclosure may unite you to the manifold origin of Being and language. Why is technological man necessarily unable to live according to such an imperative? Because it requires detachment, *Abgeschiedenheit*. The *praxis* of calculative thinking is technology, whereas the *praxis* of meditative thinking is detachment. Heidegger follows Trakl in the expectation of a new breed, "the breed, not yet carried to term, whose stamp marks future generations. The gathering power of detachment holds the unborn generation beyond all that is spent, and saves it for the coming rebirth of mankind out of the originary."[36] The protest that hastens this coming rebirth acts not through strategies but through detachment. Then the "there is," the *es ist* of the ontological difference, in its metaphysical understanding, "takes its leave" (*Abschied*). Detachment is the practical protest which eventually produces a breed detached from metaphysical ontology and its remains. After the abolition of teleology and the displacement of responsibility, detachment is the principal criterion left for verifying which path is aberrant and which is not. One has to be perfectly detached in order

36 Heidegger, *Unterwegs zur Sprache*, 67; *On the Way to Language*, 185 (with minor changes in the translation). The next quote is taken from 154 of the German, 54 of the translation.

to bring about a generation detached from metaphysics. "Protest" thus recovers its primitive meaning, which is to "testify" to truth.

(4) *Human Destiny.* Heidegger's thinking seems to be deeply concerned with the future of man. In our century the total provocation of nature has led to "the all-out challenge to secure dominion over the earth," he says.[37] Yet provocation and challenge as the ultimate forms of Western metaphysics not only reveal its essence but also point toward a new beginning: "The completion of metaphysics as the essential fulfillment of modern times is an end only since its historical ground is already the transition into another beginning."[38] Texts about the imminence of a new era—and about Heidegger's own role in it—abound. But in insisting greatly upon his concern with our future one easily misses another displacement that occurs in Heidegger's thinking, namely, that of the understanding of destiny. The displacement of destiny, away from man, can even be traced as the guiding thread throughout his writings.

In his first period, Heidegger raises the question of Being as that of the "meaning of Being." This was also the vocabulary used by such neo-Kantians as Dilthey and Rickert. But since the talk about meaning seemed to tie understanding as an existentiale to values and to valuing, Heidegger speaks, in his second period, with a less humanistic ring, of *alétheia*, "the truth of Being." Paradoxically, the displacement away from man occurs with a new emphasis on history: "recollection in metaphysics as a necessary epoch in the history of Being gives us food for thought: that and how Being determines the truth of beings in each case."[39] In this second period, Being is understood as "sending." Destiny no longer refers to man's past or future, but rather Being destines realms or epochs of possible life and thought toward man. These epochs cannot be planned or fabricated, the future is not a matter of human powers: "Recollection of the history of Being entrusts historical humanity with the task of becoming aware that the essence of man is released to the

---

37 Heidegger, *Unterwegs zur Sprache*, 212; *On the Way to Language*, 105.

38 Heidegger, *Nietzsche*. 2: 29.

39 Ibid., 481; *The End of Philosophy*, trans. Joan Stambaugh (New York: Harper & Row, 1973), 75. The following quote is taken from 482 of the German, 76 of the translation.

truth of Being before any human dependency on powers and forces, predestinations and tasks." In his third period Heidegger abandons this reference to *alétheia* and the history into which man's essence is released. Now releasement is said to be "the event of Being," it no longer refers to man at all. The preoccupation with the future of man ceases altogether: Being as the appropriating event is thought of "without regard for a foundation of Being out of beings,"[40] that is, outside of systems and theses, and not for the sake of man.

This more and more radical disinterest in man's destiny as the titles "meaning of Being," "truth of Being," "event of Being" suggest, this antihumanism in other words, has political consequences. To develop the political implications of Heidegger's thinking, as some authors do,[41] chiefly from the "setting into work" of truth (second period) misses the mutation of the understanding of destiny into the event of *Es gibt* (third period). By this radicalization "thinking stands in and before That which has sent the various figures of epochal Being. This, however, what sends us Appropriation, is itself unhistorical, or more precisely without destiny." "One cannot speak here of a why. Only the 'that'—that the history of Being is in such a way—can be said."[42]

---

40 Heidegger, *Zur Sache des Denkens*, 2; *On Time and Being*, 2 (translation slightly modified).

41 Alexander Schwan, *Politische Philosophie im Denken Heideggers* (Cologne: Westdeutscher Verlag, 1965). For Schwan, the key text is: "One essential way in which truth establishes itself in the beings it has opened up is truth setting itself to work. Another way in which truth occurs is the act that founds a political state" (Heidegger, *Holzwege*, 50; *Poetry, Language, Thought*, 61–62). Pöggeler is probably right in assuming that if in the lectures "On the Origin of the Work of Art," from which these lines are taken, Heidegger analyzes only the first of the two ways in which truth occurs, and if the analysis of the second way, the political deed, was not carried out, this omission is probably "due to the political circumstances" in 1936 (Pöggeler, *Philosophie und Politik bei Heidegger*, 122). See also n. 58, below. The expression "antihumanism," much popularized by Althusser, refers to Heidegger's "Gegen den Humanismus," in his *Platons Lehre von der Wahrheit* (Bern: Francke, 1947), 75; trans. Edgar Lohner in Richard M. Zaner and Don Ihde, eds., *Phenomenology and Existentialism* (New York: Putnam, 1973), 158.

42 Heidegger, *Zur Sache des Denkens*, 44, 56; *On Time and Being*, 41, 52. It is out of the later writings that one may challenge Harries's statement: "Heidegger's understanding of destiny rules out all attempts to draw anarchistic consequences from *Being and Time*" (Harries, "Heidegger as a Political Thinker," 651).

The event of the There is (*Es gibt*) is the extreme *symballein*. "That" which gives Being plays itself out: not in henological self-sufficiency, but in ever new topological multiplicities. The ahistorical, always finite "event" of Heidegger's latest writings, when translated by means of the symbolic difference into action, produces *playful disinterest in the future of mankind*. The event not only stops the history of Being, but it also cancels the three temporal ecstasies of existence (first period). The event brings man into authentic time, the Now. This radicalization which results from the *Es gibt* is eminently political. The event brings man into his ownmost by abolishing the last enemy of freedom, time as ecstatic temporality (first period) and as cultural history (second period). As in Nietzsche's doctrine of the eternal recurrence, the playful Now puts an end to the struggle to decide what man's next world will be like.

(5) *Anarchy*. The origin symbolized by Being and language is multiple and finite. It is not the principle of things, the one and simple *archē*. It is not a principle at all, rather it is anarchic. This same character must pertain to the practice of *symballein*, peregrine identity with the origin.

In "The Origin of the Work of Art" Heidegger explains that the word "origin" must be understood literally, as a leap (*Ursprung* means "primal leap"). In an artwork, for instance, truth sets itself into work with a leap. The artwork founds a constellation of references and thereby brings truth into being. This rise of truth in a constellation is always other and always new. *The origin is always other and always new*. As such it requires a decision from man: Do we give heed to the sway of the origin or not? In the earlier writings an either/or is urged upon our existence: whether the origin appears as manifold origination or as first causation is decided by a way of existing. Heidegger wants us to exist according to the rise of truth which is historical, that is, ever new: "Are we in our existence historically at the origin?"[43] The origin is seen as the multifarious emergence of the phenomena around us. In the later writings this understanding is modified only insofar as the historical dimension recedes. Heidegger quotes from Goethe: "Look for nothing behind

---

43 Heidegger. *Holzwege*, 64; *Poetry, Language, Thought*, 78.

phenomena: they themselves are what is to be learned."[44] In conversation he also quotes from René Char: "Give but a quick look on the wave casting its anchor in the sea." Char calls the poet "the great Beginner" whose word is the ever changing origin. "Poetry is of all clear waters the one that lingers the least with the reflection of its bridges."[45] The understanding of the origin as an appropriating event in which finite constellations of truth assemble and disassemble themselves is not monistic; to eliminate all remnants of metaphysical ontology Heidegger says that "It," the origin which grants Being, is a *neutrale tantum*. It is not Being itself, rather it grants Being in ever new articulations. The origin as "It" which grants Being defies monism.

Translated by the symbolic difference into practical thinking, the anarchic essence of *Es gibt* defies fixed social constellations. In a symbol the origin beckons man upon a road made of ever new beginnings. His practice espouses discontinuity. This has some concrete consequences, among other things, for the understanding of authority. As suggested earlier, the structure of metaphysical ontology is the same in theoretical and in practical philosophy: in either discipline beings are seen as organized in relation to a *princeps*, which means "principle," but also the "prince." If symbols point to an origin which does not satisfy the requirements of the principle of reason, that is, if the symbolic difference is essentially anarchic, then the speculative ground for the legitimation of central authority is lost altogether. The middle term between Heidegger's treatment of the question of Being and a theory of the state, of law, property, etc. would then be anarchy. His thought, if it yields this political dimension, would thus introduce radical fluidity into social institutions so as to honor not only the concrete claims made by the symbols but also the revolutionary way in which Heidegger has reformulated the question of Being. Political thinking in accordance with *Seinsdenken* would be as critical of utopian constructions as

---

44 Heidegger, *Zur Sache des Denkens*, 72; *On Time and Being*, 65-66.

45 The first quote is taken from René Char, *La Parole en archipel* (Paris: Gallimard, 1962), 152, and the second from *Poèmes et Prose choisis* (Paris: Gallimard, 1957), 94. See also my article "Situating René Char: Hölderlin, Char, Heidegger, and the "There Is'," *boundary 2* 4 (1976): 513–34. [See this volume, 77–104.—Eds.]

of central authority. In either case it would denounce an underlying static ideal. Such ideals, together with extrinsic legitimations of power, have been destroyed by Heidegger's phenomenology.

It seems to me that theoretical anarchy,[46] as opposed to the principle of reason or of foundation, becomes thinkable at the end of an "epoch." This claim can be verified at the end of the Middle Ages (Meister Eckhart) and at the end of German Idealism (Nietzsche). Heidegger himself is aware of thinking the end of the entire Western tradition understood as one such epoch.[47] Whether Meister Eckhart saw the implications of some form of anarchy in his doctrine of releasement depends to a large extent on the still unsolved problem of his links to the Begard communities, who really lived a kind of "life without why." At any rate, his time, marked by the decline of the medieval order, was one of social experimentation. As for Nietzsche, he saw these practical implications clearly. His last years show patently what it meant for him to be a tempter (*ein Versucher*) making an attempt with truth (*einen Versuch mit der Wahrheit*). Heidegger, finally, was evidently mistaken about the convergence that he believed to witness during ten months between his emerging understanding of the origin as anarchic and the establishment of the new political power. In retrospect Eduard Spranger judged "the national movement of the students [in 1932] still genuine at the core, only undisciplined in its form":[48] Heidegger's error would thus have consisted in confusing a totalitarian regime with his own,

---

46 In "thinking," as it is understood by Heidegger, the distinction between theory and practice actually does not obtain.

47 This characterization of the entire Western tradition as one single epoch of metaphysics ("a deplorable stand taken by Heidegger," according to Paul Ricœur, *La Métaphore vive* [Paris: Seuil, 1975], 395) might be nuanced by the introduction of the category of "problematic" borrowed from Althusser. In our context: Meister Eckhart puts an end to the "mystical problematic" begun with Plotinus, and Nietzsche puts an end to the "transcendental problematic" begun with Kant. This does not mean that after these periods mystical (as in Angelus Silesius) and transcendental (as in Husserl) thinking is impossible. But the one Western metaphysical tradition is made of problematics which have their time. They may occasionally reappear within an already new problematic.

48 Eduard Spranger, "Mein Konflikt mit der national-sozialistischen Regierung," quoted in Fritz K. Ringer, *The Decline of the German Mandarins: The German Academic Community*, 1890–1933 (Cambridge, MA: Harvard University Press, 1969), 439.

more antiauthoritarian and anarchic expectations, which may have been prepared by the authentic elements in the youth movement.

The Ontic and the Ontological Loss of the Origin

At first sight Heidegger's later writings seem still less concerned with politics than some earlier ones. This impression is reinforced by his frequently declared inability—or unwillingness—to see any practical implication to his thinking. On closer examination, however, the reverse has appeared to be the case: the severalness of Being as well as the "symbolic" (in the etymological sense) essence of both Being and language become thinkable only in the contexts of the History of Being and still later of the Topology of Being. Again, Heidegger's proper, although hidden, political thinking appears only from the writings misleadingly entitled Heidegger II. Ontically, that is, in a description of innerworldly occurrences, this standpoint entails the practical abolition of *archē* and *telos* in action, the transvaluation of responsibility and destiny, and the protest against a world reduced to functioning within the coordinates of causality. Perhaps Heidegger's topological interpretation of Leibniz's principle that "nothing is without reason" (*nihil est sine ratione*) reveals most clearly the anarchic essence of his political thinking: to Leibniz's metaphysical tenet that everything has a "because" (*warum*) Heidegger opposes Meister Eckhart's "life without why" (*ohne warum*).[49]

The hermeneutical dilemma is remarkable: reading Heidegger forward, from the Fundamental Analysis of Being-There to the Topology of Being, one is left with the evidence of an "idealization of unity at the expense of plurality,"[50] that is, ultimately of the *Führer* principle. Reading Heidegger backward, from the Topology to the Fundamental Ontology, the picture is quite different: instead of a unitary concept of ground, the Fourfold; instead of the praise of

---

49 Heidegger, *Der Satz vom Grund*, 68 ff. See John D. Caputo, "Meister Eckhart and the Later Heidegger: The Mystical Element in Heidegger's Thought," *Journal of the History of Philosophy* 12 (1974): 479–94; 13 (1975): 61–80.

50 Harries, "Heidegger as a Political Thinker," 669.

"the hard will" (the main theme in Heidegger's eulogy of the Nazi hero Schlageter), releasement; instead of the integration of the university into the "fields of construction" (Heidegger's article in the student newspaper of June 1933), protest against technology and cybernetics; instead of the identification between the *Führer* and the law (Heidegger's article in the student newspaper of November 1933), anarchy.[51]

Since it took several decades to appropriately work out the question of Being, there can be no doubt that only the retrospective hermeneutics produces a correct understanding of Heidegger's overall problematic. Here is one illustration of the necessity of reading Heidegger backward: until 1947 such careful interpreters as Paul Ricœur and Mikel Dufrenne were still totally mistaken about the very basic drift of Heidegger's thinking.[52]

---

51 All three texts in Schneeberger, *Nachlese zu Heidegger,* 47–48, 63–64, 135–36. Palmier, *Les écrits politiques de Heidegger,* 124, addresses himself to the ambiguity of declaring the "state of Labour" (*Arbeitsstand*) "the sole German state of life" (*Lebensstand*): "This can be understood in line with Hitler's speeches, but it can also be elucidated out of Aristotle's *Physics,*" Palmier writes. It seems to me, however, that the safest way of substantiating in a positive fashion the intimate link between these texts and "the whole of Heidegger's problematic" (ibid., 125) is the restrospective hermeneutics which replaces, as we have tried to do, the utterances of 1933–34 in the context of Heidegger's one dominating problematic, the question of Being. All other elements are correctly understood only in relation to this one problematic.

52 Mikel Dufrenne and Paul Ricœur, *Karl Jaspers et la Philosophie de l'Existence* (Paris: Seuil, 1947), 327–31, 364–72. Heidegger is said to be a nihilist (306), who, with *Being and Time,* pretends to a doctrine of Being; however, the authors say, "we want to show that it is Jaspers who has a doctrine of Being in itself, whereas Heidegger has not emerged, as yet, from his preparatory works" (327). "Heidegger has confessed himself rather than manifested man... His philosophy climaxes in the heavily subjective experience of finitude and distress before the absence of God... His universal claims are betrayed by his private presuppositions" (329-330). "From the beginning Heidegger has locked himself up in the squirrel's cage. To him, transcending is no longer a method of deliverance, but the very project of prison itself" (364). His project is "nauseating" as it only knows of "one focal point," that is "the merely existent" (*l'existant brut*) (371–72). These lines are important: they show that to fully understand Heidegger's early problematic (cf. the first chapter of *Being and Time*) one has to be aware of its very latest treatment (in *On Time and Being*). More recently, however, Ricœur has written—and one can only agree—that "it is impossible to refer to the 'first' Heidegger without taking a stand regarding the 'latest' Heidegger" (*La métaphore vive,* 388).

From the vantage point of the later writings, the anarchic element as the key to Heidegger's enduring political thinking appears even in the early work. In *Being and Time* this element shows forth in the understanding of potentiality. The authenticity of human being-there is described in relation to "potentiality for being a whole": authentic existence becomes free for its own finitude in the anticipation of its death. "Anticipation turns out to be the possibility of understanding one's ownmost and uttermost potentiality for Being—that is to say, the possibility of authentic existence."[53] Originary potentiality thus reveals itself in the anticipation of death. The anticipatory resolution of human being-there is whole and authentic only in projecting itself toward its own total negativity. "Potentiality as an existentiale is the most originary and the ultimate positive way in which being-there is characterized ontologically."[54] But what is appropriated when existence becomes authentic? The possibility of one's own not being at all, Heidegger answers. Nothing is appropriated. In seeing the chief characteristic of authenticity in potentiality Heidegger clearly wants to eliminate the teleological structure from authentic existence. To be sure, death as the object of anticipation is a concretion of the teleological structure which is that of care in general. But to speak of death as one's ownmost possibility which has to be taken over always anew introduces an anarchic element into authenticity which is absent from the description of care. Because it anticipates death, potentiality is relationless, *unbezüglich*. Death is "the ownmost, relationless, unsurmountable potentiality."[55] Heidegger thus thinks authenticity as a relationless fullness of potentiality. Reality has a why and a what-for: "present at hand," it corresponds to a viewpoint of man, and "ready to hand," it is good for some usage by man. Correspondence and usefulness are the two ways according to which reality exhibits its teleological structure. "But higher than reality stands potentiality."[56] Why higher? Because the potential is never present at hand or ready to hand. Potentiality thus does not fall within the

---

53 Heidegger, *Sein und Zeit*, 263; *Being and Time*, 307.

54 Ibid., 144; 183 (translation slightly modified).

55 Ibid., 250; 294 (translation slightly modified).

56 Ibid., 38; 63 (the translators put "actuality" for *Wirklichkeit*).

coordinates of causality, that is, within the domain delimited by *archē* and *telos*.

The political consequences of this anarchic element in authentic existence as described in *Being and Time* are suggested by the very meaning of the word *Möglichkeit*, potentiality, as opposed to *Seinkönnen*, possibility: *Möglichkeit* derives from *mögen*, in the sense of *vermögen*, being able to do something. Its full meaning is preserved in *Macht*, power (which has the same root as "mechanics" and "magic"). I submit that Hannah Arendt's concept of power[57] contains an implicit reference to Heidegger's understanding of authenticity out of potentiality. Power thus would retain the anarchic essence of potentiality insofar as it results from agreement among actors and not from constraint upon the next, that is, insofar as it is opposed to sheer force or strength (*Gewalt*). To understand power out of anarchic potentiality would mean that power has no extrinsic purpose; that playfully reaching ever new social constellations is an end in itself; that its essence is boundless interplay without a direction imposed by authority. Interpreting Heidegger's early writings in the light of his understanding of potentiality and of the "power potential" which results from it yields quite a different kind of political implication in the project of a Fundamental Ontology than establishing parallels with the inaugural address as rector of the University of Freiburg. I agree, however, that the essentially anarchic thrust appears only on the condition of reading Heidegger backward, that is, of interpreting, as he did himself, his early writings out of the later ones. "As you began, so you will remain" (*Wie du anfingst, wirst du bleiben*, Hölderlin, *The Rhine*).

Finally, the elements for "the other politics" (consistent with "the other thinking") which have been sketched here allow for further specification of the more frequently invoked notion of setting-to-

---

57 Hannah Arendt, *The Human Condition* (Chicago: The University of Chicago Press, 1958), chap. 28, for instance: "Power is what keeps the public realm, the potential space of appearance between acting and speaking men, in existence" (200; italics added). It is true that this method of isolating "themes" in *Being and Time* is as questionable in our comparison with Arendt as it is in Harries's stretching of the "theme" of resolve. Any such treatment needs to be justified in a retrospective hermeneutics, as has been said.

work.[58] The essential trait of truth is said to lie in its setting itself to work in art, religion, philosophy as well as in the deed which grounds a political state. The phenomenology of this "trait" of truth aids in uncovering the ontological structure of politics, quite as *Being and Time* uncovered the ontological structure of human being-there. To limit Heidegger's political thinking to this "trait," however, would imply that phenomenology, for all its showing of essences, would have to remain speechless before the question, "What must I do?" A much better starting point for renovating the problem of politics in this line is the symbol; indeed, here practice is not derived from ontology but is its very condition: One has to exist in a certain way—according to the five characteristics developed above—in order to understand Being out of the symbolic difference. The abolition of teleology in practice is the ontic condition for understanding ontological an-archy, that is, for understanding the destruction of a hypostatized First. But the recognition of the paradigmatic status of the region of symbols allows us to raise the question of doing ontically as well as ontologically. It does so by approaching this question otherwise than in terms of political leadership and its legitimacy.

In a culture where philosophy has so radically abandoned its task of criticism as to cooperate with the existing system by unending

---

58 Schwan, *Politische Philosophie in Denken Heideggers*, very accurately describes this setting into work of truth. However, for Schwan the epitome of such setting into work is the totalitarian state. Schwan's point of departure is well founded, although insufficient: namely, that Heidegger's phenomenological destruction pulls the rug, so to speak, from underneath traditional political philosophy. But, as Palmier puts it, "for us, what counts is to understand how Schwan, starting from correct principles, has ended with absurd consequences" (*Les écrits politiques de Heidegger*, 152). See similar remarks in Pöggeler, *Philosophie und Politik bei Heidegger*, 121–25. Dauenhauer, "Renovating the Problem of Politics," wants to start from the same principles as Schwan and then show "the delimitation of the realm of politics from other realms of human expression" (639). But he merely outlines five elements that appear when "what Heidegger says about art is translated into the question of what is the political and is then conjoined with his reflection on meditative thought and technology": the historical, irreducibly manifold, speechlike, autonomous character of political action as well as the preservation of tradition which it must effectuate. These remarks happily correct Schwan, but they stop short of indicating a kind of politics in agreement with Heidegger's destruction of metaphysics.

enforcements of its technological rationale, Heidegger's destruction of metaphysics opens an alternative way of thinking of life in society. What indeed is a more powerful challenge to the merry-go-round of reason in the calculi that have usurped the title of philosophy, particularly in the Anglo-Saxon world, than to say no to philosophy's unconditional surrender to technology? The symbolic difference allows for the elaboration of an alternative type of political thinking. This is not a theory of the organization of man into collectivities. But it is certainly not the celebration of pure interiority either. Between a system of social constitution and its negation by spiritual individualism or apolitical solipsism there is room for a thinking about society which refuses to restrict itself to the pragmatics of public administration as well as to the romantic escapes from it. The "end of philosophy,"[59] which suspends ontological justifications of domination by depriving the political deed of exterior grounds for legitimation, radically puts into question institutionalized authority. This does not eliminate the task of preservation from the political realm. But the tradition to be preserved is that of the response, in thinking as well as in political conduct, to the ever new constellations of "the truth of Being." "The rebellious element in Heidegger's enterprise"[60] led him to hail, not the chief, but radical mutability in accordance with an understanding of Being as irreducibly manifold.

---

59 The expression "end of philosophy" appears first in the title "La fin de la philosophie et la tâche de la pensée," in *Kierkegaard vivant* (Paris: Gallimard, 1966), 167. Jean Beaufret quotes Heidegger as saying: "There is no philosophy of Heidegger, and even if there were to be something like that I would not be interested in this philosophy." (Martin Heidegger, *Essais et conférences* [Paris: Gallimard, 1958], viii).

60 Arendt, "Martin Heidegger at Eighty," 50.

The Ontological Difference and Political Philosophy

> Oute archein oute archesthai ethelo.
> I wish neither to govern nor to be governed.
> —Othanes, as quoted by Herodotus

In what follows I would like to point to some consequences of Heidegger's understanding of the ontological difference. Ultimately these consequences are of a practical and political order. The present paper will be limited to suggesting what kind of middle term, what "missing link," can coherently be established between Heidegger's treatment of the question of Being and a political philosophy. An outline of the more precise categories of action that result from such a reexamination of the ontological difference has been suggested elsewhere.[1]

It is to the clarification of the nature of such a missing link that this paper wants to contribute. To do so, it will start from a reflection on symbols. Why this preference? Symbols constitute that area of reality whose understanding requires a certain way of existing. To grasp the full meaning of a symbol a certain practice is required. Unless one plunges into the waters, jumps through the flames etc., the rejuvenating, purifying, initiatory effects attached to these symbols will not be comprehended. It is out of the question to treat any particular symbolism here; rather it will be shown how the practical *a priori* at work in the understanding of symbols provides a clue for the elaboration of categories of action in accordance with Heidegger's nonmetaphysical version of the ontological difference. Of the two versions of the ontological difference, metaphysical and phenomenological, only the latter allows for an adequate understanding of the referential character of symbols (in symbols a first, apparent meaning refers to a second, hidden meaning which is

---

1 "Political Thinking in Heidegger," *Social Research*, Vol. 45, No. 1 (Spring 1978), 191–221. [See this volume, 105–34.—Eds.]

explored through practice). Symbols will appear to be paradigmatic for the phenomenological reformulation of the ontological difference; insofar as in Heidegger the ontological difference, in order to be thought of, requires a certain practice, that is, a certain way of existing, I shall speak of the symbolic difference. The missing link between Heidegger's treatment of the question of Being and a political philosophy derived from it, I shall claim, is the "symbolic difference."[2]

The reciprocity between existence and thought is already present in *Being and Time*; it becomes explicit, however, only in Heidegger's later writings. There is, of course, some irony in wanting to develop a foundation of practical philosophy from Heidegger, who is probably the most unpolitical of all philosophers. Even more, the destruction of metaphysics ruins the very foundations upon which practical philosophy would traditionally be erected. Heidegger refrained from developing his political thinking beyond a few hints here and there in his works; this is probably due to several, and complex, reasons. At any rate, in his project of raising anew the question of Being for itself and out of itself Heidegger henceforth deprives practical philosophy of its metaphysical ground and at the same time suggests only by implication from what new grounds action might become thinkable. In order to integrate his suggestions into a theory I shall first show in what sense symbolic data are, by their very nature, understandable only through practice. Then I shall present an amphibology in the phenomenon of origin and thus substantiate what will be called the symbolic difference. Finally this latter concept will be verified on a broader scale out of some of Heidegger's remarks on language.

---

2 In an earlier series of four articles, all in French, I have examined the relation between symbols and language, symbols and the sacred, symbols and poetry, and finally symbols and human action, in: *Cahiers Internationaux de Symbolisme*, 21 (1972), 51–77; 25 (1974), 99–118; 27 (1975), 103–20; 29/30 (1976), 145–69. [For the first, second, and fourth of these texts, see this volume, 7–42, 43–76, 77–104, respectively.—Eds.]

I. Understanding Symbols Through Practice

If we take a step backwards to the origin, both in the etymological and the ontological sense, of the symbol, it will appear that, because of the particular ontological locus of the symbol, such a step from interpretation to foundation has consequences for the relation between the philosophy of Being and human action. This does not mean yet another attempt to derive 'ought' from 'is'—an enterprise which, after all, has had its time (exactly one hundred and forty years in the history of philosophy: from Kant's *Critique of Practical Reason* to Heidegger's *Being and Time*). Rather such a step back will reveal the two aspects of symbols necessary for the rethinking of political action after Heidegger's destruction of metaphysics. On the one hand symbols unite being and language in a peculiar way, they are things interpreted; thus they constitute that area of reality in which the question of the origin of being and speech arises explicitly and for its own sake. In other words, they require that we think the ontological difference. On the other hand the origin so uncovered addresses itself to human practice as much as to thought. Those phenomena in which a manifest meaning points towards a hidden meaning and which therefore require interpretation, thematize explicitly the concealed presence of what the tradition calls being in beings. But the inability of the doctrines of being, that is, of metaphysical ontologies, to think of Being otherwise than in causal schemes also makes them unable to recognize the paradigmatic nature of the ontological structure of symbols and consequently to acknowledge the practical dimension that the hermeneutics of symbolic data introduces into the question of Being. Symbols gather people together for some kind of activity. As the "second sense" becomes uncovered through practice, (for instance through labor, celebration, accusation and penance, combat, etc.), each group of constituted symbolisms, each symbol even, incites a specific behavior. By this incitive nature the recognition of full symbolic meaning founds specific actions for each given symbol. Action, though, is here not only a consequence of understanding, but also its condition. To be understood the full meaning of a symbol already requires an attitude and a way of action. I shall call symbolic difference that form of the ontological difference in which Being appears as requiring a certain attitude from thinking, that is, from existence, in order to be understood.

It is this reciprocity between ontology and practice which will open an alternative approach to political philosophy. Heidegger's attempts at reformulating the ground for action—scarce though they are in his writings—are indebted to a tradition that runs parallel to, while hardly encountering, the Aristotelian and Anglo-Saxon interest in the organization and well-being of the polity. To suggest such an alternative to the predominant approach to human action does not necessarily lead to apolitical solipsism. Quite the contrary. This alternate tradition of political thinking has other objectives, other ideas about life in community. The reciprocity between ontology and practice was already at the core of Meister Eckhart's teaching: "He who wants to understand my teaching of detachment must himself be perfectly detached."[3] In order to think Being as releasement one has to be perfectly released oneself.[4] This is one way to articulate the practical requirements that Being exacts when it shows itself to thought as the "second sense" symbolized by beings. Another way, still in the same tradition, consists in saying: "The task is to live in such a way that you must want to live again—you will anyway."[5] Meister Eckhart's doctrine of releasement and Nietzsche's doctrine of the Eternal Recurrence of the Same suggest the abolition of teleology in action; they recommend action "without why," without end, or purpose. In this tradition the paradigm of action is play. The hermeneutics of symbols engages upon a similar path.

The interpretation of symbols calls for a rethinking of the ontological difference. Although Heidegger mentions the title "ontological difference" more and more rarely, the relation between Being and beings, that is, phenomenology as the science of the Being

---

3 Meister Eckhart, *Die Deutschen Werke*, vol. II (Kohlhammer: Stuttgart, 1970), 109: "Der mensche, der diz begrifen sol, der muoz sêre abegescheiden sîn."

4 In my book *Meister Eckhart, Mystic and Philosopher* (Bloomington: Indiana University Press, 1978), I have defined mysticism as the experience of a disclosure of being which requires a certain attitude from man as its condition.

5 Friedrich Nietzsche, *Kritische Gesamtausgabe*, ed. Giorgio Colli and Mazzino Montinari (Berlin: De Gruyter, 1967), vol. V/2, n. 11(163), 407–08.

of beings, remains the sole subject matter of his thinking. This relation is reconsidered at several stages throughout his writings: after the 'turn' the question of Being is no longer worked out by "making one being—that which raises the question—transparent in its own being," but "without regard for a foundation of Being out of beings."[6] If the title "phenomenology," too, disappears in the later writings, this does not indicate a shift in Heidegger's attitude. Rather than negating phenomenology, he sees it as so closely linked to the elaboration of the question of Being that the title becomes superfluous (and misleading if it is understood simply as the examination of the structure of consciousness as well as of its experiences and contents). "Whence and how is it determined what must be experienced as 'the things themselves' in accordance with the principle of phenomenology? Is it consciousness and its objectivity or is it the Being of beings in its unconcealedness and concealment?"[7]

It is only from the way in which the question of Being is dealt with in the later writings, though, that a philosophy of human practice becomes thinkable out of the ontological difference. In these writings the Difference is precisely thought of in such a way that the understanding of Being results from a certain attitude in thinking and existing. However cryptic Heidegger's essays on language may be, they are the texts from which a new determination of action is possible. It is true that for him theories of the symbol pertain to, and indicate, late forms of representational thinking. Also, in order to think the essence of Being and the essence of language as one, Heidegger never speaks of the phenomenological difference, as we shall do. Our concept of symbolic difference applies not to practical philosophy immediately, but to the foundation of practical philosophy: it is in raising the question of foundations that one is most faithful to Heidegger. Our concept wants to situate human

6 The first quote is from *Sein und Zeit* (Halle: Niemeyer, 1941), 7, trans. John Macquarrie and Edward Robinson, *Being and Time* (New York: Harper & Row, 1962), 27; the second is from *Zur Sache des Denkens* (Tübingen: Niemeyer, 1969), 2, trans. Joan Stambaugh, *On Time and Being*, (New York: Harper & Row, 1972), 2. Both translations slightly modified.

7 *Zur Sache des Denkens*, 87, trans. 79. The same attitude towards phenomenology is explained in *Unterwegs zur Sprache* (Pfullingen: Neske, 1959), 121–22, trans. Peter D. Hertz, *On the Way to Language* (New York: Harper & Row, 1971), 38–39.

action in relation to ontology: it is neither Being nor beings that make man act, but a certain way in which Being appears different from beings. The symbolic difference is a modality of the ontological difference; in it *to on* neither founds *ta onta* nor merely presents them to thought, but makes itself known through a particular kind of human doing.

One difficulty in this reflection stems from the seeming heterogeneity of types of discourse that it brings together. The status of practical philosophy is ontic whereas that of the Difference is ontologic. But what we want to understand is precisely the ontological rooting of human action. Moreover "practice" will have to be understood in a very broad sense as joining thought and existence: "Thinking changes the world," Heidegger writes.[8] In the aftermath of the Heideggerian dismantlement of metaphysical constructions, a new approach to the foundation of political action is wanting. Political philosophy, the way the West has learned it from the Greeks, has been made impossible by Heidegger. With Heidegger's subversion of the *archē*, i.e., of governance and domination, life in the community appears as literally anarchic. Where, then, does ontology encounter the origin otherwise than as *archē*? In symbols. This privileged position of the symbolic realm has been described and justified in detail by Paul Ricœur. Still, Ricœur remains more interested in the properly hermeneutic dimension of the symbol, and lately of the metaphor, than in an ontological grounding of human practice that results from its interpretation. Such a grounding would appear to him as the "short route" towards a recollection of Being, whereas the strict pursuit of the hermeneutical disciplines alone takes the "long route"[9] through linguistic and semantic considerations. So,

---

8 *Vorträge und Aufsätze* (Pfullingen: Neske, 1954), 229; trans. by David F. Krell, *Early Greek Thinking* (New York: Harper & Row), 1975, 78.

9 Paul Ricœur, *Le Conflit des interprétations* (Paris: Seuil, 1969), 10; trans. Kathleen McLaughlin, *The Conflict of Interpretations* (Evanston: Northwestern University Press, 1974), 6. In *De l'interprétation. Essai sur Freud* (Paris: Seuil, 1965) Ricœur indicates three domains of preparation for such an ontological treatment: the symbol as the locus of the double sense (17); the symbol as the region where the fullness of language can be thought (79); the symbol as a concrete "mixed texture" (476–77). Eng. tr. *Freud and Philosophy: An Essay on Interpretation*, trans. Denis Savage (New Haven: Yale University Press, 1970), 7, 69–70 and 494–95.

the matter developed here—the interpretation of symbols as the middle term that links the philosophy of the ontological difference to political philosophy—seems novel to me. No critic of hermeneutical training will take offense that the guiding question, *How do Being and language originally appear to thought if the starting point for their examination is symbolic speech and action?*, introduces the mind into a circle which produces the answer: *To understand Being and language out of the symbol results in an originary action which is anarchic, without principle and purpose.*

II. Not One Origin, Two

Etymologically "symbol" indicates an operation of joining together. Symbolon designated a Greek object of recognition, initially a simple clay tablet broken into two, the halves of which were kept by the partners of a business transaction. To prove that an agreement had been concluded or hospitality offered (*tessera hospitalis*) the two shards only needed to be "joined together" (*symballein* literally means "throwing together"). This would reenact the former relationship. The symbol thus realized the link or unity between two people that it signified. It is in this literal sense that I use the adjective "symbolic." In Aristotelian terminology the same type of unity would be called "energetic." It so happens that this primitive meaning of the verb *symballein* suggests some decisive elements that will lead to a political philosophy as I have started to describe it: 1) A symbol is ordered towards some kind of oneness. By this active reunification which is the practical recovery of its origin, the symbol differs from all conventional signs whose meanings, because they are artificially added to some preexisting speech element, do not affect existence. 2) Grammatically *symballein* is a verb, not a noun or a proposition. By that the symbol differs from a myth—a story, or at least a sentence—whose element it may become. 3) The restitution of oneness, that is, the full grasp of what is symbolized, does not abolish the symbol. Thus it differs from rhetorical artifices by which one thing is told to suggest another that remains deliberately untold. In an allegory once the signified is grasped the signifier abolishes itself, but in a symbol the signified is not dissociable from the signifier. This continuity of meaning has made the symbol available to metaphysical and religious overdeterminations. 4) The full meaning of a symbol transcends its apparent meaning. But transcendence here is present in appearance. By such immanence the symbol differs from a metaphor which points beyond itself towards a meaning that it does not contain. 5) Both as a word and as an object the symbol 'is' what it signifies. It does not simply reflect oneness, it realizes it; a symbol is more than an image.

This list of five basic determinants—origin, process, subsistence, transcendence, and being—is traditional. It shows clearly an ambiguity in our claim that the symbolic data raise explicitly and for its own sake the question of the Difference between beings and their foundation or between language and its foundation. Indeed, what seems more tempting than to declare that the second sense of a symbol is its metaphysical ground? That is, what would be more tempting than to represent the Difference according to the old pattern of an analogy of being whereby the first, visible meaning of a symbol participates through deficient similarity and formal limitation in a second, invisible meaning which is also its ultimate cause? Such a construction relies on the principle of order, and it can be shown how this principle, transferred from Aristotle's *Metaphysics* to his *Ethics* and *Politics*, is at the bottom of the traditional Western representation of a polity. The ambiguity lies in the quest for foundation itself. This quest can be carried out through reference to a First (the substance, God, the Prince, the elected government) or through a phenomenological destruction (understood in the sense of Heidegger's plan for the unpublished part of *Being and Time:* "Basic Features of a Phenomenological Destruction of the History of Ontology According to the Guiding Thread of the Problematic of Temporality"). The latter considers less *what* this or that symbol signifies than *that* and *how* they signify. A metaphysical interpretation speculates about their content. For instance, the neo-Platonists thus speculated about the most appropriate divine names that they allowed to be inferred; today, such speculation is about the 'sacred.' The phenomenological interpretation, on the other hand, attempts to bring into sight their referential character as such. The metaphysical inquiry asks: How does the visible symbolize the invisible? The phenomenological inquiry asks: How do Being and language appear *in* the spread opened by symbolization? This step backwards from metaphysical to phenomenological foundation is thus a step into an understanding of Being, not as the supreme reason or ground of all that there is but as the opening within which manifestations of a symbolic kind are at all possible. Being is now the disclosedness, and in that sense the foundation, of the process of symbolization. Being lets symbols symbolize.

The same opposition between a metaphysic and a phenomenology of Being can be described by their respective understanding of the origin. Most symbolisms seem to speak of some primitive beginning of the world whose trace they preserve. When they are expanded into a myth the second sense that they suggest is often etiological: they relate how the gods made, visited, or saved the earth. Symbols constitute a metaphysically privileged domain of reality because they point to an ontotheological origin of things; they are, so to speak, the translucid, thinned out, spot in the fabric of the world through which its invisible cause shines forth, as for the Stoics the cosmic fire shone forth through the holes in the sky which we call stars. The symbolic reality, in this perspective, produces by itself a certain understanding of the origin or the principle of the universe. Being as the metaphysical origin of the world is thus identical with the second sense to which symbols point. But to the phenomenological questioning of the difference between the apparent and the hidden sense the origin appears different from that which is symbolized. The origin is closer to us, not distant. It is present insofar as it opens the very realm of symbolic reference. The object symbolized, be it the highest conceivable, recedes behind the way symbolization occurs. So understood phenomenology does not encounter, to answer either in the affirmative or in the negative, the question of a supreme being to whose omnipresence (as Tillich and others argue) all symbols would testify.

There are thus two ways to speak of the origin of the symbol. Metaphysically the origin is the principle and cause of all that appears; phenomenologically it is the very openness in which appearance occurs. A remark on the "long route" may localize this reduction more precisely. The dismantling of contents, which leads us to understand Being out of the process of symbolization and as its own origin, also constitutes the program of contemporary structuralist approaches to symbols and myths. The detour through linguistics and ethnology can rely on the human sciences insofar as these discover 'systems' of symbolisms, that is, a homogeneous plurality of elements which are related to each other and which form by their interactions an autonomous whole. Since their inner dependencies always follow the same simple rules, such systems can be discovered in very different cultures. Their elements, quantitatively limited and qualitatively stable, lend themselves to 'models' of interaction[10] which may eventually lead to the reconstruction of an element that is missing in a given narration. Such invariable patterns are obtained at the cost of dispensing with the meaning, or the sense, that constitutes a symbol; thus they certainly disrupt any metaphysical construction of an origin of such meaning. Whether this formalization escapes metaphysical presuppositions altogether is however another question; quite the contrary appears to be the case when the formalized structure is described as if this were now the most real reality.[11]

For two reasons the formal structures of symbolism should be localized epistemologically halfway between a metaphysical and a phenomenological understanding of origin: with the former they share the pretense to an unhistorical, all-encompassing explanation out of one true reality (no longer an ontotheological reality, but still, at least so it seems, a *maxime ens*), and with the latter they share the dismantling of symbolic contents, ontic contents as Heidegger would say. In the phenomenological destruction—after the 'turn' Heidegger speaks rather of "overcoming metaphysics," but the matter remains the same—the decisive moment is the repetition, *Wieder-holung*, of the question of Being. This is not raised out of a representable meaning, i.e., out of the "second sense"

---

10 E.g. Claude Lévi-Strauss, *Anthropologie structurale* (Paris: Plon, 1958), 306.

11 The extraordinary "Finale" of *L'Homme nu*, the last volume of Lévi-Strauss' *Mythologiques*, Paris 1971, 559–621 is very ambiguous on this question. On one hand we are told that philosophy will find no food in structuralism, that myths say nothing about the "order of the world" (571). But on the other hand structuralism is said to "discover behind things a unity and a coherence which the simple description of facts can never reveal" (614) and which is so powerful that its discovery inaugurates the twilight of man (620). I wonder if this is not a step from a metaphysics of meaning to one of structure.

in symbols, but out of their referential nature as such. This is what the destruction intends when it is carried into the symbolic field. Also it does not stop with a tableau of structural interactions between models but is carried further to eliminate the very question of a most real being from its method and to locate the question of Being within the referential nature itself. Being thus appears as coming to presence in the symbolic reference. Only such a continued interest in Being, but severed from myth and metaphysics by the discovery of structures, and such a continued dismantling of meaning, but replenished by the question of Being, will allow one to ground human action upon the symbolic difference. It is this concept of symbolic difference that has to be worked out now in order to understand why the phenomenology of symbols is the middle term or the "missing link" that permits one to ground a political philosophy on Heidegger's understanding of the ontological difference.

III. Ontological Difference and Symbolic Difference

The title "ontological difference" can be understood both metaphysically and phenomenologically. In either case it wants to answer the question, "What is Being?" If one asks in the traditional fashion what a being is "insofar" as it is, this way of questioning already contains the answer. The "insofar," *inquantum*, answers the question of Being by distinguishing between things and their fact of being (*on* and *ousia, entia* and *entitas*, or again *das Seiende and Seiendheit*). The ontological difference so understood is indeed the dominant theme in the history of philosophy. Metaphysical ontology questions the sensible substance, the thing that is present to our experience, and distinguishes in it elements of composition that make it be that particular being (act and potency, form and matter, etc.). The ontological difference, understood metaphysically, results from such composition: being, *esse*, is what makes a being, *ens*, be. Thus the metaphysical concept of composition introduces being, *esse*, for the sake of a coherent discourse about this or that being, *ens*. In these constructions, though, the science of being remains "sought for," as the declared purpose of metaphysics is to understand finite beings out of a most real and self-sufficient being. Thus the very starting point of metaphysical ontology, the sensible substance, is an act of "forgetfulness of Being."

Heidegger's first attempt at raising the question of Being anew takes its starting point not from the composite substance but from that being that raises the question of Being, that is, from human existence or being-there. The key experience of thought now is that beings be there in an open space which lets them appear to thought—the key experience is "that" beings are (hence the misleading title "existentialism") rather than "why" or "what" they are. The phenomenological, as opposed to ousiological, version of the ontological difference does not consider the sensible substance as the paradigm of Being. It does not ask which is the being, *ens*, that realizes being, *esse*, primarily and fully; it does not start from the multiple uses of the copula; Being is not construed as the ultimate ground of all that there is, rather being-there is the ground for appearance in a new sense: the ground that allows for an understanding of Being out of what shows itself to thought. The Difference now is a rift between being-there to which beings appear and Being that grants such appearance. Being lets beings appear to being-there. In this account the ontological difference has to be described as letting be, granting, opening a clearing, and by related metaphors rather than in terms of causality. The goal of such an unlearning of metaphysical speculation is no longer to represent Being out of beings, but to think of it in its own truth. The truth of Being is the ontological difference so understood. To let beings appear to being-there is Being's essential, and historical, way of being. This approach is descriptive of the appearance of beings in being-there, and to that extent it remains phenomenological. It describes the truth of Being as this process of unconcealment.

Thus a new amphibology of Being manifests itself: the verb "to be" signifies both what makes beings be (their beingness, *Seiendheit*) and the truth or unconcealedness of the showing forth within being-there. The metaphysical sense of the Difference is integrated into the phenomenological sense when Heidegger speaks of "the difference between 'Being' as 'the being of beings,' and 'Being' in respect of its proper sense, that is, in respect of its truth (the clearing)."[12] These lines speak of the same—the Difference—twice. Being understood through substantial composition is the "being of beings"; this is the first twoness (*Zwiefalt*). Being as essential appearance is the truth, or clearing, of the being of beings; this is the second twoness. The quote says the same twice; but the same which is said twice is not the identical. In the first difference being is thought of as constant presence and unshakable ground of beings; in the second difference Being is the presencing, the appearance of being to thought. Being in the first sense constitutes sense objects, and such constitution has been the leading concept of ontology since Aristotle. Being as unconcealment "constitutes" thinking, but this second kind of constitution, a gathering or coming together of Being and thinking, has been obfuscated by the traditional insistence upon object constitution. The two ways of understanding Being are collected into the Difference (capitalized) which thus indicates an equivocity of titles such as 'ground' and 'constitution': in their metaphysical usage these titles are *terms*, that is, they stop and fix the process of language for the sake of defining things; in their phenomenological usage they *manifest* the way in which things appear to thinking. Composition and substance on one hand, appearance and unconcealedness on the other introduce severalness into the very heart of our knowledge of Being. Ontology can be both ousiology and phenomenology. The latter does not abolish the former, but it displaces the question. It takes a step backwards to ask how Being comes to be understood as substance, that is, as the constant presence of what is present. This step backwards, which opens up the Difference, is not taken in order to better understand either beings or beingness; rather this is properly the step towards thinking Being itself. In Heidegger's later writings, when the question of Being is no longer the radicalization of a tendency inherent in existence but when the starting point is Being itself with regard to things present and to their presence, the 'destruction' of the metaphysical quest for a constant presence ceases to be simply a project and begins to be actually carried out. The true multifariousness of Being lies in its propensity to let itself be represented as

---

12 Heidegger, *Unterwegs zur Sprache*, 110; trans., 20.

the metaphysical difference between the composite and the cause of its composition, and to let itself be thought of as the difference between what appears and the event of unconcealment or appearance itself. The multifariousness that the Difference points to is not Aristotle's '*pollachos legetai,*' said of the copula, but the severalness of beings, beingness and Being, that is, the multiplicity according to which beingness "makes" beings be and Being "lets" them appear. This Difference is the "handing over of presence which presencing delivers to what is present."[13] The 'destruction' and the discovery of the severalness of Being that results from it also displace the quest for certainty: "Where certainty is all, only beings remain essential but no longer beingness (*Seiendheit*), to say nothing of the clearing of beingness."[14] The step backwards thus occurs in two heterogeneous moments: from beings to their beingness and then into Being itself. Or again, from what is present to its presence and then to the event of presencing itself. Or finally, in the language of *On Time and Being*, from what is 'present' (*das Anwesende*) to letting 'be present' (*Anwesen*lassen) and then to 'letting-be' present (Anwesen*lassen*). This is not to be understood in the sense of a gradation towards an ever greater originality.[15] Rather what is destined to us is manifold in its very origin.

The vocabulary that most appropriately suggests the severalness of Being as it results from the step backwards into the essence of metaphysics is perhaps the opposition between "making" and "letting." Both verbs indicate primarily an attitude of man. All making has a purpose. Every making and every doing, Aristotle says in the opening lines of the *Nicomachean Ethics,* aims at an end result different from itself. This idea of making, of production, can be seen as permeating all levels of metaphysics: the Good, in Plato, is said to "make" the universe; the active intellect in Aristotle, "makes" all things knowable, it produces intelligibles; Christian philosophy stands and falls with the idea of creation; Kant's transcendental critique begins with the wonderment at how reason can "produce" a

---

13 Martin Heidegger, *Holzwege* (Frankfurt: Klostermann, 1950), 337; trans. David F. Krell, *Early Greek Thinking*, 52.

14 *Nietzsche* (Pfullingen: Neske, 1961), Vol. II, 26.

15 *Zur Sache des Denkens*, 48; trans. *On Time and Being*, 45.

priori syntheses; Hegel's World-Spirit is the very notion of fecundity ... In Heidegger's view this poietic essence of metaphysics is carried to the extreme and thus revealed by technology, where the identification between Being and making and between beings and being-made still goes unquestioned. The metaphysical difference is constructed according to the relation between producer and product, i.e., according to the pattern of causation. Calculative thinking which today "captivates, bewitches, dazzles, and beguiles man"[16] suggests that—except for some rare historical figures that this is not the place to mention[17]—philosophers have represented Being out of the difference between making and being made, between cause and effect.

The ascendancy of the representation of causation over philosophy becomes questionable when the primary attitude of thought is "letting" rather than "making." This reversal most deeply affects the schemes of teleology: the beginning (efficient and material cause) and the end (formal and final cause) are no longer the most revelatory categories to describe a phenomenon. *Whence* and *why*, the questions of beginning and of purpose, recede behind the acknowledgement *that* there is being. I should like to suggest this shift in a more descriptive fashion. As the analysis of letting-be and of its consequences will mark the transition from the ontological to the symbolic difference, this step of reflection is crucial. The shift can be sketched in many ways, but the most appropriate seems to be the description of an experience directly opposed to that of making as well as to Whence and Why. This other experience is that of a path. Symbols, by the semantic structure derived from their double sense, precisely open a path to human existence by which their second, hidden meaning lets itself be explored out of their first, apparent meaning. Symbols put man on the road of a distinctive experience of Being. But there is no "end" to the peregrination imposed by a symbol upon its hearer.

---

16 Martin Heidegger, *Gelassenheit* (Pfullingen: Neske, 1959), 27; trans. John M. Anderson and E. Hans Freund, *Discourse on Thinking* (New York: Harper & Row, 1966), 56.

17 Meister Eckhart is one of these, cf. my "Trois penseurs du délaissement" in *Journal of the History of Philosophy*, Oct. 1974, 455–77 and January 1975, 43–60, as well as "Heidegger and Meister Eckhart on Releasement," in *Research in Phenomenology* III (1973), 95–119.

To travel a road means first of all to leave one place in order to reach another. The wanderer experiences the succession of places and locations. The curious bystander who sees him pass and questions him about his ways will mostly be interested in the two extremes of his itinerary: Where does he come from, and where is he going? If the wayfarer answers these two questions with satisfactory precision his stopover is accepted. One will offer him lodgings and may recommend a shortcut or a means of transportation which will spare his strength and allow him to arrive at his destination safely and quickly. But if he travels without Whence and Whither, he is suspect. Curious consciousness has learned everything about a road when it is informed about its starting point, the traveler's wherefrom, and its end, his whereto. The succession of places, which is the road proper, is not considered for itself, but only for its usefulness in regard to whether it furthers or hinders the progress towards a destination. For curious consciousness a path appears as nothing more then the shortest passage between two geographical points; its ideal would be to accomplish the transition in zero time.

Such an understanding of the road results from an excessive preoccupation with Whence and Whither, that is, with Why. Where does the road come from, and where does it lead? The two questions arise from the same anxiousness, the desire for reasons. Why the path? Spontaneous consciousness, anxious as it is about causes and goals, does not see the path in itself. Just as there are words for general consumption—all words insofar as they vehiculate a sum of information and not as they symbolize a calling—thus there are also roads for general consumption: all roads if they are comprehended out of provenance and attainment. The question arises whether Whence and Why are sufficient categories to yield a full understanding of the phenomenon of a path. There are experts in itinerancy whom we might question (Parsifal or Wilhelm Meister, "The Cherubinic Wanderer" or "The Winter Journey"...), but we can turn to ourselves. Indeed, already and always we are ourselves engaged upon a road. Where do we come from? Where do we go? Only if we unlearn to question peregrination in this fashion will it show its essence. Whence and Why conceal what peregrine existence knows. The condition for the path to show itself out of itself is to journey without a why and to let be whatever there is: to let be "the lime tree by the fountain at the gate," "the mooncast shadow, my companion," "the organgrinder beyond the village," to let "the wind play with the weathercock" and let "the crow fly hither and thither above my head"... (all quotes from Wilhelm Müller's *The Winter Journey*). A wanderer who has unlearned preoccupation with Whence and Why, who travels in releasement, experiences itinerancy in itself out of itself. His experience follows another 'method' (*meta ton hodon*, along the way) than knowledge through the causes. The attitude of letting, of letting-be, effects a translation from causal discourse into an existential course. Such abandonment to the path produces a convergence between the order of existing and the order of understanding.

The recognition of a human attitude as a condition for the understanding of Being, that is, the reciprocity between letting-be and thinking,[18] has some consequence for the ontological difference. The foundation of a phenomenon is no longer extrinsic as in the metaphysical difference that results from composition, but is intrinsic. To say that in a phenomenon which is 'left' to itself the foundation appears as 'letting-be,' implies a particular kind of appearance; this is neither epiphany nor delusion, but the visibility of the visible itself. Letting-be or releasement is thus the phenomenological attitude. In a phenomenon understood through letting-be the foundation shows itself to be nothing other than letting-be, although not in the sense of a human posture. It is the depth of whatever shows itself to human releasement.

It is essential for the establishment of the symbolic difference to see how letting-be or releasement grounds again the identity between Being and thinking. The specter of ontological monism that such a formulation implies has been dissipated above. The ontological difference, when it is thought of in a phenomenological fashion, reveals Being not as a selfsame universal, but as multifarious, as several. We spoke of the severalness of Being in *On Time and Being*. An analysis of what Heidegger calls the *Geviert*, the fourfold, would again illustrate the destruction of monism. If

18 In Heidegger the prerequisite for the thought of being is to "let technical devices enter our daily life, and at the same time leave them outside, that is, let them alone," *Gelassenheit*, 25; *Discourse on Thinking*, 54.

the decisive step in the questioning of Being is indeed that from 'making' to 'letting'—beingness 'makes' beings be (the metaphysical moment), and Being 'lets' beings appear (the phenomenological moment)—then releasement, or letting-be, turns from an attitude of man into the essence of Being. What seems to be a simple requirement for man to understand his world[19] becomes the way of being of this world itself. A human way of being turns into Being's way of being. Releasement can be an attitude of man only because it is primarily the truth of Being. This reversal from a disposition of thinking into one of Being, the reversal from man's resoluteness into Being's "resolve," discovers beings themselves as showing forth "without why." This discovery of letting be as the identical truth of thinking and of Being actually overcomes what in the history of metaphysics is called a philosophy of identity. Together with speculative monism this discovery also renders impossible the defense of any practical philosophy derived from such totalitarian monism. If positing is no longer the paradigmatic process of ontology, there are neither speculative positions for thinking left to hold nor any political positions that may ensue.

To formulate now what is meant by the symbolic difference we have to keep in mind what happens in reflecting on the path: at first sight the experience of the path in itself seems to be a simple prerequisite for seeing the things of our world better as they show forth, without reference to Whence or Why. The "without why" at first sight is an attitude, and so is itinerancy. But then Being appears to let beings be, and in a reversal "without why" becomes Being's own way of being. The same reversal affects itinerancy. We remember that a symbol, as the word suggests, unites actively, "throws together," a sign and what it signifies; it unites in an event the manifest and the hidden meaning in a symbolic action, object, or word. I call symbolic difference that way of being of Being itself by which it appears as actively enowning, "throwing together," the beings that it lets be. The ontological difference says how being shows itself to thought; the symbolic difference says how it calls upon existence and thought as upon its own. This calling pertains

19 See the quote from Meister Eckhart above, note 2.

to the very structure of symbols: their second sense calls upon the interpreter and lets itself be explored by way of a renewed existence. The symbolic difference thus says more than the ontological difference, as it speaks of Being insofar as Being itself urges thought (that is, man) upon a more originary road. Neither the ontological difference nor the symbolic difference are speculative constructions for the sake of some theory of man, although each allocates to man his proper place: the Difference is the place where Being comes to rest and where man comes to himself. The essence of Being appropriates man just as the meaning symbolized by symbols makes man *its* own. In this sense Being is essentially peregrine. When Heidegger writes that Being leaves itself to thought, that it gives or grants itself, it is no longer man who is seen as committed upon a road. Being as the origin (*oriri*, to rise, to come forth) of appearance commits itself to a coming, and thus to becoming.

The difficulties that accompany such a rethinking of the ontological difference out of one highly revelatory domain of reality, the symbol, are numerous. They should however be seen in the light of Heidegger's own development. Indeed, what is here called the symbolic difference would have remained unthinkable without the temporalization of Being as undertaken first in *Being and Time*, then under the title of "history of Being," and finally with regard to language and its essentially historical way of speaking. It should be understood also that such a rethinking would have remained impossible without a reference, sometimes implicit, to Nietzsche's thought that "becoming must appear justified at every moment"[20] as well as to Nietzsche's fellowship with Heraclitus.[21]

Before carrying this reflection into an examination of language as is now due, another trait of the political philosophy that results from the interpretation of symbols is to be retained: quite as the

---

20 Friedrich Nietzsche, *Der Wille zur Macht*, n. 708, ed. Peter Gast and Elisabeth Förster-Nietzsche (Stuttgart: Kröner, 1964), 479; trans. Walter Kaufmann, *The Will to Power* (New York: Random House, 1967), 377.

21 Heraclitus' concept of becoming, Nietzsche says, "is clearly more closely related to me than anything else thought to date," *Ecce Home*, "Die Geburt der Tragödie," n. 3, trans. Walter Kaufmann, *Basic Writings of Nietzsche* (New York: Modern Library, 1966), 729.

severalness of Being uproots rational certainty, so the peregrine essence of Being uproots practical security. The words seem to suggest this: the experience (*Erfahrung*) of such peregrination (*Fahren*) is full of peril (*Gefahr*). The groundwork for an alternative to organizational political philosophy will have to be so multifarious as to allow for an ever new response to the calling advent by which Being destabilizes familiar patterns of thinking and acting.

IV. The Symbolic Difference in Language

The phenomenological difference becomes thinkable only on the condition of a displacement of inquiry, that is, on the condition that philosophical reflection ceases to be primarily concerned with securing a most real reality, be that the sensible substance, the divine subject, or human subjectivity. If in place of substance, subject and subjectivity we turn our attention to language, this is not to proclaim yet another most real reality—the reassignment every other century of an *ens realissimum* will never allow for an overcoming of metaphysics. Rather language is that experience of ours which aims at nothing other than manifestation. Speaking is in its very essence *phainesthai*; it is nothing but showing. As such it provides natural moorage for the phenomenological difference. But what is closest to thought is also the hardest to think. Language is so close indeed to our very being that thinking has to search for a particular area of language in which its manifestative essence may become thinkable for its own sake. This privileged area is that of symbols. Since they are always, in one way or another, dependent upon interpretation, symbols are not only primarily phenomena of language, but they are also the primary phenomena of language.

The most extreme forms of manifestation through language are the most revelatory of what happens in speech as well as writing. We shall again remain decidedly descriptive and look at the case of a derided text in which some general features of language appear clearly. Language is Being that can be understood. Although language occurs originally as the spoken word, a written text provides easier access to the basic characteristics of language than does conversation. A text detaches language from its living process and makes it distinct; it makes it both removed from ourselves and more clearly seen. To narrow down the scope of inquiry still further we question an extremely simplified form of writing: brochures of cheap fiction for easy consumption as they are available at railway stations and similar places. What does language do in schmaltz? It captivates. The romance of hearts and flowers is accessible without much hermeneutic effort. It carries the reader into an illusory elsewhere which at the same time is the lightest to understand—lighter, precisely, than his own reality. As these texts assimilate us to their world, a peculiar kind of conformity, *adaequatio,* comes about. The illusion "works" because it develops a possibility of being in language, hence in the world, with the least amount of interpretive exaction. We have already understood the content of these brochures before reading the first line. The elsewhere that they propose is only the most familiar of fantasies—so familiar that their reading is actually unnecessary. The traveler in the train who nevertheless leafs through them is thus first of all neither with their heroes nor in a means of public transportation: he is first of all with himself in a mode determined by the words he looks at. Language establishes here a mode of being in the world that is simpler than one's own, and it tends to substitute itself for one's own. The *roman du cœur* is highly efficacious in momentarily reducing being in the world to utter simplicity. Language thus founds a way of existing. Fundamentally a great work of literature which leaves indelible traces in us does nothing different. In closing such a book one is no longer exactly what one was when opening it. Something similar may happen in conversation. Wherever it occurs, language performs a transformation of reality. The text interprets the reader, literally verifies him. *Verum facere,* to make true, appears to be an essential trait of language. A partner's distraction in dialogue is not only a discourtesy, it is an untruth. The truth is that man may hear, even that he cannot but hear. He cannot remain indifferent to language.

Words thus carry a claim, an urgency. Such a claim is altogether missed when they are reduced to their psychological impact. This results clearly from the case just described: in maudlin works the authorship does not count, and their understanding does not result from sympathy with the author's mind, as the Romantics would have it. But neither does the claim or address in language stem ultimately from the matter communicated. Not all subject-matters make existential demands. The character of appeal is rather a structural element of language itself. Language is naturally irresistible.

The character of appeal is made explicit by and defines a particular region of language, that of symbols. In symbols a second sense calls upon the hearer who responds to it with renewed existence. Thus the symbols only make obvious what language does always and everywhere, even though it conceals its own clarity behind the sum of contents. This essence of language, the openness into which historical existence is called forth, is what a metaphysics of sign and signification cannot think. The essence of language as calling man over to itself remains occultated in metaphysics. To say that the semantic structure of symbols—a scission in meaning and a call to overcome this scission—is paradigmatic for all of language, is not to identify the essence of language with the full meaning, or the second sense, of symbols. What symbols symbolize is not the ontological essence of language, but ontic contents: freedom, rebirth, peace, brotherhood, purity, etc. In the hermeneutics of symbols the second sense is an object of knowledge; but in a phenomenology of language the unthought essence of speech and writing can never be represented as an object of cognition. In speech and writing the essence of language both manifests and hides itself, quite as the full meaning of symbols manifests and hides itself in the apparent meaning: water is more than itself, it "is" also the matrix of the universe, life-giving as well as destructive, producing a second birth or a second death, formless origin and return to formlessness, it purifies and regenerates and therefore "is" health, a new creation, another world. The second sense so uncovered requires interpretation and practice. Likewise speech and writing are more than themselves: they are vocal sounds and letters, phonemes and morphemes, but they also "are" the presencing of the essence of language which they conceal and reveal. Such an inner difference is constitutive of language as it is of symbols. In both of them the *mode* of signification, or the structure of revelation, is the same: the scission between the absence and presence of the origin, and the call to overcome this scission.

From such a reduction of language and Being to the same essence, that is, from the discovery of the origin which grants both, some consequences result. Firstly, "Being itself" is several, and so is language. Being lets beings be, and language lets words speak. The severalness of language appears in a regression similar to the one developed earlier (beings —beingness—Being): the reason of words is their meaning, just as the reason of beings is their beingness; and language lets words be grounded in meaning just as Being lets beings be grounded in beingness (words—meaning—language).

Secondly, the *symballein*, the peregrine "throwing together" which had appeared essential to the symbolic difference, now characterizes the Difference altogether, both in its ontological and its linguistic aspects. The origin that discloses and conceals itself in language, as it does in Being, puts man on the road. When thought of in reference to the symbolic difference, human being and human speaking have the same essential structure—upstream peregrination. The same source that shows forth in Being and speaking urges a practice upon man. This common *Ursprung* cannot be construed metaphysically as beginning, principle, or cause, but it appears phenomenologically as a claim to exist anew, as the claim to a leap, *Sprung*. The origin "sets over" towards man only if man "sets over" to original Being and speaking. The *Satz* of the origin requires human *übersetzen*, translation or transference. When practice so becomes *symballein* the severalness of Being is no longer the traditional philosophic fragmentation of the single mystery of Being into the secrets of man (anthropology), the secrets of the world (cosmology) and the secrets of God (theology). Rather the symbolic essence of the Difference solves the age old question of the One and the Many by showing intensities of presence: representational thought and existence fix what is present; "heartier" thought speculates about presence; the "heartiest"[22] thought, however, lets presencing be. Thus the heartiest human practice is neither manipulation nor speculation, but releasement.

---

22 Heidegger, *Gelassenheit*, 27; *Discourse on Thinking*, 56. The translators put "courageous" for *herzhaft*, which misses the nuance of polemic against calculative representation and production as it is further explained in a brief commentary on the "heart" according to Pascal: *Holzwege*, 282; trans. Albert Hofstadter, *Poetry, Language, Thought* (New York: Harper & Row, 1971), 127–28.

Thirdly, *symballein* is the truth both of Being and of language. The symbolic difference is the phenomenological difference. To be sure, symbols constitute only a region within Being and language; but the symbolic essence of the Difference is not regional. This results from the way in which Being and language appear linked together: a thing "is" when language delivers it from *léthé*, from concealment. Wherever language is missing, but that is properly unthinkable, nothing can be. Thus neither language nor Being are given; however, they give. Understood in their truth, *alétheia*, they are the same. Being symbolizes itself in beings, and language symbolizes itself in speech and writing. To things the Same (the origin or "It") gives presence, and to thought it gives openness.

It now has to be shown briefly how the vocabulary of the later Heidegger does suggest what we have called the symbolic difference. Heidegger, it is true, would take exception to this title. The word "symbol" is indeed laden with scientific as well as artistic resonances that turn its concept either into a convention among researchers or into an artifice among art producers. What we have called symbol in its original and etymological sense is expressed differently by Heidegger. To circumscribe this matter he has recourse to words like *Gebärde*, *Wink*, *Brauch*, *Spur*. Some remarks on these words will help suggest why the symbolic difference, with the demand for authentic existence which it implies, is the appropriate tool towards founding human practice anew after "the 'true world' finally became a fable" (Nietzsche).

a) *Gesture*. In the dialogue about language between Heidegger and a Japanese the visitor imitates a gesture (*Gebärde*) from a 'No' play. By a single movement of the arm and the hand this gesture makes a mountain landscape appear on the empty stage. Is such a gesture more powerful, more imaginary than words? Does it indicate something about language that words do not immediately show? Indeed, our marvel is at the promptness with which such a gesture brings the mountain scenery before us. The thing evoked is borne to presence, bears itself towards us. "Gesture is the gathering of a bearing."[23] But what is it that so gathers? A gesture forces noth-

23 *Unterwegs zur Sprache*, 107; *On the Way to Language*, 18.

ing, it only brings to presence. As such it more clearly does what language always does. But, the Japanese says, that which grants the gesture is empty, nothing. The gesture arises out of the void. It signifies "out of that essential Being which we attempt to add in our thinking, as the other, to all that is present and absent."[24] In the gesture the origin of Being and language shows forth in such a way that it signifies a mode of existence: it gathers beings, absent or present, into a unity. What unites them arises from nowhere. The cipherless origin of Being and language is here called emptiness. It is nothing, but it gathers things into one and thereby calls upon existence. *It calls for a "counterbearing"* (*Entgegentragen*). The originary unity is a void, no thing, it differs essentially from the objects analyzed by sciences.[25] It is quite significant that this meditation about gesture is found in a dialogue: the call for renewed existence occurs most vividly in the living word of conversation. Speaking among humans is responsible only if it is a response to the origin of language, a "counterbearing" to its address. Bearing and counterbearing then are one in a process, in *symballein*.

b) *Hint*. In the same dialogue is found the second word, *Wink*. It refers to the structure of concealment-unconcealment: "the hint is the message of the veiling that opens up."[26] The Japanese tries to translate a word from his language which tells of the origin of speech. The fundamental trait of this word in Japanese, we are told, is the hint. Not that the word itself hints at anything or signifies anything; rather the process of signification is reversed: in that word, the origin from which language arises—"the veiling that opens up"—hints to the speaker. The hint points out a path of existence. That which hints to us in language urges us to go closer to the source of language and Being. This source discloses the space in which words and beings are possible. But it also denies itself in words and beings, it stays veiled. As the "beckoning stillness" (*die rufende Stille*) *it addresses thought and existence for a response in thinking and existing*. The hint beckons man upon the originary

---

24 Ibid. 108; trans. 19.

25 *Was ist Metaphysik?* (Frankfurt: Klostermann, 1960), 45; trans. R. F. Hull and Alan Crick, *Existence and Being* (Chicago: Henry Regnery, 1949), 384.

26 *Unterwegs zur Sprache*, 31; *On the Way to Language*, 44.

path. It invites the same unity in process as bearing and counter-bearing.

c) *Usage.* This word is again taken from a dialogue, although of a different kind. It stems from Heidegger's interpretation of the Anaximander fragment, one of his most difficult and controversial essays. We shall not discuss whether "usage," *Brauch*, is an appropriate translation of *chreôn*. Rather, with this translation Heidegger wants to think of an involvement. "Usage" indicates not only utilization and usance, but also a way of recognizing the presence of a thing and of enjoying it, of "being pleased with something and so having it in use." By its usage a thing enters into its proper relation with other things, it comes into its essence. The usage of a thing brings forth its essential being. This coming forth happens through the user's preservation, through his "keeping in hand." The user, Heidegger writes, lets be present what is present. As have the two previous words, "usage" becomes a name no longer for man's attitude but for the way in which the origin of Being and language lets beings be present and lets language speak. "Letting" is not a causal relation, just as use is not the cause for the thing's appearance. "Usage now designates the manner in which Being itself presences as the relation to what is present."[27] This relation is an active process which is here called "approaching" (*an-gehen*) and "becoming involved" (*be-handeln*). To receive what approaches him thus is for man to become involved with the origin. Usage suggests *an originary movement towards man which elicits involvement.*

d) *Trace.* That which does not appear, but which lets beings be and language speak, leaves its trace, *Spur*, in all that appears. This word is directly related to peregrine identity with the origin. In the opening pages of "Nietzsche's Word: 'God is Dead,'" Heidegger speaks of the mittence (*Geschick*) of Being: the traces of the historical mittences must be trodden by thinking and existence. "To each thinker is enjoined one path, his own, whose traces he must tread to and fro, again and again."[28] These traces are the manifold marks of the other of all things and words, in things and words.

---

27 *Holzwege*, 339; *Early Greek Thinking*, 53.

28 Ibid. 194–95; trans. William J. Lovitt, *The Question Concerning Technology and Other Essays* (New York: Harper, 1977), 55.

They do not belong to the thinker or any existence, and they lead nowhere. They are "woodpaths." But on them the origin lets itself be experienced. The thinker has to tell what he has experienced on his way to language, i.e., on his way to Being. Such a response to the mittences of Being requires an active tread of a particular kind. Woodpaths arise from nowhere. *To be trodden, the traces of the origin require an aimless gait.*

To disclose the origin of Being and language Gesture, Hint, Usage, and Trace all ask for a way of thinking which is indistinguishable from a way of existing. Only on the condition of a new turn in thinking and of a return in existing do they disclose the truth of language and being "symbolically," that is, by uniting man to what makes a gesture and a hint and what uses him and leaves its traces. The origin can be understood only upon the condition of a certain practice.

Conclusion

The question of the origin as it is raised by Heidegger, particularly after the 'turn,' undercuts metaphysical constructions not only in thought but also in action. The phenomenological destruction, if it is thought of within *symballein*, has concrete consequences that reverse the metaphysical way of grounding a practical philosophy. Such reversal becomes thinkable upon the condition that the origin of Being and language, their identical coming-forth, be not represented as the ultimate foundation of both theory and practice; that is, that the quest for one ultimate foundation be abandoned altogether. Then the essence of foundation undergoes a reversal: it is not beings that call for a ground, but Being as the groundless ground calls upon existence. In this sense Heidegger's 'turn' literally operates a subversion: the reversal of the essence of foundation is an overthrow (*vertere*) from the base or ground (*sub-*). The middle term that carries the phenomenological destruction into practical subversion is the symbolic difference. It translates the 'turn' in thinking into an 'overturn' in action. In a culture where philosophy has come to cooperate with the existing system to the point of radically abandoning its task of criticism, Heidegger's insistence on releasement and "life without why" as the practical *a priori* for the thought of Being opens an alternative way to think of life in society. The symbolic difference allows for the elaboration of an alternative type of political philosophy.[29] This is not a theory of organization of man into collectivities. But it is certainly not the celebration of pure interiority either. Between a system of social constitution and its negation by spiritual individualism or apolitical solipsism there is a place for a thinking about society which refuses to restrict itself to the pragmatics of public administration as well as to romantic escapes from it. I should agree, though, that if theories of collective functioning and organization are alone to be called political philosophy, then it is better to abandon this title for the practical consequences of the thought of the symbolic difference. This article simply wanted to elaborate the notion of symbolic difference as bridging the gap between the question of Being and that of action.

---

29 In the article mentioned above in note 1, I examine five elements towards such an alternative political philosophy:
1) the abolition of the primacy of teleology in action;
2) the abolition of the primacy of responsibility in the legitimization of action;
3) action as a protest against the administered world;
4) a certain disinterest in the future of mankind due to a shift in the understanding of destiny;
5) 'anarchy' as the essence of the origin as well as of originary practice.
These same five elements have been sketched more briefly in "Questioning the Foundation of Practical Philosophy," *Human Studies*, I, 1978, 357–68, followed by a reply from Prof. Bernhard P. Dauenhauer.

On Judging and its Issue

"A new science of politics is needed for a new world" wrote de Tocqueville in *Democracy in America*. Taking up his call, Hannah Arendt sought to inquire anew into the realm of human affairs, into the *vita activa*, the active life.*

In *The Human Condition*, Arendt mapped out the method of that sought-for-science—that philosophy, as it turned out. It would situate the modem age in relation to the Greek *polis*; it would mark off the public from the private realm; and it would trace the web of what she considered to be the fundamental human activities: labor, work, and action. These topics outlined a "new political philosophy."[1] It was "new" in that she wished to counter the *déformation professionnelle* of all Western philosophers, who preferred to speak of Man as a universal rather than of the human plurality. Therefore, in subsequent writings, she applied her framework to such concrete issues as totalitarianism, revolution, democracy, and republicanism. So adamant was her desire to restore the dignity of the singular that at times she denied being a philosopher—a denial she did not mind retracting in her last project. When she died in 1975, she had completed two out of the three volumes that were to complement her theory of active life by a theory of the *vita contemplativa*, "The Life of the Mind." These two volumes are entitled *Thinking* and *Willing*, respectively. The third was to deal with *Judging*. On this topic, however, we only possess posthumously published lecture notes, which I will discuss further below.

In this introduction I shall first trace, albeit critically, that attempted rehabilitation of the singular in Arendt's post-Kantian theory of judgment. Then, at my own risk, I shall look at Kant himself to see how in his critical system the singular turned into the very issue for judging. (This can best be shown by exhibiting the two senses of being in Kant, being as *Position* and being as *Setzung*, one articulating synthesis and the other dispersion). After this, I

---

* This text was originally published as the introduction to an edited collection. We have omitted the passages that refer merely to its context of publication.—Eds.

1 Hannah Arendt, *The Human Condition* (Chicago: The University of Chicago Press, 1958), 298 n.

will argue that there are good reasons not to gloss over, paste up, or drown in exegetical charity the ontological rift laid bare by Kant. Finally, I shall return to this collection of essays and describe briefly the scope of its theme and the order of its composition.

"Meeting the Phenomena Head-On"

> What if *differing* rather than consensus were the issue for thinking?[2]
>
> —Jean-François Lyotard

To judge is to apply a law to some fact or occurrence. There can be no judgment unless the law exceeds the fact in scope and unless it somehow grounds it in depth—unless, in comparison to the fact, the law is universal in both extension and comprehension. Theories of judgment necessarily spell out a relation of subjection whereby one evaluates a particular that is the case using a universal that measures the case. We make the most modest claims to judgmental universality when we have recourse merely to some paradigmatic instance of a particular, as when we say, "As courageous as Achilles," or "As strong as Samson." A given particular, Achilles or Samson, finds itself endowed with exemplary universality as it serves to measure other particulars. The claim is modest in scope since examples apply only to selected facts, for example, phenomena of courage or strength; it is also modest in depth since it entails only comparisons, no groundings. Indeed, any exemplary standard can in turn be measured by higher standards, as when one asks, "What is better, courage or strength?" The least modest claim to judgmental universality, on the other hand, would aim at securing one standard immune to further evaluation, one supreme referent. The history of philosophy offers a supply of such ultimate representations that should satisfy even the most voracious metaphysical appetite. From Parmenides to Husserl,[3] philosophers have been the

---

2 Jean-François Lyotard, *Le Différend* (Paris: Minuit, 1983), 127.

3 "We are the functionaries of mankind," Edmund Husserl, *The Crisis of European Sciences and Transcendental Phenomenology*, trans. David Carr (Evanston: Northwestern University Press, 1970), 17.

covert civil servants whose expertise has secured the (legitimating) law of (juridical, ethical, and discursive) laws. As technicians of subsumption, they have varied the *judgmental difference* between one hegemonic fantasm and the many facts or occurrences covered by its extension and anchored by its comprehension.

We say we *differ* on something whenever two (or more) conflicting claims cannot be subsumed under the same covering law. Both claims may be legitimate in their respective orders of validity, yet they may be heteronomous falling under diverse *nomoi* because those orders are incompatible. When two opposing parties enter a litigation, they thereby acknowledge the pertinence of one law under which they seek to be judged. Their dispute can therefore be settled. To enter a litigation is to bring one's case, as particular, under the relevant law as applicable to that case and hence as universal. No settlement can be reached between *differing* stands, that is, when the conflict amounts to a *différend*. In such a case, the mechanics of subsumption get out of gear. Lyotard, from whom I borrow the term (but only the term), cites the position of contemporary historians who deny the existence of extermination camps under National Socialism. These authors argue that they would recognize only testimony from victims—who, by definition, can no longer give it. What common law could settle such a disagreement? From the very start, the case for grievance is robbed of all possible arguments. Lyotard also cites the French officer at Verdun who shouts "Charge!" and leaps out of the trenches; his infantry men shout back "Bravo!" and do not move. A conflict of so-called values, too, is a *différend*.

It may well be that, since Aristotle, the irreducible diversity of the sciences has entailed something like a scattergram of styles and methods, in as much as the measure-giving science remains "sought for." First principles would then govern such regions of phenomena as ethics, politics, physics, and so on, but not the constellation of these regions, not phenomena qua phenomena. Aristotle would have opened the *différend* between disciplines. No regional science is conceivable without the subsumption of particular facts under universal statements. What, then, would a radical *différend* be? It would be one in which coercion under a principle would be matched by an equal dispersion among singulars. The 'particular' is always a case of some universal, while the 'singular' merely is the case. In a radical *différend*, we stand equally exposed to laws unifying the particular and plurifying the singular.

Below I shall try to show how, in the *Critique of Judgment*, Kant not only acknowledges such a radical conflict among phenomena but also gives an ontological account of it. His discovery of reflective, as opposed to subsumptive, judgments culminates in the recognition that the singular alone—not the particular—"is." What I have called the judgmental difference between the normative one and the normed many takes on in Kant the form of two senses of being. The 'one' that serves as the law for all synthetic judgments is being as the thinking "I": the hegemonic fantasm of earlier modernity. The dispersed 'many' to be conformed to that highest unity is made up of the appearances. In reflective judgments, however, we do not determine the "existent in nature" so as to grasp it through a concept. We only mirror it. In these judgments, then, the normative force of being as one, for being as the many, breaks down. In subsuming intuitions under concepts, we constitute what is to be known and, by right, can then reach a consensus about what is to be done. No such remedy to dispersion is within our reach if 'to think being' means to reflect disparate singulars. Then, as surmised in the epigraph above, the issue for thinking may indeed be differing rather than consensus.

The strongest reading of Kant's third *Critique* as a theory of noncognitive judgments has been given in Arendt's posthumously published lectures.[4] In a homage, however critical, to her attempt to rehabilitate the singular in political philosophy, I shall discuss the affinity she claimed rather peremptorily between aesthetic and political judgments:

> The reason why I believe so much in Kant's *Critique of Judgment* is not because I am interested in aesthetics but because I believe that the way in which we say "that is right," "that is wrong" is not very different from the way in which we say "this is beautiful," "this is ugly." That is, we

---

4 Hannah Arendt, *Lectures on Kant's Political Philosophy*, ed. Ronald Beiner (Chicago: The University of Chicago Press, 1982). Page numbers in parentheses refer to this book.

> are now prepared to meet the phenomena, so to speak, head-on, without any preconceived system. And, please, including my own![5]

We should certainly heed Arendt's twofold advice in these lines: to read the *Critique of Judgment* as a work of political philosophy, but also *not* to read it with what she calls her own preconceived system.

Arendt was fascinated with what she called the "rare moments of freedom" in history, the moments of interregnum when one order of rules is about to vanish and a new one has not yet entirely come into place. Such intermittent times of deep breathing are literally times of anarchy, of absence of governance. In the modern period, these were the months of the Paris Commune with its attempted revival in May 1968—when one could read on the walls of the Sorbonne, "Long live the workers' councils extended to all aspects of life"—as well as the weeks of the Russian Soviets and the German *Räte* at the end of the First World War, revived also for a moment in Budapest in 1956.

Arendt obviously never dreamt of participating in political action. She was, in Kant's terms, the enthusiastic spectator co-constituting the events, but for the reading public. It is not difficult to imagine that she would have had strong moral objections to picking up cobblestones and throwing them at various living targets, but equally evident was her aesthetic delight in the elusive meaning given to these events by another graffito at the Sorbonne: "*Dessous les pavés c'est la plage*" ("Underneath the cobblestones is the beach"). The point is that writers of wall inscriptions and editorialists, together with their readers, contribute more decisively to the public realm than those who fight battles and sign treaties. The storytellers contribute more to it than those about whom the stories are told.

Aesthetic delight is what, according to Kant, the individual beautiful object gives to the beholder. Arendt's project in her recently published lectures consists in showing Kant's discovery of judgment as an independent faculty along with understanding and will-

5 Hannah Arendt in an address to the American Society for Christian Ethics, quoted in Elisabeth Young-Bruehl, *Hannah Arendt, For Love of the World* (New Haven: Yale University Press, 1982), 452–53.

ing; her project is furthermore to expand that faculty's competence to the political domain. Kant, she says, "did not recognize the political and moral implications of his discovery" (107). She undertakes, then, to outline Kant's "unwritten political philosophy" (7 and 31). It is entirely a philosophy of the singular.

Knowing what is right and willing what is good are indeed insufficient credentials for entering the public realm, just as they are insufficient for appreciating works in a museum or on a stage. If what was needed for public performance, whether aesthetic or political, was merely knowledge, then intellectuals would make the best politicians. But, Kant observed, such is not the case: "It is not unusual to meet learned men who in the application of their knowledge betray an original want: ... deficiency in judgment is just what is ordinarily called stupidity, and for such a failing there is no remedy."[6] Intellectuals are poor politicians because they make it their profession to subsume each particular occurrence under some general truth. Subsumption under universals is their occupational hazard. But politics is the art of the particular. It is, Kant says, even the paradoxical art of "thinking the particular" (quoted on 76)—paradoxical since we have learned from Aristotle that we can only think in concepts, that is, in universals. Only in what Kant called reflective judgments do we then "meet the phenomena head-on," that is, as *singular*.

Arendt thus shows why judgment is irreducible to cognition. She also shows why it is irreducible to will. Willing, as she understands it, is by nature single-minded, oblivious of contexts. She liked to quote Bergson in this respect: "The will acts like a *coup d'état*."[7]

If cognition was all that was needed in the political sphere, then politics would be reduced to management, to sheer administration—the substance of which was for Arendt "the social." This prepolitical nature of social phenomena appeared most clearly to her in contemporary mass cultures: "The fundamental contradiction of the country [the United States] is political freedom coupled

---

6 Immanuel Kant, *Critique of Pure Reason*, B 172 n.

7 Hannah Arendt, *The Life of the Mind*, 2 vols. (New York: Harcourt Brace Jovanovich, 1977) I: 213, and elsewhere.

with social slavery."[8] If, on the other hand, the will was all that was needed in the public realm, we would be living in a world of perpetual *coups d'état*—under the "triumph of the will" she had known through first-hand experience.

The originality of Arendt's political theory after Kant lies in this topology of specifically political phenomena. They are located neither within the reach of knowledge, compelling it to true statements, nor within that of the will, impelling it to appropriation. Rather, their phenomenal site is akin to that of aesthetic objects. Just like the world of the performing arts, the world of politics *would not exist* if there were no spectators. With a predilection for overstatement that caused her trouble on more than one occasion, Arendt did not hesitate to write: "The public realm is constituted by the critics and the spectators, *not* the actors or the makers" (63). The point is that the spectators alone are in a position to decide which singular act is noteworthy and which is not.

Concretely, if the French Revolution was, in Kant's words, a "phenomenon that cannot be forgotten," this is due not to such actors as Danton, Marat, Robespierre, and others, but to the "reading public" all over Europe and its "outspoken partiality." One feels partiality for this or that deed, this or that object; one cannot feel partial for universals. Kant adds, "This revolution finds in the hearts of all spectators a wishful participation that borders closely on enthusiasm." In *judgment* we cannot but approve of the storming of the Bastille, but in *moral* reasoning, Kant goes on, our disapproval has to be equally unmitigated. Right and wrong, or just and unjust, are consequences of the self-given law of freedom, hence universal. "The people may not pursue its rights by revolution, which is at all times unjust." "It is *sweet* to think up constitutions that would correspond to the demands of reason; it is *foolhardy* to put them forward seriously; and it is *punishable* to incite the people to do away with the existing constitution."[9] Kant's well-known ambivalence toward the events of 1789 illustrates most strikingly his delineation of two phenomenal regions: that where we are merely

---

8 Quoted in Young-Bruehl, *Hannah Arendt, For Love of the World*, 166.

9 Immanuel Kant, *The Strife of the Faculties*, A 143, 148 n., and 159 n.

onlookers and that where we are actors. It illustrates his distinction between two faculties, that of judgment and that of the moral will. It instantiates despite terminological fluctuations in both Kant and Arendt the irreducibility of the singular to the particular. The singular needs to be looked at, appreciated, and judged; the particular needs to be conceived through subsumption, determined by concepts, and known.

Concerning Arendt's account, it is clearly much too partial for Kant's praise of partiality. The expanded competence she gives reflective judgments should not be taken as doctrine. We would be wise in seeking, as she did, Kant's political philosophy not only in his writings explicitly devoted to it but also in his texts on aesthetic judgment. But where we should not follow her advice to the end is in what she described as her "preconceived system": in this context, the all too sweeping disjunction between the moral and the political, as well as a certain disdain for history that pervades her thinking. Both tendencies result from her fascination with the singular.

A clear-cut disjunction between moral and political philosophy is impossible for Kant, if only because the stakes are the same in either discipline: *enlightenment* through reclaiming the subjective autonomy that had been lost under the sway of ultimate metaphysical representations. "Enlightenment is man's release from his self-incurred tutelage."[10] In matters of science, to become autonomous is to prescribe transcendental laws to nature; in matters of morals, it is to submit freely under self-given imperatives; and in matters of judgment, it is to esteem things beautiful and things political for their own sake. Contrary to Arendt's repeated claim, in all these attempts at enlightenment, subsumption is indeed operative, except that judgmental standards are taken from experience as when we say that someone is "as brave as Achilles" (77) and exercised in communication with others. Political judgments are formed through experience and persuasion just as judgments of taste are formed through education. In the absence of such exercise and education, we run the risk of life-long embarrassment in aesthetic choices and, more dangerous, of lifelong mistakes in political

---

10 Immanuel Kant, *What is Enlightenment?*, A 481.

choices. The terminological fluctuations between the 'particular' and the 'singular' stem from the peculiar status of the aesthetic and political objects: They are subsumable, not under universals, but under standards nevertheless.

Arendt's disdain for history—which she treated as one more "metaphysical fallacy" (127)—results from the same fascination with singularity as she construes it from her overdrawn parallel between the aesthetic and the political judgment. The "rare moments of freedom" are unique, irretrievable. Today's superpowers may eventually relive something of the slow decline the British Empire has suffered since World War I, but we will never relive the Paris Commune or May 1968. As a consequence of her fascination with singulars, politics turns into something other than the pursuit of realizable, but common, ends. That is left to what Kant called "the mechanics of nature," by which even "a race of devils" will eventually be forced to enact a republican constitution.[11]

What remains for the public realm is one's being seen and heard by everybody in speaking about the common good. What Achilles is in respect to courage, namely, the paradigmatic instance, the revolutionary general assembly is in respect to politics. The political realm is opened up wherever participants in a community speak up: always *hic et nunc*. How strangely disembodied such a notion of the political turns out to be appears from the underlying time concept, which is more akin to the medieval "standing now" than to Kant's secularized "providence."

On the positive side, her extreme, rarified understanding of the political allows Arendt to cut through the old dilemma, whether it is an active or contemplative life that makes man happy. Had she lived to write the third volume, *Judging*, of her *Life of the Mind* she might have had to take back her earlier siding with Aristotle's *Politics* when she summed up her theory of the *polis* saying, "Acting is fun."[12] From the Kant lectures it appears inevitable that she would have had to shift her emphasis and identify *eudaimonia* neither with action nor with contemplation, but with judgment. Her

---

11 Immanuel Kant, *Perpetual Peace*, A 60–61.

12 Hannah Arendt, *Crises of the Republic* (New York: Viking Press, 1969), 203.

Kantian revisionist reading of the Greeks might have compelled her to conclude, judging is fun.

On the negative side, however, such a shift leaves no room for the genuinely Kantian conviction that history is the locus where we emancipate ourselves from our self-incurred tutelage "over a long, perhaps incalculable series of generations, each passing its enlightenment to the next."[13] Construing a sharp either-or between Kant's trust in progress and his discovery of nonteleological judgment, Arendt concludes, "The very idea of progress ... contradicts Kant's notion of human dignity" (77). As a result, she denounces "the pseudo-divinity named History of the modern age" (131). In Kant himself, no such either-or is possible, be it only because the two terms that she separates are actually held together by the ideal of the noumenal republic. This ideal generates moral imperatives that make her separation of the political from the moral look artificial as well. It is true that, at times, she does acknowledge the link between the two, but only to pull even the moral over to the side of the singular, of our choice and judgment of it: "In the last analysis ... our decisions about right and wrong will depend upon our choice of company, with whom we wish to spend our lives" (113).

The thrust toward rehabilitating the singular, as Arendt has traced it in Kant's theory of judgment, goes to the heart of his critical system. This last quotation indicates, however, most strikingly that she tried to run that rehabilitation program on impracticable tracks. To make right and wrong depend on one's choice of friends amounts to metabolizing the good into an object of chance encounter and selection, the way one encounters and selects a life companion. Such hit-or-miss morality turns the prestige of the singular against Kant's very letter and spirit.

Along which tracks, then, is one to pursue Kant's doctrine of the singular as he adumbrates it in his theory of aesthetic judgments? It is no more than an adumbration since aesthetic appreciation puts only conceptual, not paradigmatic, subsumption out of function. As the singular appears under the guise of one given particular gauged by one exemplary particular, it is not entirely set free from

---

13 Immanuel Kant, *Idea for a Universal History*, A 389.

comprehensive measurement. Still, there exists a line of inquiry in Kant that articulates not only the judgmental difference but also the *différend* by which the one and the many impose on us their contradictory claims. This is not some argumentative strategy among others; it is the most traditional of issues in Western philosophy, a question Kant consistently shuns while answering it equally consistently: *Ti to on*; "What is being?"[14]

Synthesis and Dispersion

Kant is said to have substituted a merely formal act, apperception, for all ancient substantive referents held capable of ordering a cosmos inasmuch as they were conceived as eminently present to it. However, Kant did not quite abandon the ancients' quest for an ultimate *mensura*; he merely directed it away from the demiurge or Creator measuring his works to reason measuring its acts. He is, therefore, said to have replaced dogmatic metaphysics with critical metaphysics, the metaphysics of experience. Yet he, too, seeks an "originary" *thesis*, positing, by which we can discriminate between what is and what is not. To be sure, his transcendental egothesis cannot be "ontological" in the sense of a highest degree of being. The ultimate self-positing of thinking sought by Kant has to satisfy only the requirement of a highest condition for experience. As such, it is nothing entitative—"no thing," not a subsistent referent of which one could predicate, for instance, simplicity or eternality. Still, it has to be "originary," "an act of spontaneity," be it only as "the highest point to which all employment of the understanding must be attached."[15] Apperception is the source of mental func-

---

14 I have developed the various senses of being in Kant from a different perspective in "Legislation-Transgression: Strategies and Counter-Strategies in the Transcendental Justification of Norms," *Man and World* XVII (1984), 361–98. [Republished in Reiner Schürmann, *Tomorrow the Manifold. Essays on Foucault, Anarchy, and the Singularization to Come*, ed. Malte Fabian Rauch and Nicolas Schneider (Zurich: Diaphanes, 2019), 77–120.—Eds.]

15 Kant, *Critique of Pure Reason*, B 132 and 134.

tions, not the origin of subsistent beings. Through one of the functions emanating from it, we declare what is.

To "declare" or "accuse" is *kategorein* in Greek. In Kant, being is a category: that which tells us not *what* we experience, but *that* we experience something. As such it is one fundamental mode of synthesizing data into the unity of objective experience. Just as every other category, being is not only a law for all actual experience but also inseparably a form of all objects actually experienced. It has objective validity when gathered with the pure forms of intuition, time and space. In conjunction with these forms, the dynamic category of *Dasein* co-constitutes whatever can become a phenomenon for us. Such is Kant's doctrinal answer to the question of being. It is doctrinal inasmuch as for him anything that can be proved without recourse to appearances, anything that can be demonstrated or deduced *a priori*, is part of a doctrine. Kant's discovery of the categorial status of existence allows for a *critical doctrine* (the two terms are not mutually exclusive) of being.

A second concept of being is, however, also operative in Kant, which precedes the revolution in his way of thinking and remains operative at each major step in his critical system. It may be called his countervailing concept of being since it avails or prevails against the doctrinal notion. The 'vail'—value or worth—of this other notion equals that of the category. It pulls Kantian ontology into the direction not of the uniting one, but of the disparate singulars. It thereby opens the rift between the one and the many as equally binding for us. It opens the *différend*.

In his precritical treatise on the sole proof for a demonstration of God's existence, Kant wrote, "Being is not a predicate, nor a determination of any thing."[16] It is usually held that this early work is incompatible not only with Kant's later criticism of the ontological argument, but more generally with his transcendental method as such. That is assuredly the case—except in one respect, which is related to the understanding of being operative in the treatise. Being has nothing of a predicate since it adds no thought content to what-

---

16 *Der einzig mögliche Beweisgrund zu einer Demonstration des Daseins Gottes* (1763). For what follows, see particularly A 1–16.

ever we conceive. Kant's starting point is reminiscent of Leibnizian idealities (propositions in logic, mathematics, and pure geometry) among which universal and necessary connections obtain. The young Kant reasons not from 'real things', as the Scholastics did, nor from 'being' as a necessary thought content, as Descartes did, but from the universal *possibilities*, the formal presuppositions for anything real. His argument is *a priori,* based neither on observation nor on a trusted correspondence between concepts and things, but on connections among concepts. Absolute existence is attainable from that rationalist starting point—the system of rules for thinking—insofar as *that system of rules is given*. If there are any rules whatsoever for connecting concepts, be it only the opposition between "true" and "false," then material existence, too, is assured. "If all existence is canceled, then nothing whatsoever is posited, nothing at all is given: no matter for anything thinkable, and any possibility vanishes entirely." The point is that the real and the possible can very well be negated together without any ensuing contradiction. It is, however, contradictory to hold that the real exists without the possible, or the possible without the real. *What* is being thought does not lead then, as in Descartes, to apodeicticity, but rather *that* there are thought contents ruled by necessary connections. There would be no thinking at all if these particular kinds of givens—possibles—were lacking: "That there is anything possible and yet nothing real is a contradiction since, if nothing existed, nothing thinkable would be given."[17] Being as the position of anything follows from the givenness of ideal entities.

The steps by which the early Kant argues the existence of God—stepping from any thing's givenness to absolute givenness and from existence to essence—have no direct bearing on his understanding of being. The anticipation of the transcendental method in the early treatise is, however, remarkable: without givenness as its starting point, all knowledge would remain impossible. To be sure, after the critical turn givenness is no longer that of a system of idealities. Therefore, being is then no longer understood as absolute, but only as relative positedness, that is, relative to our experience. The

---

17 Ibid., A 19.

first feature one has to retain of the other concept of being in Kant, other than the category, is givenness as such. That concept cannot be analyzed any further; it can only be determined negatively. Each major section of the *Critique of Pure Reason* contributes to such negative determination whereby givenness will appear as precognitive, precategorial and prepredicative. The most revelatory issue is that of the existing I, of how the I is given to me.

Kant claims that the Transcendental Aesthetic "establishes already of itself the objective reality of noumena" (A 249) insofar as, in experiencing, we necessarily experience something.[18] On the level of a simple encounter, what is experienced yields no knowledge yet. We cannot say what it is that we come upon. It yields however its own certitude of objective reality, namely, that something is there whereby we are affected. Contrary to some ambiguous formulations in and after Kant, this affectedness, or facticity, cannot be construed as "posited" by consciousness. It precedes all acts of the mind. Such is the very starting point of the Aesthetic: the preeminence of intuiting over thinking is due to the immediacy of the sense data. As is well known, that starting point of the *Critique* made Friedrich Jacobi complain, "*Without* that presupposition (of the noumenon) I cannot enter the *Critique*, while with that presupposition I cannot remain in it."[19] Sense affection provides obviously no knowledge of the noumenon qua noumenon; as a mere sensation, it is "blind." Nor has the being concept implied in sense affection anything to do yet with the formal constitution of objects. It is merely the concept of a datum as such, the critical descendant of the "data of possibility" in the earlier treatise. In the Transcendental Aesthetic, ontological givenness is determined negatively as precognitive.

Kant specifies his understanding of being as givenness in the Transcendental Analytic. "The 'I think' expresses the act of determining my existence" (B 158n). Affection and givenness are here self-affection and self-givenness in inner sense. "My existence" can-

---

18 This and all subsequent references in parentheses are to Kant, *Critique of Pure Reason*.

19 Friedrich Jacobi, *David Hume über den Glauben oder Idealismus und Realismus* (Breslau, 1787), 222–23.

not be given either to intellectual intuition or to formal consciousness, since it is to be determined by the "I think." The existing I cannot be either the noumenal or the transcendental I. But neither can it be the empirical I as observed in our mental life. For such observation—for self-experience—the intuition through inner sense would have to be joined to a pure concept of the understanding. But, Kant adds, "existence here is not yet a category" (B 422). As a mere sensation, existence precedes, he says, any experience and therefore any synthesis. In this context, then, the "I think" is turned into a proposition of existence independently of any recourse to categories. This is not, in Kant, a momentary lapse into Cartesian metaphysics. He explicitly justifies that step by describing the existing I as "indeterminately given" (B 423n), impossible to reify into a thinking thing. At this stage, it has already become impossible to maintain that existence, as the second category of modality, accuses being that is given to the senses. If such were the case, how could Kant claim that "existence here is not yet a category"?

Conversely, and for the same reason, the category cannot stand for the being (*Existenz*) of beings. If in givenness existence is not yet a category, then given beings have their being in themselves and do not receive it from the bestowing agency of the spontaneous rational subject.

How is one to construe the determinacy of the 'I think' so that it can in turn determine my existence? Obviously its *Bestimmtheit* cannot result from the pure concepts of the understanding. As the source of all determinations, the logical subject of thinking cannot itself be determined categorially. Determinacy is its very nature; it is utter spontaneity. It reigns supreme as the sole agency of configuration in experience. And yet, for it to "determine my existence," it has to be equiprimordial with givenness. The existing ego designates the as yet *indistinct* presence of an indeterminate sensation to thought. As their protosynthesis, it lacks conceptual articulation.

The dilemma, and eventually the *différend*, is more complex than the conflict between a 'mentalist' and a 'realist' ontology. The question is not: Does being lie in the mind or in the things? The question as it arises from Kant's examination of the I, is rather: Is "my existence" the indeterminate content of sensation or the determinate act of consciousness? Kant remains perplexingly hesitant on this crucial point. He does justify the step from transcendental logic to transcendental ontology ("existence here is not yet a category"), but he does not in any way thematize the precategorial sensation of existence with which, however, in his own words, experience sets out. His hesitancy shines through when he states that, prior to any act of experience and any synthesis, there occurs the givenness of the indeterminate "something real" that is "designated as such in the proposition 'I think'" (B 423n). Could it be that the "unknown root" (B 29) of our faculties is existence as sheer presence of ourselves to ourselves? If so, this is not only a fragile root, but a fractured one. Its brokenness appears from closer scrutiny of the way such primitive self-presence comes to be determined.

In order for the existing subject to function as the stage for all beings, making them appear through representation and thereby granting them categorial being, it would have to be thoroughly determined. This is, however, not the case. Indeterminate presence proves to be a distinct moment that precedes not only knowing but also thinking and apperception. Otherwise the "I think" could not determine my existence. The originary nomothetical act, the act of legislation from which both theoretical rules and practical norms are derived, is the imposing of the I as a law unto myself: We have to "presuppose ourselves, entirely *a priori*, as legislating with regard to our own being and also as determining this existence ourselves" (B 430). Self-presence is indeterminate since in it my existence is not yet articulated. Presence precedes consciousness (apperception) as well as introspection (experience). *Being as indeterminate presence precedes being as schematized category.* The subject thus shows itself to be broken. On the one hand, there is the determinative "I think" that posits itself and unfolds into twelve categories, and on the other, "my existence" which stands in need of determination. Kant's second being-concept disrupts critical ontology inasmuch as indeterminate existence, given to inner sensation, opposes a counterpoint of ignorance to apperception as the highest point of consciousness. It opposes a counterstrategy of indistinctness to the originary strategy of supreme formal synthesis in the *cogito*.

The determinate "I think" arises from indeterminate presence and in turn determines it. Without this double strategy, there would be no subject at all. By the same token, however, determination or self-possession does not result from what Kant describes as ontologically first, "my existence." As a consequence, Kant gives two answers to the question, What is being? His doctrinal answer (existence is a category) centers being on the spontaneous I, but his countervailing answer (existence is presence) disperses being among the givens received in sensibility (of which the existing I is only the paradigmatic case). Kant's first answer to the being question follows the strategy of synthesis toward the one. His second answer hints at an undertow toward plurification or dispersion.

In these conflicting answers, something entirely different than an insufficiently worked out ontology is at stake. One has to view that break as a displacement of the old metaphysical difference between *einai* and *on*, or *esse* and *ens*, and one may speak consequently of a transcendental difference in Kant. All forms of the ontological difference, whether metaphysical, transcendental, or phenomenological, spell out an ambiguity that lies in the present participle: the English participle *being* can mean both the noun *a being* and the verb *to be*. Due to the Copernican Revolution in Kant, the transcendental difference exhibits the peculiar feature that the inherited terms of the difference are inverted. In Kant it is not the verb, not *Dasein* as a categorial act or as conceiving, that stands for indeterminacy, but the noun, the unknown something encountered in a sensation. In the transcendental difference, determination is a human doing, the act of categorizing. The verb expresses subsumption under predicates. Both in Aristotle and in Heidegger, on the contrary, the verb stands for indeterminacy and the noun, for determination. An entity determines—"forms" (Aristotle), "stops" (from *epechein*, Heidegger)—the neutral being-process. Kant's inverting the poles of determinacy and indeterminacy is the consequence for ontology of what is described today as the modern triumph of subjectivity. Determination is a subjective doing: categorizing. But the inversion is ineffectual; the subject's pretense to universal determination remains shot through with indeterminacy. Hence Kant's broken ontology, broken between verbal *kategorein* and nominal fact.

Kant's self-congratulatory comment that he has drawn up "exhaustively" the architectonic of pure reason and has solved all conflicts to "complete satisfaction" (A XII) forbids filing his broken ontology under the rubric of unsolved issues. His two answers to the being question must be taken in their *heterogeneity*. In them, Kant acknowledges the condition that makes us mortals. His analysis of the existing I shows that indeterminacy and self-determination are two equally indispensable moments of our being. Their equiprimordiality is sufficient reason to read him as articulating more than the harmonious depth-structure of *Differenz*, namely, the disharmonious surface-rupture of *différend*. As Kant subverts his doctrine of being as a category, the subject stands torn between the pull toward synthesis and the pull toward dispersion. The doctrine of being as concept (from *con-capere*, holding together, just as *Begriff* stems from *greifen*, to grasp), that is, as the act of uniting the pure sensible manifold, is subverted by his systematic need for being as givenness, as indeterminate, and as precategorial. Primitive self-presence, the starting point for experience, throws the subject's quest for self-possession out of gear. Its "ground" or "essence" (B 430) places full presence forever out of reach.

The best known formulation of Kant's countervailing concept of being occurs in the Transcendental Dialectic. The formulation is reminiscent of his precritical writings: "'Being' (*Sein*) is obviously not a real predicate" (B 626). 'Real' does not here refer to the first category of quality any more than 'being' refers to the second category of modality. We know empirically what something is when we know its 'real' predicates or properties. In the case of the supreme being, these properties would have to be known *a priori*. If such were the case, the properties—what the medievals called 'perfections'—of that supreme being would allow for its "thorough determination." Its concept would then be rendered concrete as the "set concept (*Inbegriff*) of all reality" (B 605). But *Sein* is obviously not a real predicate once being is understood as the sensible givenness of a physical fact, to the exclusion of intellectual affection. As to the category of *Dasein*, although it is thinkable *a priori* and although it is a predicate, it does "not in the least enlarge the concept to which it [is] attached" (B 266). It is not a *real* predicate either. It gives us nothing to think. *Sein* differs from *Dasein* (or *Existenz*) in that it is not thinkable *a priori* in any way, neither formally as all categories are nor materially as the supposed divine perfections would have to be. To refute all attempts at an ontological proof of the existence of God, Kant then repeats his precritical equation between being and positedness (B 626). Translated into the critical context, that equation points most decisively to being as the precognitive, precategorial, prepredicative givenness of singulars.

The being of the singular remains only hinted at in the first and the second *Critique*. It comes fully to the fore in the third *Critique*, where Kant, as Hannah Arendt had sensed, addresses it as the very issue for judging. That issue remains distorted, however, as long as one does not place it within the itinerary of the being question in Kant. The itinerary begins with the precritical assertion that being is no predicate at all; it leads to the *Critique of Pure Reason*, in which being is negated as a 'real' predicate, to be affirmed only as the copula (B 626); and it concludes with the express recognition of the two strategies in being, in the *Critique of Judgment*.

The divergent strategies toward synthesis and dispersion are expressed there through the distinction between 'position' (*Position*) and 'positing' (*Setzung*). The first addresses the possibility of things, the second, their actuality. The 'position' indicates merely the mind's ability to represent phenomena to itself, that is, to gain access to them. The term must, therefore, not be confused with the same term in the first *Critique*, where it designates the exact contrary: the "being outside my concept," for example, the actuality of a hundred thalers in my pocket (B 627). In the third *Critique*, such actuality is called *Setzung*. "The actual ... signifies the positing of a thing in itself (outside our concept)."[20] 'Position', then, marks the relation of a representation to the understanding and 'positing' that of an existing thing to our sensibility. *Setzung* results from chance encounter. It is, as Kant adds, "contingent." Furthermore, representations are universals; 'position' denotes the strategy toward synthesis, toward the one. Contingents, on the other hand, are singulars; 'positing' denotes the strategy toward dispersion, toward the many.

Throughout his writings, Kant understands being as givenness. But only after the discovery of aesthetic judgments, by which we

20 *Critique of Judgment*, B 340.

address the unprecedented, does givenness clearly mean for him the *there* of singulars irreducible to any representation. In calling that givenness 'positing', Kant calls attention to the act of reception in sensibility. Receptivity, as he explained already in the Transcendental Aesthetic, is an act. It does not mean passivity. 'Position' and 'positing' articulate, then, the acts of understanding and of sensibility, respectively. Kant's two ways of answering the being question result from his dualist ontology, which splits the subject into "two entirely heterogeneous pieces."[21] According to one line of argument, being is a category, a concept, the act of unifying the manifold in the understanding. According to the other line of argument, it lies "outside my concept." It is the sporadic singular, encountered by chance in sensibility and acknowledged by equally sporadic acts of compliance.

Tragic Sobriety

"That mountain there! That cloud there! What is 'real' about that? Just subtract the fantasm and the whole human *contribution* from it, my sober friends! If only you *could!*"[22] Fantasms are what Kant calls representations. Nietzsche invites his sober friends—presumably the adherents to enlightenment—to acknowledge the singular as such, without judging it as beautiful, as purposive, or as spectacular in Arendt's sense, without turning it into a particular. All fantasms subtracted, we would "meet the phenomena head-on." Judgment would be transvaluated into thinking. We would think the singular in its being. We would be entirely sober and enlightened at last. But, "If only you *could!*"

It seems that we can*not*. Aesthetic and teleological judgments are reflective. In them, the universal is not pregiven, as in determinative judgments; it is to be sought and can be retained only in the mode of an 'as if'. Neither Kant nor Nietzsche believe that we can disintoxicate ourselves from universal representations to the point

---

21 Ibid.

22 Friedrich Nietzsche, *The Gay Science*, bk. II, sec. 57.

of thinking no more than the singular in its being (both Kant and Nietzsche would therefore be mislabeled as 'nominalists'). But both have seen the push-and-pull that tears all human experience: the push toward unity under some representation, coupled with the pull toward dispersion among singulars. Not unlike Nietzsche's, Kant's—reluctant—statements about being arise from a deep insight into the human condition. Unlike Nietzsche, however, he shied away from what he saw. The human condition is to stand under the twofold law of collocation and dislocation, without recourse to any supreme locus from which would proceed all allocations.

As a category, concept, or fantasm, being gathers beings into one; its script is a monogram. As "outside my concept," it disperses beings into the many; its script is a scattergram. Kant never attempts to elaborate a theory of the singular. Yet throughout his writings, although mostly in passing, he recognizes that rift between being as univocal and being as plurivocal. He does more than just recognize it. By his dualism he justifies it expressly as inscribed in our very constitution. Only in one line of inquiry is there no hint, as far as I can tell, of the undertow toward plurification, and that is in his moral doctrine. There the monovalence of the law triumphs over all polyvalence. Indeed, which axiologist could sustain the fervor of an absolute value that is *prescriptive morally*, while asserting as equally *prescriptive ontologically* the counterstrategy toward "that mountain, that cloud"? Such sobriety could only deflect the subject from the orbit of implacable necessitation. It would be an exorbitant sobriety.

From the aesthetic and the teleological point of view, the counterstrategy toward the monadic appears in Kant's third *Critique* as the very issue for judging. Yet sheer compliance with monadic givens exceeds our capacity. To say how much I like that mountain, that cloud, I say, "It reminds me of ...," and already the singular is lost to subsumption. Already the judgmental *difference* is put to work. On the other hand, from the ontological point of view, our allegiance is as much to monadic, centrifugal dispersion as it is to centripetal synthesis. In all our activities investigated by Kant, we put to work the ontological *différend*, or rather that *différend* puts us to work. In all our endeavors it ties us in one stroke and necessarily to consolidation as well as to dissolution. The retraction toward chaos, which Kant's critical turn was meant to stem, appears as no less normative ontologically than the attraction toward order. The most enlightened insight is into that double bind. There is no greater sobriety than to recognize and live that conflict, without dreamt-up sublation.

Kant's split ontology argues an insight that is as old as Homer and the Tragics. Achilles, the most shining of all heroes, delights in his splendor, feeds his anger, savors his vengeance, is more alive than anyone else, all the while knowing his imminent death. Antigone and Oedipus are not victims 'crushed by the terrible wheel of destiny.' Rather, they enact and affirm the dissolution at the very heart, art of all configuration. The tragic insight does not affirm life *against* death, it affirms death *in* life. To think to its end the *différend* in being, which Kant preferred to skirt, would amount to breaking the age-old contract whereby the philosopher acts as the expert of deep anchorage and, therefore, as our most indispensable civil servant. His promotion to that worthy rank coincided with the decline of the Greek tragedy, when the noblest task came to lie in the ministry of consolidating the city and consoling the spirit. The *différend* unmasks that twofold edification as redundant hubris.

Kant with Aeschylus, then? Inceptively so, yes. In the age of Aeschylus, Greece lost once and for all its archaic smile. One century later, Democritus discovered a new pleasure. He has been called the laughing philosopher. He said he found greater joy in understanding a causal relation than he would have had in occupying the imperial throne of Persia. Nothing, indeed, protects normative edifices better than causal representations from dissolutive encroachments. In the reliability of causes, Democritus found his peace of mind and Greece, a comfort by which we have lived ever since. The *différend,* on the other hand, neither consolidates nor consoles. The inescapable, though contradictory, allegiance to both synthesis and dispersion ties us not to the edifying radiance of a cause but—like Oedipus blinded and *sophos*—to an excess of light which is the horror of night.

Discursive Types

There were strong reasons why Hannah Arendt borrowed from Malraux the title of her first major work, *The Human Condition*. In that book, she located all human experience at the conjunction of two determinants in our lives, natality and mortality. As conditions, these are not equatable with birth and death in the sense of the occurrences that open and close a life span; rather, the term *condition* has to be taken in its technical transcendental sense as designating *a priori* traits. The double-bind in which natality and mortality place us marks the *vita activa* as inescapably tragic. This starting point of her inquiries accounts for the peculiar untimeliness of her attempted new science—that is, philosophy—of politics within the contemporary types of discourse about the public realm.*

Within the so-called Continental tradition, there exist, indeed, today two predominant discursive types in political philosophy. One type presents itself as prescriptive. From various quarters one hears that a theory of praxis is not worth its label unless it establishes first foundations. This claim has been put forth for some decades now from both ends of the political spectrum. On the Left, it has been couched in the discursive type of a critical theory that would secure, or rest on, some form of 'ultimate grounding'; on the Right, it has produced notorious attempts at rehabilitating the prestige of 'classical' teleology.

The other predominant discursive type in political philosophy today remains more modestly descriptive. Its modesty is, however, deceptive: Phenomenologists trust that a pertinent insight into the human condition suffices to assure the necessary and sufficient premises for practical intervention. They need neither ontology, nor deontology; they have no use for operations such as deriving 'ought' from 'is'; yet they are far from dismissing the question, "What is to be done?" Rather they consider that, inasmuch as they succeed in bringing into view the life-world with its given potential, this question is already being answered.

---

* Here and in the subsequent paragraphs of this section we have omitted Schürmann's synopses of the contributions to the edited collection to which this essay served as an introduction.—Eds.

If we now look back briefly at Arendt's attempted rehabilitation of the singular, it becomes obvious why the new political philosophy for which she meant to lay the groundwork had to remain and still remains untimely: Neither the normative nor the phenomenological discourse about the public realm address the singular as *unhintergehbar*, impossible to subsume. To be sure, prescriptive and descriptive universals make for heterogeneous subsumptions—as heterogeneous as are standards imposed on action and categories read off the life-world. Still, both of these discursive types make it impossible to retain the issue for judgment she wished to hold on to, namely, the singular in its being. Not that she did not have use for either normative or phenomenological questions; in fact, she answered both [...]. But her answers to these questions could and can only infuriate the practitioners of both the prescriptive and the descriptive discourse. What did she have to say about norms? That the "rare moments of freedom" in history were those in which compelling rules for action were temporarily suspended! Such anarchism does not sit well with social scientists convinced that the heritage of the Enlightenment stands and falls with their ability to secure the one type of rationality by which communicative action would find itself necessarily placed under some universally obligatory *a priori*. And what did she have to say about descriptions? That they amount to comparing individual deeds to individual deeds: this agent X acting as bravely as that agent Y. In the private realm, "our decisions about right and wrong depend on our choice of company, with whom we wish to spend our lives"; in the public realm, they depend on persuasion. Partner-choice and rhetorics, however, do not sit well with phenomenologists looking for originative categories in the acting subject 'as such.'

Technicity, Topology, Tragedy: Heidegger on "That Which Saves" in the Global Reach

> The technicity of modern technique follows from a mutation in the essential way to be of truth. [...] From aletheia's conflictual way springs the possibility and the necessity of "tragedy."
>
> —Heidegger, *Parmenides*

The organizers of the symposium at the same time raised and chased the specter of what one may call technological essentialism.[1] In so doing, they placed themselves in good company. Michel Foucault wrote a *History of Madness* and later a *History of Sexuality*, only to tell us that neither 'madness' nor 'sexuality' designated enduring essences but rather problems that have their dates of emergence and their age of pertinence.

Likewise our hosts. They raised that specter in as much as the general title, "The Problem of Technology in the Western Tradition," suggests that we were invited to wrestle with a unitary issue that may have assumed various forms over the ages. In that, they have conventional wisdom on their side. Common sense would indeed have no qualms about distinguishing *kinds* of technology, for instance, pertaining to, or at least contemporaneous with—I quote from the titles of essays in this series—classical thought, Christianity, modern philosophy, Romanticism, and American liberalism. We do speak of Stone Age technology and DNA technology. One is then perfectly justified in suggesting that technologies come in the plural, that is, in various species subsumable under one generic concept. At the same time, however, we were there to discuss the technological project for the control and mastery of nature, clearly an exclusively modern project. Here the problem of

---

1 [This essay is based on a talk Schürmann gave at the "Symposium on Science, Reason, and Modern Democracy" at the Department of Political Science, Michigan State University, in 1989–90.—Eds.]

technology is pertinent to one age alone. Control and mastery as projected by Galileo and Newton are not pertinent to the premodern world. The caveman's club has its *specific* technology; so do the medieval crossbow and today's MX missile. But the modern quest for mastery does not *specify* technology. When Descartes conceived a method "to render ourselves masters of nature,"[2] and inasmuch as modern technology realizes that project, one is clearly no longer speaking of some universal concept specifiable according to kinds. Between the plural of, say, warfare technologies and the singular of modern technology there exists a mere homonymy, the same word being used with diverse semantic functions. The specter of essentialism is thereby chased.

I wish to show some implications of the distinction thus suggested between technology as, on one hand, the common name for innumerable techniques and, on the other, the proper name for modern universal *mathesis*. A technique, the know-how that the Greeks called *technē*, is operative whenever humans make some goal-directed use of their hands. As to modern mastery over nature via a universal mathematical project, this is something different from know-how. It is one epochal project of truth, best described as 'technicity.' Because I was asked to discuss Heidegger, I first develop a few traits of technicity so understood. Then I suggest that the discourse of epochal configurations, or stamps—diachronic topologies, such as Foucault's—cannot be Heidegger's last word about truth in technicity. As stamping our world today, technicity reveals something that saves. It reveals a more originary truth: the tragic condition of being.

An Epochal Truth

Heidegger's description of modernity as the age of global technicity is probably well known. I therefore remain content here with enumerating a few thematic points—not Heideggerian theses but

---

2 René Descartes, *Discourse on Method*, pt. 6, *Œuvres de Descartes*, ed. Charles Adam and Paul Tannery (Paris: Vrin, 1965), 6:62.

short cuts connecting some of what he called his 'ways' of thought. He has indeed followed diverse ways of thinking about *technē* and technicity, as well as about technology (in the sense of the *logos*, that is, the peculiar mode of gathering proper to technicity) and about technocracy (the regime imposed by technicity on thinking and acting). From his most explicit text[3] about these issues the following reminders can be spelled out.

An essentialist difference. "Technique is not the same as the essence of technique" (*QCT*, 4). Any modern procedure based on quantification requires a technique. But the essence of such techniques—'technicity'—is not itself technical. One may call this the technological difference, as quantification gathers (*legein*) phenomena into their way to be. The difference is clearly modeled, albeit for modern mathesis only, after the generic notion mentioned earlier. The essence (*Wesen*) of technique, Heidegger indeed says, is comparable to "the essence of a tree" (ibid.), which is not any particular tree. Likewise, technicity is not any particular technique, not this or that quantificatory procedure. The technological difference describes technicity in analogy with the subsumptive concept I began with.

A historical difference. "Enframing is destined to us as one mode of unconcealment" (*QCT*, 29). With this, modern technicity is now placed outside of generic descriptions. The displacement results from another sense of *Wesen*, other than Platonist: "Thus far we have understood 'essence' in the usual meaning it has [...] in the academic language of philosophy" (ibid.). The other sense of technicity, however, accessible to an 'other thinking'—other than subsumptive and opening, as we shall see, an 'other possibility'—inscribes our age within a concrete historical destiny. *Wesen* here is a verb. It designates the way epochs have unfolded in the West. In each, everyday stuff revealed itself situated within one finite constellation, one definite mode of unconcealment. Thus the crossbow does not belong in the age of technicity but in what Heidegger else-

---

3 Martin Heidegger, "The Question concerning Technology," in *The Question Concerning Technology and Other Essays*, trans. William J. Lovitt (New York: Harper, 1977), 3–35, hereafter cited as *QCT*. I do not always follow this translation.

where calls the imperial-imperative epoch.[4] The stamp (*Prägung*, *Gepräge*) that marks our own age is described as *Gestell*, 'enframing' or 'positionality.' It differs from things, not logically, as a species differs from the cases it encompasses, but phenomenologically, as one pervasive mode of manifestation differs from what it makes manifest. Enframing is not a universal. Nor is it a particular, in any way subsumed or subsumable under some universal. It is our *singular* site. By way of anticipation, let me add that tracing the epochal stamps by which the West has lived is one task incumbent upon topology.

Phenomenality. "Modern technicity [is] an unconcealing that requisitions" (*QCT*, 17). This answers the question of how, under the exclusive mode of manifestation that is technicity, phenomena are constituted. Modern phenomenality is due to a certain hegemonic trait in self-disclosure, which Heidegger calls 'requisitioning' (*Herausfordern*). Phenomena appear, summoned as it were by the all-encompassing regime of method in the sense of Descartes.[5] Stated negatively, nothing can become manifest that does not conform to the project of global mastery. Nothing has being unless it enters into the system of quantification with its consequences, such as experimentation, production, circulation, consumption—in a word, unless it is objectified into "standing reserve" (*Bestand*; *QCT*, 17). This epochal requisitioning designates "the way in which everything comes to presence" (ibid.). It includes therefore the subject as well, which is why in the age of hegemonic technicity man becomes properly a phenomenon to himself only via the human and social sciences. Phenomenality no longer results from the intuitive grasp of an essence or species but from the probative grip on a specimen.

Truth as event. "In enframing happens the event of unconcealment" (*QCT*, 21). Throughout his writings, Heidegger sought to understand truth as a process of unveiling rather than a state of

---

4 For the entire Latin-speaking age and beyond, the "fundamental relation to beings as such was administered by the sway of imperium" (Martin Heidegger, *Parmenides* [Frankfurt: Klostermann, 1982], 65–66).

5 See also Heidegger's commentary on Newton's First Law of Motion in *What Is a Thing?*, trans. W. B. Barton Jr. and Vera Deutsch (New York: Henry Regnery, 1967), 76–80, 85–88.

conformity. *Alétheia* is the originary condition beneath received normative notions of truth. Thus, when the norm is sought in 'adequate' propositions about data, or in the 'agreement' of a thing with its form, or again in some 'assimilation' of the soul to the true, the philosophical gaze remains riveted to things disclosed rather than moving back to the process of disclosure. With this step back from the manifest to manifestation, Heidegger steps out of the realm of metaphysics. As there have been various modes of manifestation in the West, truth has a history. The condition of that history is an event: truth always occurs as an unconcealing. This relation between condition and conditioned in history was the one issue Heidegger kept pursuing in his middle period. It can be described as the difference between two disparate singulars: the unfolding of truth epochs and the ever-new truth event. Contemporary technicity is one such differential configuration, one epochal figure of manifestation as it differs from everything manifest. In it happens our epochal truth.

Conflictual Truth. "The essence of technicity is ambiguous in an elevated sense. Such ambiguity points into the mystery of all unconcealing, that is, of truth" (*QCT*, 33). Normative truth stands and falls with univocity. Indeed, received standards of conformity had to be unambiguous, simple. How else could they have normed performances of adequation, agreement, or assimilation? Understood as event of manifestation, on the other hand, truth is inescapably conflictual. A strategy toward concealment asserts itself in all modes of unconcealment. This ambiguity entails decisive consequences for the law as well as for being, affecting the very ultimacy of *Sein*. In terms of the law, a transgressive strategy works within every legislative strategy. In terms of the event that is being, an expropriating strategy (*Enteignis*) disperses all appropriating strategies (*Ereignis*) as they constitute constellations of phenomena. To render fully what Heidegger takes to be 'the Greek experience,' *alétheia* then needs to be understood as unconcealment-concealment; the law, as legislation-transgression; and being, as appropriation-expropriation. The originary duality indicated by the privative *a-* and the verb *léthein* (to dissemble) is in no way symmetrical. Despite their lexical parallelism, unconcealment is not the determinate negation of concealment. Unconcealment is of entities, but concealment is of being qua being. Truth and untruth therefore remain irreconcilable. The two strategies in truth, Heidegger adds, "draw past each other like the paths of two stars in the sidereal revolutions" (*QCT*, 33). With this disparateness at its very heart, truth loses its univocity. Again by way of anticipation: retrieving the event of disparate, conflictual truth will be the other task assigned to topology.

That which saves. "Where danger is, also grows that which saves" (*QCT*, 28, 34, 42). In his investigations into technicity, Heidegger liked to quote this line from Hölderlin. What is that which saves? It can only consist in the express retrieval of truth's conflictual way to be. Hence this highly polemical either-or: *either* "pick up all standards" from among the unconcealed available stock, *or* "letting oneself be taken into the essential way to be of the unconcealed and of its unconcealment" (*QCT*, 26). This either-or sets "the other thinking" apart from all normative, subsumptive, entitative, univocal thinking. It sets 'the other possibility' apart from technicity as today's actuality. The other thinking and the other possibility indicate that which saves, namely, that man place himself expressly within the double bind that is truth. "As yet unexperienced, but perhaps more experienced in a time to come, [man] may be needed and used to preserve truth's essential way to be" (*QCT*, 33). Since that essential way to be is conflictual (from *fligere*, to 'clash'), polemical (from *polemos*, 'strife'), agonistic (from *agonia*, 'contest'), there is agony in salvation. In the words of the epigraph quoted at the beginning, that which saves resides in the possibility and necessity of tragedy.

From Topology to the Tragic Condition of Being

This is obviously not the place to propose a theory of Attic tragedy. Suffice it to say that it always displays a clash, a strife, a contest between irreconcilable laws: for example, between those of Antigone and those of Creon.

Tragedy traces out something like a path of sight. The hero *sees* the laws of the city and of the family in conflict. Then he *blinds himself* to one of them, keeping his gaze fixed on the other. Nations and other communities have lived and continue to live within the shadow of this blindness. All normative single binds result from such self-incurred blinding. Then follows a catastrophe that *opens the hero's eyes*. This is the moment in which tragic truth is recognized. The vision of irreconcilable differing among laws *takes his sight away* (even gouges his eyes, as was the case for Oedipus and, in another way, for Tiresias), and it singularizes the hero to the point that the city no longer has room for him. From denial to recognition, blindness is transmuted. His orbits empty, Oedipus sees a normative double bind. He sees tragic differing. In *Oedipus at Colonus*, he is shown embracing it, reduced to silence but granted apotheosis, that is, deification, and receiving tutelage over Athens.

Heidegger's topological inquiry into the epochal stamps by which the West has lived, and of which technicity is the latest, models its itinerary after that tragic crisis.[6] It looks back toward beginnings that have initiated epochs and discovers in them an ambivalence breeding hubris. Then it seeks to grasp—again in the words of the epigraph above—the mutations in the essential way to be of truth. Heidegger seeks to retrieve the critical 'thrusts of time,' as he also calls the reversals in the history of truth, which set epochs apart. Finally, topology finds its own task in keeping alive the question of a possible *there*, a possible topos in which humankind might prove experienced enough to sustain the tragic condition of being.

That topos would respond to the early Greek. Here are a few lines on the Greek beginning, as well as on the other beginning in which tragic knowledge might save us in—not from— global technicity:

---

6 That model is most notable in Heidegger, *Beiträge zur Philosophie* ("Gesamtausgabe," vol. 65 [Frankfurt: Klostermann, 1989]) cited hereafter as *BzP*. The present article is fully understandable only in conjunction with three related papers on *BzP*: "Ultimate Double Binds," *Graduate Faculty Philosophy Journal* 14 (Fall 1991): 213–36 [Reprinted in Reiner Schürmann, *Tomorrow the Manifold. Essays on Foucault, Anarchy, and the Singularization to Come*, ed. Malte Fabian Rauch and Nicolas Schneider (Zurich: Diaphanes, 2019), 121–149.—Eds.]; "A Brutal Awakening to the Tragic Condition of Being," in Karsten Harries (ed.), *Art, Politics, Technology*, ed. Karsten Harries (New Haven: Yale University Press, forthcoming) [See Karsten Harries and Christoph Jamme (eds.), *Martin Heidegger. Politics, Art, and Technology* (New York: Holmes & Meier, 1994, 89–105.—Eds.]; and "Riveted to a Monstrous Site," in Joseph Margolis and Thomas Rockmore (eds.), *The Heidegger Case: On Philosophy and Politics* (Philadelphia: Temple University Press, 1992), 313–30.

"All inceptions are in themselves what is complete, unsurpassable. They escape historicist recording not because they are trans-temporal and eternal, but because they are greater than eternity. As *the thrusts* of time they place the openness for being to conceal in. The proper founding of this time-space is called *being*-there" (*BzP*, 17).

Topology is an inquiry into topoi, places. In Heidegger, these are the epochs in our history as they have led up to the age of technicity. Topology shows the deep historical roots of today's global reach. As it traces the places that have been ours, are ours, and can be ours, it is recapitulatory, critical, and anticipatory.

Recapitulatory topology asks, What has been the form of conflictuality—of the tragic—that in its Greek, Latin, and modern ministry the philosophical civil service[7] had both to see and to deny? In this its retrodictive task, topology spells out the double bind marking epochal inceptions. These are 'in themselves what is complete, unsurpassable.' Yet they are never simple. In his more nuanced readings of the tradition, Heidegger tries to show how any *instituting* discourse remains faithful to the phenomena, that is, in his words, to the disparity of unconcealedness and concealment. Epochal institutions 'place the openness for being to conceal in.' They point up the legislative-transgressive double bind, analogous in this to the opening of the dramas of Creon, Agamemnon, Eteocles, and others.

Any *instituted* discourse, on the other hand, represses dissension. As Heidegger diagnoses it, such repression is the fantasmic work of 'logic.' Following his less nuanced readings of the tradition, the reign of logic repeats the hubristic moment in tragedy when the heroic edict brings the conflict between city and family under one law. The order so established, however, never fails to prompt the return of the repressed. In the same way, even as it sustains an epoch, every hegemonic referent unfailingly also calls for singulars to assert themselves against subsumption, whereby it calls for its self-destitution.

---

7 "We are the functionaries of mankind" (Edmund Husserl, *The Crisis of the European Sciences and Transcendental Philosophy*, trans. David Carr [Evanston: Northwestern University Press, 1970], 17).

In its recapitulatory work, topology inquires about the places—the phenomena, the regions of experience—that philosophers have retained to the exclusion of others and that they have absolutized so as to deny originary strife. Among these topoi have figured mathematics (Plato), motion (Aristotle), the observation of consciousness by itself (Descartes), and many more. From the elevated position of these strongholds, like Creon settled in his royalty, the normative *chargés d'affaires* have been able to legislate. They have exalted one representation beyond measure, hubristically declared it the standard of all measurement, and thus turned singulars into particulars subjected to it.

Critical topology. Here one topos only asks to be situated and described. It is that caesura place from which speaks the topologist of the present who asks: How can the double bind once glimpsed (the repressed 'having-been' of Greek tragedy) today appear imminent (the 'to-come' that saves and is a matter to safeguard)? In this literally decisive place, phenomenology does not, to be sure, turn into yet another instituting discourse. Rather, it addresses a transition. What is at stake is how "the essence of technique [...] can be led into the transmutation of its destiny" (*QCT*, 39). In that *krisis*, some problems disappear, while others, and formidable ones, emerge. All have to do with the status of a discourse trying to remain faithful to the singular that is happening to us and that is not simple.

What disappears is the very possibility of obliterating originary strife. The hypothesis of an epochal closure gives to the tragic double bind that singular feature, never before seen, of archie-anarchic monstrosity. Such bifrontal character of our site results from a 'thrust of time.' The phrase answers to the perplexity before singulars, in which historical thinking begins: things are one way, then suddenly in an entirely different way. In topological terms, we find ourselves inscribed within one horizon, one "time-space," and then suddenly reinscribed within another. This perplexity involves nothing but singulars: a *terra deserta* that is no longer ours, a *terra incognita* that is not yet ours, and a transition in which an entire collectivity lives as if holding its breath. No encompassing *nomos* governs this nomadism where allocations, assignments to discontinuous planes, follow one another without warning or mediation.

Reinscription, however, institutes a possibility that remains to be seized upon. To *whom* can and ought the "proper founding" be entrusted? Not to any particular hero. The possible concerns precisely the way to be of the entire age of technicity. To the question, Who? the answer in Heidegger is a desubjectivized self, that is, a site (not a subject, which would answer instead to the question, What? What is man?). The transmutation of blindness about technicity, as described, cannot be forced. One can only let oneself be assigned to this conflictual site. Such an assignment may happen or not. It eludes willful conquering. When in a crisis, which may be ours, such allocation occurs, the originary condition of what we are living becomes thinkable. Univocal ultimates (*archai*) then appear as having covered up an an-archic originary condition; technical expertise proves to feed on the denial of tragic knowledge; global technicity reveals 'that which saves'; and in Heidegger's idiom of the mid-1930s, being-there (*Dasein*) comes to be. Since it is conflictual, the *there* of *Dasein* can only be tragic.

Yet the discourse of this historical crisis—critical topology—also encounters formidable difficulties. To trace the break between the univocally archic terrain and the tragically anarchic, it cannot but speak two languages. To think about the faultline (*de linea*) where epochal history terminates[8] requires *one* discourse uttered from within, as well as *another* uttered from without, that closure. It requires an epochal bilingualism. Thus we have yet to become, Heidegger says, "dwellers along the [abyss] in the time-space from which the gods have fled" (*BzP*, 52). The age of global technicity is readily described as one of great destructions, and not to subscribe to this diagnosis would take a hopeless case of anorexia toward reflection. But if to think is to stop at the conditions of what one is living, then it is worthwhile asking, How did we get here? To this question, the topology answers by pointing out the *krisis* around which the history of being turns, which enables us to become the dwellers along the abyss that we are. Critical topology implies that in the twentieth century the double bind beneath every monofocal

---

8 "The history of Being is at an end for thinking in the event of appropriation" (Martin Heidegger, *On Time and Being*, trans. Joan Stambaugh [slightly modified] [New York: Harper & Row, 1972], 41).

posit becomes obvious, which in turn implies that the tragic denial at the foundation of order makes itself all the more violent. Institutionalized brutality of a magnitude never seen before, error and errancy, an isomorphism in everyday life that stifles reflection; then the critical turning that moves outside of the same and its laws; lastly the lesson learned from devastations, the vision of empty sockets and the silent affirmation of originary differing: this tragic itinerary becomes accessible only to a bifrontal phenomenological thinking. The topology that frees dissension is a thinking, since Heidegger does no more than linger upon the site and its conditions; it is phenomenological, since it gathers what shows itself there; and it is bifrontal, since it looks back at the collapse of normative epochs (strictly speaking, a redundancy: an epoch always results from an idea that puts a stop to questioning, from a fixed idea, a half posited, a decree, and, in that sense, from a norm) and looks ahead at a constellation that is anarchic because it *lacks simple ultimacy*. What shows itself is the kenosis that makes possible, while deferring it, the tragic *there* of being-there.

The difficulties have less to do with the circular character of this topology (which surmises a transition at work and then discovers symptoms verifying the surmise). Not every hermeneutical circle is vicious. The difficulties arise rather from the fact that topology can be retrospective and critical only because it is essentially anticipatory. In the vocabulary of representation, the promoting agency behind all standards, both the meta-narrative instructing us about the stage whence we come and the semi-narrative about the possible *exit* we are living (semi-, since narration remains suspended as philosophy runs out of representables) have their condition in a discontinuous sense in which all actors today find themselves enrolled.

As this is a temporal discontinuity, the preeminence of the possible over the actual[9] requires a "headway in order to reach our 'location' in being itself and thereby our history" (*BzP*, 501). We learn about our past and our present only via the contingent future, that is, via the eventual, eventlike topos. As long as the tragic *there* has not been

---

9 Martin Heidegger, *Being and Time*, trans. John Macquarrie and Edward Robinson (New York: Harper & Row, 1962), 63. The key section on the mathematical project as well as on the genesis of the theoretical gaze is sec. 69, trans. 401–18.

seized upon as our ownmost possibility, one will never "measure what has happened in the history of metaphysics: the prelude to the event itself" (*BzP*, 174). This prelude has from all time deferred the tragic *there*, as well as the differing whose possible site it is.

Heidegger is not saying that soon, perhaps in the year 2000, we shall reach our conflictual location in being and thus be saved from the global reach of technicity. He is saying that the tragic *there* is possible, that it always has been, that it has become even more clearly so in the age of worldwide cataclysms that is our own, and that there is no bearer of salvation (*salvus*, as 'whole' as tragic vision becomes after the crisis) other than that possible. With the deferred *there*, nothing gets postponed until later. Deferment, rather, describes originary differing itself.

Deferred in what way then? The question is one of anticipation.

Anticipatory topology. This deals with a possible historical locus: one already given, yet still to be occupied. Its description is first of all negative since topos here no longer signifies any region of entities whose relations can be maximized to produce some archic referent. "In the other beginning, it is no longer either some entity or some region and realm, any more than entities as such, that can set the standard for being" (*BzP*, 248). The difficulty consists in understanding anticipation without associating any utopian or millennial postponements. This requires some clarification of the negations in the lines just quoted.

Clearly what is being denied under their obvious apophatism is the hyperbolic use of one entity-proper (doubtless the Platonic 'good'), regional (doubtless Aristotelian 'physical' motion), or general (doubtless Leibniz's perplexity about why there are 'entities in general') posited as normative. They are aimed against representational maximization. What is excluded is the transition to another genus as Hegel had described it. The "great men," Hegel said, "see the very truth of their age and their world, the next genus, so to speak, which is already formed in the womb of time."[10]

---

10 G.W.F. Hegel, *Reason in History: A General Introduction to the Philosophy of History*, trans. Robert S. Hartman (New York: Liberal Arts Press, 1953), 40.

But what is thereby being denied more broadly is a certain phenomenology of simple manifestation, the kind one may be tempted to read into Heideggerian 'giving.' Such a phenomenology, answering the ancient question of being qua being, would run like this: Heidegger relates *geben* to the Greek *phain-* and *phy-*, the radicals for 'showing' and 'rising,' hence to manifestation; then he inverts the relations of grounding (as attested to by the lines quoted), anchoring not manifestation in one entity that shows itself most noteworthy but rather this entity as well as all others in manifestation. Being qua being would consist in simple giving (*Es gibt*) as underscored by these verbs in the middle voice: 'to show forth,' 'to rise.' To respond to the question of being, presencing would have to be retained as such, regardless of any consideration for present entities.[11]

This is all well and good. Still, reconstructions such as this say nothing about the *intrinsic contrariety* of being, nothing about the originary strife for the sake of which Heidegger never ceased renewing his idiom. Being is indeed showing, rising, manifesting, presencing, giving; but it is all that in a 'fissured' mode, in 'dissension,' as 'unconcealment-concealment,' 'appropriation-expropriation,' in the 'struggle' by which the No asserts itself against Yes and death declares itself against life. Whatever apophatism there remains in Heidegger, it does not hide some negative haplology (*haploon*, 'simple').[12] It puts simplicity out of operation. With their negations, the lines quoted do suggest that being alone is *maßgebend*, setting the standard. But "Yes and No are an essential property of being itself, and the No even more originally than the Yes" (*BzP*, 178). With essential properties like these, how would apophatic utterances ever exalt a simple standard, retrieve a simple condition beneath epochal regimes, prepare a simple dwelling site? The *thought* of the double bind that is being may indeed be simple

---

11 Heidegger goes rather far in formulating this disregard: a "knowing seriousness" would "no longer be bothered by good and bad, by decay and rescue of the tradition, by benevolence and brutality" (*BzP*, 242). See also *On Time and Being*, 2 and 24.

12 For one recent attempt to read into Heidegger just such a negative haplology, see Jacques Derrida, *Of Spirit: Heidegger and The Question*, trans. Geoffrey Bennington and Rachel Bowlby (Chicago: The University of Chicago Press, 1989), 108–13; and *Psyché* (Paris: Galilée, 1987), 535–36.

(*einfach*, *schlicht*, etc.), just as the sight of Oedipus blinded alone could be simple, whole, safe.[13] But if, in the other beginning, it is no longer any entity that ultimately 'gives'—gives (sets) the standard, gives (provides food for) thought, gives (brings about) a site—nor any thesis about being that binds uniformly, then Heidegger's great awakening after the compromises of 1933–34 led him outside of all *simply normative* regimes. Anticipatory topology leads toward a conflictual normativity, the knowledge of which is more ancient in the West than any theticism of the same—the theticism most effectively deployed with contemporary global technicity.

To speak of the deferred tragic *there* is to sustain the possibility that the denial of the transgressive other in what philosophers ascertain as ultimate may reveal itself exhausted. Such denial has provided the impetus to every figure of the legislative same, while its exhaustion has always secretly shattered normative power. To attempt the possible means here to destabilize affirmation, the firm, firmness, and to rehabilitate under the Yes the pull of the No. The possible undercuts the effects of positive, that is, thetic discourse. Hence the silence of the tragic hero fleeing into that *nonplace* for the ancients, the desert; a nonplace (*ou-topos*), not moving (like the island of some messianic society) into an ever-greater distance as a result of a poorly calculated arrival, but deferred under the mode of the possible and therefore differing with itself. No utopia here, and quite another apophasis. Negating and questioning are all that remain to anyone seeking to retain the disparate: for Heidegger, a negating that posits no dialectical nescience and a questioning that presupposes no maieutic prescience. The topology of the possible does not work with a theodolite. Like the desert where Oedipus wandered, the anticipated conflictual topos is closed to prospection. In the *Beiträge*, it is described through 'fissuring' (*Zerklüftung*), a word that stresses time more than space. To be deferred is the very temporality of the tragic *there*: the discord of phenomenal presencing and of a singularization always to come (see below). This is

---

13 Oedipus blinded "has one eye too many perhaps...To live is death, and death too is a life" (Friedrich Hölderlin, "In Lovely Blueness," in *Poems and Fragments*, trans. Michael Hamburger [modified] [Ann Arbor: University of Michigan Press, 1967], 603–604).

the originary strife whose vision blinds one and whose knowledge strikes one silent.

Now if such is the originary condition as Heidegger has come to view it after his brutal awakening from reliance upon univocal "originary rootedness,"[14] then why state it in the future tense? Witness the proliferation of topical postponements: at present, we can at most prepare the "place of questioning" (*BzP*, 85), where "those to come" will prepare themselves, who in turn will prepare "new standpoints in being," from which alone can "the strife of earth and world be sustained" (*BzP*, 62), a strife out of which may issue the tragic *there*. This series of sites—*Frageort, Standort, Da*—has nothing to do with a speculation on happier morrows. In anticipatory topology, the emphasis remains on the possible site and its discontinuity rather than on actual terrains and their contiguity. Statements in the future tense concern a potential that is given now. They are not meant to put off indefinitely the other beginning, but to aggravate here and now the discontinuity between regimes of the same, whose institutionalized hypertrophia Heidegger had just helped in promoting, and the event of differing by which he henceforth understands being—to aggravate, in his words, the temporal difference between illusory full presence and fractured presencing.

Providing a Place for the Originary Double Bind

If topology is concerned with the place where the conflictual event can be sustained, at least one misunderstanding regarding Heidegger is excluded. One might indeed object: if he advocates express compliance with an originary strife modeled after Aeschylus and Sophocles, then what is there about his model that *saves*? Is such a possibility not more disruptive than even global subsumption under univocal standards?

The objection is meaningless. It reduces the guiding category of modality, the possible, to what derives from it, the actual. One

---

14 *Ursprüngliche Verwurzelung* (not *"primordial roots,"* as the translators put it), *Being and Time*, 429.

worries about what will happen to public order *if* the legitimating referents were to turn out fractured. This amounts to misconstruing the status of the possible, since conflictual being already grips and breaks us, just as it has always gripped and broken us: "We are already moving, although still only transitionally, within another truth" (*BzP*, 18): within the other truth which, in the epigraph quoted at the beginning, was described as the very condition of tragedy. In hardening the reign of rule-governed technicity, we would merely be once again answering the possible with denial. Planetary totalitarianism—Creon's worldwide and ultimate triumph—would only extend and deepen the actual. Creon forces and enforces the public order by denying its transgressive other; but what would there even be to deny if the tragic double bind did not hold him always and already? The conflictual possible is *to come* only because it is our most ancient condition. It breaks with the actual as the event breaks with constant presence; as the singular, with subsumption; as originary strife, with any one focal meaning of being; and as the acknowledgment of what is (letting the tragic *there* be) breaks with thetic repression (positing fantasmic figures of firstness).

In order to see in what sense the originary double bind "saves" in technicity, it suffices to ask, As opposed to all thetic ultimates, what is phenomenologically ultimate in everydayness? Ultimacy is the property of a condition that cannot be sidestepped or stepped behind. A condition is ultimate if it is not determined by some yet more originative condition. In everydayness, only our coming-into-being and out ceasing-to-be satisfy that requirement. What is phenomenologically ultimate are not precisely birth and death as two biographical facts, one having occurred and the other yet to occur, but two pervading traits—two pulls on the present—originating in them. Hannah Arendt called the first of these traits 'natality'; it is "the new beginning inherent in birth," "the principle of beginning" "in which the faculty of action is ontologically rooted." Primal institutions are good examples of that originative trait, but so are drafting parliamentary legislation, founding the United Nations, sitting down to begin a book, or choosing a life partner. Arendt called the second trait, our being-toward-death, 'mortality.' It is what ties us to one definite sequence of events, bound eventually to lead to our extinction. Mortality is therefore a description of our utter singularization to come. Natality and mortality are what we all know, yet poorly. Since they are given only mediately, these two traits are what stand most in need of rigorous clarification. As phenomenological ultimates, they, more than any immediately given phenomenon, call for *diasozein ta phainomena* ("preserving that which shows itself," Eudoxus of Cnidus).

The double bind of natality-mortality is phenomenologically first in the sense of the *origin* of each and every experience. It is not first in the sense of *principles*, not foundational in any way. Principles and affiliated representations arise only from the subsumptive violence that turns whatever is the case into a case of whatever universal. Global technicity is the most effective translation of principial thinking into everydayness.

Now whenever philosophers ask, In the name of what? they refer facts and deeds to principles, which bear common names. Heidegger, for his part, seeks to step back from principial referents to what is originary and does not bear a common name. Natality and mortality, as mine, are singular traits. Topology is thus a discourse about *singulars* not only as it narrates the sequence of epochs in our history but more decisively as it seeks their condition in the originary double bind of natality and mortality. The one great possibility never to become an actual economy—which is why there is no salvation *from* technicity—would be to comply equally with the claims of singulars and the fantasms of the common: to comply with the temporal difference. Topology does not legitimize facts by referring them to a name. It legitimizes the feasible in anticipating the one nameless possibility, the event of appropriation-expropriation. What common name indeed would fit differing laws? In Heidegger, the whole issue of legitimation gets transmuted. The site of norms is to become what it has always been: the locus of the event, a locus to which we have always been allocated already and whose evidence gains as principles collapse into the isomorphic: "Being happens as the event. This implies that a singular site has unexpectedly befallen us, alienating us toward the instant and only thus spreading" (*BzP*, 260).

It is true that the locus thus anticipated can no longer guarantee any tranquility of order. Yet this is not to say that its topology justifies anything and everything. Its criteria of responsibility were set forth not only by Aeschylus and Sophocles but also by Heraclitus and Parmenides. It heeds other imperatives than do normative signifiers: “The things that are absent, behold them nevertheless as firmly present.”[15] In the thetic impulse of natality behold the undertow of mortality. In the site mapped out by the law behold the singularization to come, which no law can subsume and which alienates us from the lures of normative presence.

“Must we then not think otherwise, anticipate zones and yardsticks and modes of being that are entirely other, so as to belong to the necessities that are dawning here?” (*BzP*, 204). Such is the onus of anticipatory topology. It is a matter of belonging to the originary possible, more powerful than any actual denial. But in this possible, a ‘not yet’ stands out from the ‘already.’ The instrumental nature of normative single binds has become obvious at least since Marx, Nietzsche, and Freud, but there is ‘not yet’ a readiness to acknowledge tragic double binds. Hence: “The locus of decision still remains to be founded” (*BzP*, 187). But also: “To think this way already requires, to be sure, a standpoint where it will no longer be possible to be lured by all the ‘good’ and the ‘progressive’ and the ‘gigantic’ that are being achieved” (*BzP*, 140). In what passes for good, progressive, gigantic—which probably means: in the technological giganticism that passes for progressive and hence for good—arise necessities that compel one to think otherwise. The everydayness that breaks with the cluster ‘good’ (again, Platonic), ‘progress’ (early modern), ‘giganticism’ (late modern) is already ours, already a necessity in the sense that everyone is living it, but it still remains for us to seize. The possible always grafts some *not yet* on an *already*, thereby breaking the order of proper temporal sequence. To say a cataclysm is possible is to say that at present things are holding up, but that the conditions of their collapse are already there. Heidegger: the conditions—the zones and the yardsticks and the modes of being—are there for the illusion to collapse due to which values, progress, and technicity appear to us as preg-

---

15 Parmenides, in *Die Fragmente der Vorsokratiker*, 6th ed., ed. Hermann Diels and Walter Kranz (Berlin: Weidmann, 1951), frag. 4,1.

nant with normativity. Insofar as they remain still to be grasped, these conditions are situated ahead of us (*ante*), whence anticipation. They fissure the subjectivist topos that continues to pass for rock bottom, whence topology.

To establish oneself expressly on the fissured ground is what in the mid-1930s Heidegger understands by 'being-there.' Such establishing marks the other beginning. Its implications appear from a disjunction—a twofold disjunction—that Heidegger was to attempt ever anew over the forty years to follow.

On the one hand, the *fundamentum concussum* remains to be disjoined from any foundation seeming *inconcussum*. That disjunction devolves on a recapitulation, or an archaeology, which frees plateaus in collision from under the numerous foundations posed since the Greeks; which frees, he says in some texts, the strife between world and earth. On the *world* map of fantasmic dominions he traces out especially the modern enclosure, freeing under the discourse established since Descartes and Kant the *earth*bound dissensions that have torn each of the great founding discourses. This labor of archaeological disjunction is incumbent on historical critique. It has its site and its hour: the 'thrust of time' making us, the subjects of technicity, feel the collision of plateaus that are presupposed beneath every foundation posed.

On the other hand, the forces in collision themselves remain to be disjoined. Heideggerian responsibility consists in a response to that destabilizing thrust in which normative posits suffer their deposal. The 'thrust of time' brings into light the disparate beneath every referential construct. To respond to what is happening to us then means to lay bare forms of the originary double bind: appropriation-expropriation in the event; the strife world-earth; the conflict gods-humans in history; that of unconcealment-concealment in truth; the discord of phenomenalizing-singularizing in manifestation… These polemological disjunctions fall upon anticipatory critique. It separates the dislocating strategies so that being-there can belong to its originary locus, that is, (Heraclitean) *polemos*.

The self-incurred stultification in technicity shows just how far away we still are from responsibility belonging to the originary locus so understood. Whence the appeal to "found the historical place for the history to come" (*BzP*, 60), to "create that space-time, the site for the essential instants" (*BzP*, 98). Later Heidegger was to describe the instant that founds history in an abbreviated form as the "entry into the event"[16] (abbreviated, since the phrase does not say the event results from mutually hostile pulls). This entry would be as compact as all beginnings have been. What interests the topologist in this compactness is the conflictuality glimpsed, then infallibly repressed, at the inception of every single epoch in our past.

Stultification gets squared in the consumer of ideas who has seen and read everything. There may be something charming about a blase gymnasium student; later, it is better to have learned how to read. For example, on truth and its site. "The truth of being [has still] to find a site that comes to be in being-there" (*BzP*, 90). Having leafed through Heidegger, one may vaguely recall that, at least when read in translation, he liked to speak of authenticity; that this doubtless has something to do with truth; and that there were decades when fashion required that one 'be true.' Speed reading may, however, make one miss the essential—here, the conflictuality without sublation which is truth. Unconcealment-concealment has yet to find its site. 'Being true' then means something more disquieting than genuine or veridical existence, as it may seem at first reading. It means the condition for which both Hölderlin and Nietzsche "had to leave prematurely the clear of their days" (*BzP*, 204). The site of truth is "the there in its abyssality" (*BzP*, 240). Thus the conflictual provides the place for the abyssal.

Such places are imparted rarely. It is one thing to describe the conflict that broke tragic heroes first, Hölderlin and Nietzsche later. It is another thing entirely for an age to find itself allotted the double bind. Topology carries out the description; the event, allocation.

Providing a place is then not primarily a human achievement. Here again, misconceptions lie in wait for the reader of Heidegger. One of these has to do with the desire for favor. To 'provide a place' (*verstatten*, e.g., *BzP*, 278) means, to be sure, to impart, assign, permit, grant. But *to what* does the event accord a place? If it is to

16 Heidegger, *On Time and Being*, 41 (translation modified).

unconcealment-concealment, and if the event is itself appropriation-expropriation, then our site (*Stätte*) is never accorded to us in a mode other than that of discord. To allow oneself to be charmed by the Heideggerian 'there is' and 'favor' amounts again to reading poorly. Each place is allotted with grace, but never without disgrace either.

Another misconception has to do with the desire for a solid ground. Heideggerian nostalgia would want to attach the people to its soil, as the Athenians were attached to Attica. And, indeed, does he not celebrate rural rootedness? Yet the history of being knows no privilege: no *lex priva,* no law that is private, that is, deprived of its transgressive other. The 'there is' occurs always, and always the giving is taken back as well. Always the *Es gibt* sunders one's dwelling site. Metaphysics was born from a desire wishing away allocation-dislocation as unbearable. Since the classical Greeks, denial has intervened normally, equipped with the apparatus of norms and the normal. In Aeschylus and Sophocles, undoing it took an act of parricide or fratricide. To us, it seems, even a world of technicity on the way to self-destruction does not suffice to undo tragic denial.

These two misconceptions suggest the difficulty of the topology. It is again a matter of desire, as Heidegger's 'other thinking' is being challenged to succeed where theticism could only fail. Having heard of metaphysical closure, one expects an investigation of contiguous historical spheres; and, remembering his exhortations to keep oneself ready for a 'gift,' one expects the demonstration of an entry into the good graces of fate. But Heidegger describes laws that always fracture the unconditioned. Gift, granting, grace, 'that which saves,' and so forth are thus to be thought of other than as healing. The thrusts of time bring no therapy to the truth of being, which is tragic strife.

Remaining riveted to a monstrous site (in accordance with the very hypothesis of closure), one expects at bottom a 'philosophy of the one' capable of edifying. Heidegger shows, however, that—and how—edification has proved hubristic and the floor it presupposed anything but solid. This is, as it were, the advantage of our epochal monstrosity: coming from afar, taken already by the polemical truth of being, how can we persist in the tragic denial from which were born all normative posits, including that of global technicity? Just like any other force of repression, the force of denial that sustains theticism works destruction. Its illusory edification is built upon the ruins of singularity.

What remains to be seen now is how the earth can be thought of other than as standing reserve for technicity; how, in other words, a singularizing pull always breaks up any pull of phenomenal contextualization into a world. "Why does the earth remain silent in this destruction? Because it is being denied the strife with a world as no place is provided for the truth of being" (*BzP*, 277–78). (Heidegger's suggestion in these lines that the earth's destruction would become utterable only with the recognition of originary strife should guard one from co-opting him for some ecological cause.)

The Tragic Condition of Being: Contextualization-Decontextualization

> What is, when the struggle for standards is dying out?
>
> —*BzP* 28

If technicity, today's epochal stamp, obliterates originary strife even as it hardens it to the extreme, then 'providing a place for the truth of being' does not amount to as obscure a program as it may sound. Nor does it amount to that all too familiar program, dialectics: as if, speaking of what saves, Heidegger were expecting that positioning (or enframing, *Gestell*), when pushed to its extreme, would prompt its own negation. He is not claiming that the oppositional logic of the world spirit will grant some remedial antidote to theticism. In the mechanics of determinate negation, theticism triumphs.

What is being asked of our age for the sake of 'salvation,' it seems, is to *undeny* a twofold pull in whose grips technicity places us more brutally than has any other epoch. Technicity contextualizes things and humans under the most efficacious universal ever seen, yet it also singularizes them without world or context. Such is the conflictual condition by which it functions. Knowing that condition is what saves. Technicity can instruct us in being's law,[17] which is ultimate without being simple. It can teach us that to rely on univocal ultimates is to cover up contextualizing-decontextualizing. These two strategies account for being qua event. How do they function?

Isomorphic contextualizing. If the task of the philosophers has been to ensure subsumption of all possible phenomena under one universal thesis of being, then today we have all become functionaries in Husserl's sense: all experts, that is, in treating whatever is the case as one more case to be subsumed under the modern primal institution (*Urstiftung*, which for Heidegger always results from a 'thrust of time' establishing a new focal sense of being). Such is the scientistic *a priori* by which we live. As Heidegger views it, modern science is never a disinterested inquiry. It is the tool for a highly interested posture we cannot avoid epochally in all our moves. Turning outward, we find but natural resources to be harnessed, and turning back upon our past, only cultural curiosities to be marketed. Turning inward, I no longer find, as did Augustine, the immutable light of truth, but rather neuroses awaiting treatment; and turning upward, more resources—perhaps uranium on Mars—awaiting exploitation.

As an epochal project, contextualization through technical-scientific mastery leaves no residue. When that project instituted the modern age, why indeed did substances facing the subject need to be termed 'extended,' if not to make them an equal (*iso*) in their forms (*morphē*), that is, uniform, isomorphic? According to Kant, the uniformization of phenomena is obtained through the inner sense. This means that only what can be temporalized is a datum and that only what can be ordered in calculable succession or simultaneity is temporal. As for the acts of the understanding, there are powerful reasons why the first of these acts must concern what can be mea-

---

17 "In enframing we glimpse a first, oppressing flash of the event" (Martin Heidegger, *Identity and Difference*, trans. Joan Stambaugh [slightly modified] [New York: Harper & Row, 1969], 38). We glimpse the event, namely, of appropriation-expropriation; we glimpse it in a flash, since technicity pushes both subsumptive universalization and dispersive singularization to their extremes; that flash is *oppressing*, as technical universalization institutes global violence; yet the glimpse is a *first*, hence there is salvation in global technicity.

sured and calculated. Since the subject knows only perceptions that are measurable in their spatial and temporal extendedness, the first Kantian category has to be that of quantity. Thus the uniform and the quantifiable must not be considered mere consequences of the modern 'Copernican revolution' toward the legislating subject. Quite the reverse: only because every phenomenon has to be accessible to calculation—because its phenomenality is summed up in its calculability—does the subject have to occupy the place of central legislator. Establishing itself as the spontaneous source of the laws of being, the subject will be certain that these laws are the same everywhere.

The modern regularity of phenomena results, then, from an act of anticipation, from an *a priori* positing, a thesis. For Heidegger, the spontaneous subject is defined by this very theticism alone. "*Positing* a rule ahead" (*BzP*, 161) is the one posture that constitutes both the autonomous agent and the datum uniformed by him; both the self and its other. Now a rule prescribing what ought to be is called a 'norm.' The isomorphic is the *normal*. To the Baconian and Cartesian institution of the project of normalization responds its full-blown success in the twentieth century. To Heidegger's question "What is, when the struggle for standards is dying out?" a first answer is obvious: struggles, for example, ideological ones, belong to the past, as there remains only one standard, contested neither East nor West—universal isomorphism. This is what being-in-the-world has come to mean in our age. The contextualization of phenomena, that is, the way they become phenomenalized, is everywhere the same.

Dispersive decontextualization. Yet as that very mode of phenomenalization, technicity also singularizes them without any agent of reconciliation. Be they phenomena of nature or of culture, subjective or objective, encountered outside or inside, they have lost their respective worlds. Natural resources, neuroses, archaeological or literary curiosities *are* inasmuch as they answer the question: What can be made with this? And making, *poiesis*, is always of singulars.

The point is decisive. As long as one does not see the enduring strategy of *making* at the heart of the age-old mechanics of subsumption—at the heart, therefore, of 'logic'—the counterstrategy of singularization is bound to remain incomprehensible, and with it the originary double bind that Heidegger seeks to rehabilitate.

This can be shown with regard to the ancient notion of *phusis*. Just as the English 'nature,' Greek *phusis* means two things: on one hand, a certain region of phenomena and, on the other, a principle of production. It designates the region of things not made by human hands, and it is the principle by which the things belonging in that region—plants and animals—are produced. The semantic ambiguity can be illustrated by a nasty two-sentence joke that circulates in London about a member of the royal family: "Princess Anne likes nature very much. That is astonishing if you consider what nature has done to her." She likes nature, namely, that region of phenomena where she finds trees, meadows, and horses, not buildings, streets, and cars. As to what nature has done to her, she, like every other biped, is also a product of that principle of production by which trees, meadows, and horses grow, a cause whose products can be more or less attractive. In Aristotelian terms, *phusis* denotes both a kind and a cause: the kind of things other than artifacts and the cause other than art (*technē*).

For Heidegger, this ambiguity shows that being has always been understood in terms of making, producing, causing. *Phusis* has all along been conceived according to its polar opposite, *technē*: first rather covertly, designating the sum of "those beings that produce themselves out of themselves," later overtly, *natura* designating beings in their totality as "the created" (*BzP*, 126). Throughout our history 'to be' has meant, in one way or another, 'to be caused.' By what? By such ultimate representations as "the Suprasensory World, the Ideas, God, the Moral Law, the Authority of Reason, Progress, the Happiness of the Greatest Number, Culture, Civilization," all standards qua causes. Heidegger adds that in the age of technicity these representations have "lost their constructive force and become nothing" (*QCT*, 65). At the moment when making remains the sole standard, all standards *for* making whither. The global reach so unfettered is what Heidegger calls "operational machination" (*Machenschaft*, *BzP*, 126).

To the question, "What is, when the struggle for standards is dying out?" the answer now is: there are only singulars, as each object for operational machination sets its own procedural standard. In the mid-1930s that assertion of singularity was understood by Heidegger as having brought about 'the highest danger,' precisely operational machination in America, the Soviet Union, as well as Nazi Germany, and at the same time 'that which saves,' namely, the knowledge of the originary differing of contextualization-decontextualization. "Being—the remarkable erroneous belief that being should always 'be.' ... Being is what is most rare because most singular, and no one guesses the few instants in which it founds a site for itself and unfolds" (*BzP*, 255). Being is ultimate, yet singular and rare, as the event of contextualization-decontextualization (Heidegger says 'appropriation-expropriation,' *Ereignis-Enteignis*) is not simple. Its site is the tragic *there*. Hence this other question: "Entering into being-there, its instant and its place: how does this occur in Greek tragedy?" (*BzP*, 374).

The double bind that saves. Heidegger neither deplores nor applauds the loss of enduring standards in global technicity. He reads that loss with the eyes of a symptomologist, and it reveals to him the self-assertion of the singular within, against, and at the basis of all normative posits. The analysis of technicity thus allowed him to translate into the ultimate condition of being what had earlier appeared as *man*'s condition: the double bind of natality-mortality.

To the question, "What is, when the struggle for standards is dying out?" he gives this answer: in every normative posit the strife of singularization against universalization *is* the standard.

Conditions of Evil

In philosophy it is advisable to state where and how one begins. One popular way of beginning appears in meta-remarks often heard and read such as this: "If I argue that X, then the result will be undesirable; therefore I shall argue that Y." This amounts to an acknowledgment, touching in its candor, that the starting point is desires, and the argument their legitimation.

Desires, however, are as notoriously unreliable as they are inescapable. They make one argue the maximization of now this, now that preference. One may suspect imagination at work as some object of desire gets promoted to the rank of ultimacy.

In what follows I shall try to examine a certain maximizing strategy in philosophy, as well as what after Kant may be called an "expanded way of imagining." In such maximization and such expansion, imagination will prove incongruously turned against itself. In its *arraying* strategy it posits standards more normative than which nothing can be desired, while in a *disarraying* counterstrategy it lets itself be given singulars. These discrepant workings may shed some light not only on the origin of desirable standards, but also on what common opinion explains as violation of just such standards: namely, evil.

The general title chosen by the organizers of this conference[1] mentions "the politics of transformation." In attempting to spell out conditions of evil, I have been guided by the ambition to learn more about certain sufferings that the West has inflicted upon itself before the middle of this century. The natural metaphysician in us might pick up those conditions—a plural not to be effaced—with one shovel and treat them summarily as negation of standards.[2] It

---

1 This paper was originally delivered at the Cardozo School of Law in New York City in September 1991, at a conference on "The Politics of Transformation and the Limits of Imagination."

2 Goethe, spokesman in this for the natural metaphysician in us, has Mephistopheles describe himself as "that spirit which always negates" (*ich bin der Geist, der stets verneint, Faust*, First Part, I. 1338). That spirit negates the good, whereby evil not only becomes knowable but also proves akin to the good: "As the opposite of the good, evil pertains to the order of the knowable as well as of the good" (*malum ex hoc ipso*

seems to me that one can sort out that shovelful and, in the process, gain some precision both about ultimates and about the way they allow for the possibility of evil.

Such sorting out goes not without pains. On the one hand, it has to deal with collective and individual hysteria, with leaders of formidable efficacy, with long lasting hatreds and short memory, with vendetta conventions and sham treaties, economic depression or boom, etc. Assortments of this kind may help explain mini-chains of events (perhaps the electoral victory of 1933). They hardly yield an understanding. On the other hand, trying to sort out conditions of the large-scale pathologies of our century, it is difficult to avoid entering precisely the sphere of standards, values, and the like. What may be gathered there is the fallout from principles betrayed: democracy, human rights, freedom ... Of course values and principles were betrayed. But what intelligibility about conditions does one gain from bemoaning a sellout? Concerning the first part of the title chosen by the organizers, I draw this conclusion for my purposes: attempting to think politics of transformation, it is advisable to stay clear not only of neo-positivist management of facts, but also of paleo-idealist assertion of standards.

As to its second part, "The Limits of Imagination," the incongruous strategies of imagination mentioned—positing standards, letting singulars be—will allow one to follow a road other than positivist, idealist, or of some pragmatic in-between. The starting point in philosophy may then not be simple, as the natural metaphysician's impetus toward norms keeps asserting itself in all experience and as singulars ask to be let-be. The task that I wish to describe consists in expanding thinking beyond, or outside, normative theticism, toward *diasozein ta phainomena*: toward remaining faithful, while giving thetic desire its due, to singulars as they show themselves.

---

quod bono opponitur habet rationem cognoscibilis et boni, Thomas Aquinas, *On Truth*, q. 2, art. 15, 2nd reply). In metaphysical theticism (a pleonastic phrase anyway), the other is always the other of some primary posit.

Differing Ultimates

If it is agreed that philosophy can do more than plead interests, be they libidinal or institutional, where and how to begin cannot remain optional. Here are some criteria to help keep clear of both the instrumentalization of thinking and its speculative disconnection from phenomena. A starting point that neither abandons ordinary experience nor trans-substantiates it into the extraordinary will have to be looked for in something everyone is familiar with, however poorly; it will have to be a knowing[3] that is not episodic, not contingent; a knowing whose seat is everydayness; from which other experiences and types of knowledge arise; and which does not in turn depend on some more primary knowing. To avoid making argumentation minister unwittingly to desires, one will have to grasp irreducible traits in everydayness and put them to the test of a historical-systematic investigation. Let us call such an inquiry into conditions a *phenomenology of ultimates*. Why phenomenology and what ultimates remains to be seen. To the claim, voiced right and left, that we need norms in order to understand, judge, and act, a phenomenologist's response has always been and should be: To learn what is to be done, no more is needed than insight into ultimate conditions of what shows itself to ordinary experience.

Ethics, then, does not belong to philosophy, no more than to imagining some politics of transformation. On the other hand, inasmuch as expanding imagination—that is, thinking—bears upon ultimates, such expansion is philosophy's essential task.

To attempt a non-ethical, non-moral, discourse about evil, one may mimic the Gnostics' question (mimes being experts in demythologizing) and ask: How did evil enter the world? Such a discourse begins not with some narrative of a primordial fall, but with a certain primal scene with and through which it has to work. The scene is the conflict of heroic and democratic laws in fifth cen-

---

3 There is no equivalent in modern English for the distinction between *wissen* and *kennen* (or *erkennen*); in French *savoir* and *connaître*. Whenever the context is not clear, one has to supply a distinction such as between "prior knowing" and "actual knowledge."

tury Athens, as represented on stage by Aeschylus and Sophocles. Agamemnon slits Iphigenia's throat *in the name* of what is called "values": nation (more than the *polis*, less than the state), army, honor of course, plus perhaps Greek expansionism and the Ionian colonization ... One cuts, so as to promote a common name capable of setting the law. But by the same slitting, Agamemnon also cuts himself off from the law of the Atrides. He decides for one clear cut law: *for* the one at Aulis, *against* the one at Mycene where other obligations would have compelled him to cut and decide differently. At Aulis, his public function inserts him into a world that bestows on him a meaning as head of the armies. Yet also at Aulis, the undeniable allegiance—yet an allegiance denied—to the family lineage singularizes him as well. The allegiance to his blood line expels him in advance from the world of weapons and battle ships, the world that in sacrificing his daughter he extolls as unequivocally normative. Knowing the expulsion and singularization that accompany clear cut normativity makes any univocal meaning meaningless. That knowing, made explicit, is tragic knowledge.

Here then are ultimates that we know, however poorly, in everyday experience: the *maximization* of some name fixing our bearings and contextualizing a world; but also, incongruously conjoined with it, the *singularization* within any such constituted world, which results from the pull of other actual worlds to which I belong.

How did evil enter the world? Not in a narratable coming, not by that erstwhile king too cowardly to sustain the double bind of discrepant laws. Evil comes in an untold move, when singularization is cut off from one's constituted world, when one blinds oneself against it; when in the name of a jealous fantasm capable of subsuming everything that can become phenomenal one "comes down on one side" of the discrepant binds; when such a fantasm is made to command exclusive allegiance; when it integrates doing, acting, and knowing in a frame that can be mastered and in this sense appropriates the world; when expropriation from that world is denied.

Was sacrificing Iphigenia right or wrong? It is more instructive to see that it is the battery of values that makes one commit acts of that kind. The primal scene does not allow "the problem of evil" to be confined within "morals" because, from the point of view of ultimacy, evil cannot be a matter of *mores*, of conduct and habit, or of inner disposition and intention. It therefore does not reveal itself to a theory one might juxtapose, for instance, to a political theory, thus rendering conduct and intention accessible to investigation or speculation. Theorizing evil—saying "Morally he was wrong," "Politically he was right"—amounts to passing off classifying for explaining. From the bird's eye view on secondary types of discourse, types not grounded in themselves, how is one to adjudicate what is good, what is evil, if not by recourse to some primary discourse, which treats of one grounding principle? Such principles, however, in the name of which issues fall into kinds, are the ones that owe their sovereignty to an act of tragic denial.

A metaphysical discourse about ultimates differs from a phenomenological one, as negation (*Verneinung*) differs from denial (*Verleugnung*). Negating standards is a metaphysical operation since it depends on a prior positing of the standards negated. Denying a knowledge, on the other hand, involves no such theticism. Its analysis devolves on a phenomenology.

As suggested by the primal scene of the doctrine of principles, the pull dispossessing us of any given phenomenality remains systematically operative in every positing of a law, which is thus in advance suspended, struck with interdiction. Such is the dubious charm of theticism: to argue positions amounts inevitably, forcibly, to both recognizing and silencing the dispossession that always pulls on phenomena as an undertow, always depriving them of their world.

In order to think evil one is left with, on the surface, a host of questions to which everyone keeps returning: What is the good life? What are proper conduct and right intention? ... as well as, in depth, a dispossessing which keeps returning. Are death and evil then to be charged with that dispossessing? At first sight, nothing would seem more plausible. Both death and evil disown us of the good life, love and the like. In ordinary experience we do know better than to exalt now this, now that colossal referent, and like dwarfs to put our trust in it. We know better than to rank evil among the special issues dealt with in a special branch of philosophy, itself one branch of the human sciences in the shadow of the modern hegemonic referent—subjectivity[4]—posited to integrate (at least by right) knowledge claims as it is to integrate life worlds.

As to the deep answer, it is hardly more enlightening than the superficial one. Something in us, to be sure, applauds when with resignation we are told: evil is a special problem indeed. Were it not, it would be everywhere—a thought more difficult still to resign oneself to, unbearable. But something in us agrees as well that the "problem" in question does not belong in any discipline of knowledge, as the problem of motion belongs in physics and as the study of insects does in entomology. Indeed, we possess a prior knowing, but no clear knowledge of it. Deep etiologies have this superficiality about them that they promise they will consummate prior knowing in actual knowledge—a promise impossible to keep. Instead of fulfilling what they promise, causal accounts end up postulating some appellate jurisdiction. They have had to enlist into that service a breathtaking parade of names and standards.

Insight, then, is to be expected neither from surveys nor from deep burrowings. I see little else but a phenomenology of ultimates, conjoined with an historical topology of normative double binds, that may help one toward it. To carry out such a conjunction, the irreducible traits of maximization and singularization need to be gathered from everydayness and then put to historical-topological tests. Borrowing from Hannah Arendt (who on this point corrected, not without irony, Heidegger), one may call the traits of ultimacy "natality" and "mortality."[5] The first, the archic trait prompts us toward new commencings and sovereign commandings. It makes us magnify standards. The second always pulls us back from the world of such archic referents. It is a singularizing, dispersing, desolating, evicting, dephenomenalizing, exclusory trait. The two do not pair off. They are originary, yet not binary traits. They are

4 Concerning hegemonic referents, I can only refer to the work in progress from which, with minor modifications, this paper is excerpted. In that work, a topology of normative binds will be attempted. [This refers to Reiner Schürmann, *Des Hégémonies brisées* (Mauvezin: Trans-Europ-Repress, 1996, republished: Zurich and Berlin: Diaphanes, 2017), published in English as *Broken Hegemonies*, trans. Reginald Lilly (Bloomington and Indianapolis: Indiana University Press, 2003)—Eds.]

5 Hannah Arendt, *The Human Condition* (Chicago: The University of Chicago Press, 1958), 246–47.

not jointly exhaustive of one genus. In other words, they do not divide one first posit that would yield to one encompassing discourse (*oppositorum eadem est scientia*).[6] As incongruent, they derail experience. There exists therefore no better heuristics than the daydreamy wonderings about how I can ever have come to be and how it is possible that I shall cease to be. The larger the design of these traits, however, the more legible will they be. This is why a topology of the normative double binds[7] by which the West has actually lived needs to turn to the pages where the impulse of natality appears colossal: the pages in which bastions against temporality have been erected, greater than which nothing can be desired. Those bastions never failed, however, to crumble under the return of the denied.

As to good and evil, they cannot parallel those phenomenologically originary traits gathered from everydayness. How could natality equal the good pure and simple? The fantasmic maximizations, to which it incites imagination and thought, kill. Nor can mortality, which ties us back to singulars,[8] be equated with evil. That those equations, tempting though they may be to the natural metaphysician in us, would be wrong is suggested by the primal scene; it is confirmed by the fate of the hegemonies, illustrated by the exhaustion of certain ideologies; and it is proven by ordinary ambivalences toward death. The last decade of this millennium has its own peculiar way of calling us back to the senseless that we know, namely, that a meaning is not something one posits or composes; but that it

---

6 The axiom is current in scholasticism (e.g. Meister Eckhart, *Die lateinischen Werke*, vol. I, ed. Konrad Weiß, [Stuttgart: Kohlhammer, 1937], 149). "Actual knowledge" results from recourse to one such generic science or discursive type. "Prior knowing," we will see, seizes disparate opposites, without a genus. To step from *Wissen* to *Wissenschaft*, the ultimates of tragic knowing need to be subjected to the principles of non-contradiction, of identity, and of the excluded middle.

7 See supra note 4.

8 An argument relating evil to good as mortality relates to natality, would do no more than disguise phenomenologically a metaphysics of identity. If evil amounts to a singularization that is equi-originary with the good, then how is one to avoid relapsing into some gnostic dialectic? That such a dialectic would be non-viable appears from singulars' *differing* with particulars. Singulars remain impossible to dialecticize. They are opposed to universals, neither contradictorily nor contrarily, but rather incongruently.

comes about as a world phenomenalizes itself, and that we always receive it only to find ourselves in advance expelled from it.

As if the lesson of those institutions of which nothing more magnificent can be conceived and which for a while go without saying before collapsing under the return of the denied—as if that lesson from history were not crass enough, the twentieth century has indeed outperformed previous ages. It has incurred a voidance of standards such that one cannot help wondering if in the end it will not suffice to pull us from denial and teach us the Yes to dispossession. Who, "us"? There has been no lack of moments in history in which a Yes to the universalizing-singularizing double bind was lived by all.[9] Who then still needs to learn that of which he possesses a prior knowing? The thetic metaphysician in us will have to learn tragic thinking.

To the thetic impulse of natality we owe our normative referents. It is the tie that sets us free. Is it not a bit hasty, then, to assert that this impulse does not amount to the good as such? It is the impulse that unifies life. Correlatively, is singularization—the retraction, subtraction, by which we incur loss of love, of home and country, of health and life—not the most plausible candidate for evil as such? These correlations fed the gigantomachia concerning ultimacy when, in the nineteenth century, normative argumentation began to savor of desire's labor. The young Nietzsche still held keenly that out of unification comes the good and out of individuation, evil. We must consider, he wrote, "the state of individuation as the source and the originary ground of all suffering. … The mystery doctrine of tragedy: the fundamental knowledge that all that there is is one; the consideration of individuation as the originary ground of evil."[10]

Evil would equal being dispossessed of some fundamental unity that allows for communication. The equation also fits all too well with the common opinion held in each of the linguistic eras of philosophy. For the Greeks, evil meant to be dispossessed of the good,

---

9 Cf. the enumeration of "the rare moments of freedom" according to Hannah Arendt, *The Origins of Totalitarianism*, [Cleveland and New York: Meridian Books, 1958], 497 and elsewhere).
10 Friedrich Nietzsche, *The Birth of Tragedy*, § 10.

at the very bottom of the ladder crowned by the one; for the Latins, it meant the dispossession of telic continuity which whoever acts against nature brings upon himself; for the moderns, it meant a dispossession of enlightenment which turns one radically away from self-consciousness. Each time the good posits itself, which is why it determines what holds as law. So long as otherness remains conceived as negation and denial itself is denied, evil can only stand opposed to such self-positing. It arises when the one, nature, or self-consciousness are deprived of their full normative presence. It is nothing but a misuse of those principal foci which life's first sufferings should have taught us to let shine in their splendid evidence. "Evil is to evilly use the good."[11]

A historical topology of normative double binds (which this is not the place to develop) teaches one something altogether different. Philosophers cannot think in our place. They can show us ways of thinking that we did not anticipate. Is it not thetic desire yet again which speaks through the wish that self-positing, hence normative evidence, may shine? Such desire has posited all *single binds*. The simplicity of singly binding referents proved however to be not given, but rather made by a bold stroke—the stroke of an ax. Concerning the non-simplicity of the good, there is therefore a truth that we know but which we do not fully understand. It teaches us that by its very positedness the law extenuates its subsumptive power (inasmuch as *das Gesetz* is always *das Gesetzte*). Such knowing should prevent us from fidgeting if the good shows an affinity with double binds. Let us therefore bracket the popularity of good and evil. It is about evil that a phenomenology of ultimates can teach us something.

The first, perhaps, who in the nineteenth century thought differently than in homage to a form of "unitary ground" (although to render homage to ethics instead), and who thought otherness differently than as determinate negation, was Kierkegaard. "Any discourse about a superior unity that would reconcile absolute

---

11 "*Malum est male muti bono,*" Augustine, *On the Nature of the Good,* bk. I, ch. 36 (PL vol. 42, col. 562).

contradictions is a metaphysical assault on ethics."[12] Instead of metaphysical grounding, there is to be ethical seriousness. Now "seriousness is: the singular."[13] The good is no longer met anywhere on the subsumptive scale—neither at the top, to be beheld universally, nor particularized at the bottom. Instead of the good's evidence, there remains "the dread of the good."[14] Dread, since the serious good demands of me that I singularize myself, just as Abraham singularized himself sacrificing Isaac. Who, then, is speaking when individuation is treated as evil? The natural metaphysician is speaking again, dreaded this time but hushing dread promptly by desire's megalomaniacal therapy. Desire cannot bear seriousness. It cannot but deny such inversion of the primal scene. Still, from one sacrifice to the other, from Iphigenia's to Isaac's, the function of simple ultimacy passes from the common to the singular.

With that translocation, now, the wherefrom of evil becomes difficult to fathom: does it arise as universal principles get obfuscated in their simple evidence, or rather as singularizing dread gets muzzled—like Iphigenia gagged—by tragic denial? A narrator of epochal hegemonies might arbitrate without metaphysical hardship. He might say: until normative self-consciousness began to wane (roughly, until the deaths of Hegel and Goethe), singularization and individuation smacked of evil. Then, with the destitution of the modern referent, masters of suspicion appeared who inverted everything. Not unlike Kierkegaard, they placed the singular at the top of the ladder of values and the universal, the one, every fantasm of unity, at the bottom. Yet the hegemonies cannot be recounted as one recounts periods in factual history. They do not stretch time into duration. Theirs is not the historian's history. Here again, therefore, what intelligibility concerning ultimate conditions of evil would be gained with the piece of information about normative inversion in the last century? None.

---

12 Søren Kierkegaard, *Diary*, entry dated August 1, 1835.

13 Søren Kierkegaard, *Gesammelte Werke*, vol. 30, ed. and trans. Emanuel Hirsch (Düsseldorf: Eugen Diederichs, 1960), 9.

14 Søren Kierkegaard, *Der Begriff Angst*, trans. Christoph Schrempf (Jena: Eugen Diederichs, 1923), 117ff. and 135ff.

In truth, if natality and morality are phenomenologically originary, we do know what to make of the inversion thesis (a thesis it is). To report that after about 1830 values got inverted, the bottom of the ladder now counting for the top and the top, for the bottom—such storytelling is not exactly free of any interest. It allows one to classify one's neighbor, if he locates high what is ultimate, as "still a metaphysician": for two centuries now, the *ultimate* insult. But the interest in simple ultimacy makes this verdict, "still an X," in its turn a thoroughly metaphysical insult. Let us rather say that, in Kierkegaard's words, the voice of dread beneath that of desire then made itself heard. Discordant voices became listened to, voices by which it is useful to let us be instructed. Through their discordance speaks tragic knowing. They testify to the *orietur* which always attracts us toward some focal meaning, as well as to the *morietur* subtracting us from it.

The two incongruent functional clusters, attraction-natality-maximization-appropriation and subtraction-mortality-singularization-expropriation, then the denial of this whole second cluster as well as the exaltation of attractive, maximally normative, theses: these then are conditions of evil other than ethical, moral, or onto-theological.

There are to be sure others, and more that we do not understand than ones we do. At least for a phenomenology of ultimates, *the* condition of evil does indeed not exist. No more, one may add, than exists *the* way of demonstration or the method in phenomenology. It would therefore be non-pertinent to object: You set out from the premises of natality-mortality, only to step from the descriptive to the prescriptive and so end up with normative double binds. The objection is beside the point. First, philosophy's point consists in submitting to rigorous thinking elements of experience of which we do have prior knowing; an argumentative circle is thus not vicious if it allows one to understand conditions better. Furthermore, it would be one thing to state first propositions held to be true, but it is quite another to begin from originary traits with which everyone is familiar; natality and mortality are thus not premises for deductive reasoning. Lastly, those traits cannot be described like givens; the conditions of evil just mentioned thus do not result out of a metabasis from the describable.

Kierkegaard can help one undo entanglements, knitted by a long tradition, which tie evil back to the singular: to individuation, and also to one single condition which would account for evil. But in order to descry the originary dissension that ruins from within any normative posit, an analytic is needed that brings an historical topology to bear on daily knowing.

Of Impossible Normative Simplicity

That analytic, varied according to the natural languages and the epochs on which each put its stamp, can be schematized here only by a few pointers. Firstly, singulars and singularities follow phenomenologically from singulariza*tion* (from the pull of mortality). Furthermore, as originary, singularization works on normative posits from within, thus depriving us of any appellate jurisdiction. Also, recognizing the singular as irreducible to the particular and hence to subsumption—a recognition that remains oblique under the hegemonies and has shown to provoke either dread or elation at their limits—in no way means that one can somehow escape from under norms, deposited though they are in advance by their singular extraction even as they are posited as sovereign. Lastly, simple focal meanings are not *evil-gotten* (their positing follows from the very attraction of natality), but the equation "the ultimate is simple" kills, since it decrees as if singularization were not. Of these pointers the first directs attention to the to-come; the second to a certain anarchy; the third to the tragic double bind that persists throughout historical dispositions; and the last to the tragic hubris of simple sways.

"Develop your singularities," one was told not long ago in Paris as well as in California. The exhortation entailed and entails analytically: "Respect singularities." Yet here is what was not said and is however needed if philosophy's task remains to render explicit the prior knowing that we have of conditions: Whence such an imperative? What renders it possible? Accordingly, no time was lost in Frankfurt to retort: "In the name of what? Spell out your validity arguments." Now names and values, as well as the subjective (or intersubjective) competency on which critical theorists rest such arguments, under topological inspection turn out as products, brought into being by theticism.[15] Just as any other thetic referent, the one invoked in the name of consensus through discursive rationality, or through communicative action, can be posited only at the cost of denying the foreignness of singular references. These references enter enabling strategies that are entirely other than subjectivist. They can be detected, provided one ceases maximizing self-consciousness, be it for the sake of a universal pragmatics. In order to reach an origin other than posited and positive, there is no abundance of methods. I need to return to what I always know, though poorly: namely, my singularization *to come*.[16]

Polymorphous singularities constitute themselves,[17] and monomorphous theses get destituted, not to be sure by time as such. That would amount to declaring yet another magnitude rather than gathering a trait. Only the expropriating retraction toward my death, hence time as *contretemps*, corners singularity. The singular I implies therefore neither fullness nor ownness. It is not the achievement of autonomous freedom, not the self. Rather it comes about with the dephenomenalizing strategy in ordinary experience: with expropriation from the world as mine. Social theorists have always acknowledged such constitutive disownment, albeit indirectly, when they say that the world—community or collectivity, family, civil society, state—does not come about through accumu-

---

15 The words "value," *Wert*, *valeur* pass from the vocabulary of political economy into that of philosophy, about the times of Hume and Kant. That idiom is not only contemporaneous with the institution of the modern hegemony, it is one of that institution's immediate effects. Values come into being, in valuations performed by the originarily spontaneous subject. Trying to develop "arguments of validity" from communication, one does therefore not cease turning in circles in the arena of hegemonic self-consciousness. With such arguments, it is still subjectivity that sniffs its own traces, i.e. the values it has posited with the transcendental turn.

16 This phrase is used here to underline in what Heidegger called being-towards-death the temporal pull of imminence, as well as the subtraction from the world induced by that pull.

17 It would be no less a thetic operation to speculate on *the* sexual difference, as if singularities were safe as long as one proves capable of counting up to two and posits no longer the (male) one, but the (female) other. In speaking of sexualities, common names such as "feminism" can only perpetuate binary models and hence the most crudely metaphysical antitheses.

lation and that, in all idealist rigor, the individual has no being. For a thinking that recognizes originary time in expropriation to come, there are singularities only as dispossessed. They are nothing to flaunt since, inasmuch as my world is always about to expel me, they owe their being to the temporality of imminence. I am I, singularly dispossessed.

As differing ultimates, natality and mortality bear thus unequally on futurity. Death as dealt—this is not a popular thought, as from all sides norms and values are clamored for—results from the impulse of natality, at least when dealt "in the name of ..." It has been said that there was an aspect of banality to exterminations. One may add: evil becomes banal, once a common focalization is posited and singularization denied. The other's death turns out to be easy as soon as a fantasm has carried the day and has come to obsess everyone's visual expanse. From the trait of mortality, on the other hand, results only death as suffered, presently imminent.[18] Maximizations will never stop being invested in, unless philosophy is trusted in its ability to dissolve the *hubris* behind any simple normative meaning: that is, to analyze it, decompose it into its elements, detect the denial, and thus beneath the prestige of names rehabilitate the temporality by singularization.

In philosophy, indeed, one may just as well put one's pens away if inquiring into ultimate conditions of experience is to be renounced. But one ceases to so inquire if some *a priori* is posited by maximizing one or the other representation that happens to enjoy prevalence. Such theticism meets one's wishes, which makes it essentially gratifying. It crowns one's fantasmic investments with a paramount guarantee, not unlike the way the FDIC guarantees bank investments. There exists today a whole philosophical industry, administered by the "functionaries of mankind" (Husserl), to sanction institutions and usages. But something unsteady remains about gratifications, since for the interval they last they require that I blind myself against negative experience. Such is the secret that

18 On the discrepancy between death about to be dealt on a large scale, banal as a consequence of a common belief, and death as imminently suffered, see the novel by Christa Wolf, *Cassandra*, trans. Jan van Heurck (New York: Farrar, Straus and Giroux, 1984). Nothing I know illustrates better the two incongruent kinds of futurity.

accounts for the ascendancy of archic posits: they condense the true, the beautiful, the good to their extreme. And how could desire not find its fulfillment—its pleasure and climax—in such compactness? It would be hard to imagine an exaltation literally more marvelous than the ascent to ideals, including of course the ideal of undistorted intersubjective communication.

Yet it is concerning just such marvels that in everydayness we do know better. If pleasure demands that I deny negative experience, then this kind of experience has already been recognized. Otherwise there could be no denying it. In addition, everyone knows that it will have, and therefore already has, the last word. But then the platform from which fantasmic maximizations take off, and from which ascend therefore normative arguments, has in advance been cut out to serve more and less magnificent—because more and less magnifiable—interests.

Last century's Objective Idealism recognized the systematic need to trace the conditions of negative experience back to the "ground" (for Schelling, freedom). However, it is not difficult to see that by splitting the sovereign principle into originary ground and non-ground (*Urgrund* and *Ungrund*), one only applies to evil the same subsumptive exaltation to which we owe all hegemonic fantasms. Evil gets in turn maximized and introduced into the master referent. Thus, in Schelling, the absolute will universalizes ends and reasons, while also singularizing itself in original sin. Coupling evil absolutely with the good, one has hardly found a way out of theticism. For that it is necessary to remain faithful to the irreducible phenomena: the traits of natality and mortality. With such faithfulness, however, the ultimate condition can no longer be absolutely simple and in that sense archic.

Whether explicitly or tacitly and whatever its variant, a doctrine of principles cannot do without a concept of anarchy. In such a doctrine, this concept only sums up the axiom that forbids stepping back indefinitely towards more and more primitive conditions. Within theticism, the first *archē* will have to be anarchic, since it would no longer be first if in turn it had its *archē*.

Quite different is the anarchy that appears as one tries to unlearn truncating the phenomenologically originary conditions. Then singularization shows itself to impair any normative posit from within. The call to remain faithful to singularization jars with the call of simple principles establishing the law. Such ultimate dissonance deprives us, and has always deprived us, of any appellate jurisdiction. The origin thus proves *anarchic because in dissension with itself.*

The eras of philosophy, set apart by the languages in which it has been spoken, can best be described through fantasmic theticism. A thetic fantasm always regulates a given epochal array. The way these arrays are articulated on their regulatory posits mutates ceaselessly. Just as varying in every epoch is the destabilizing undertow by which singularization to come brings these normative arrays into disarray.

The topologist does, however, more than describe shifting territories and the breaks between them. Were he to stay content with descriptions, the very search for conditions would be blocked. Now if these conditions are not simple, how are they to be understood and told? It seems to me that they are most easily read in the elementary functions of maximization and singularization that traverse the history of referential theses. I have suggested that these functions reproduce in large script the traits of everyday experience. If that is so, then—whether the counterstrategies issuing from morality are recognized or denied—we remain faithful to the *polemos* of ultimates in everything we do and can do. Whatever the epochal order it conditions, the originary condition thus proves to be polemically turned against itself. There is more at stake than recognizing "beneath the rule: abuse" (Bertolt Brecht). Rather transgression occurs at the very heart of legislation, in its essence and its instances. Not that agents always abuse the rule, but always, as it regulates, the rule abuses itself. To rule and regulate is to speak in the name of the common. It is to simplify the manifold, produce evidence, and thereby make oneself understood. The tragic authors saw an unruliness as part and parcel of the rule, a "dark light" (Hölderlin) at the core of evidence. They tell us: *You cannot understand. You must understand.* What? That any name laying down the law contains in it its own forces of abandon. That we always inhabit a fugued world, one about to withdraw even while it shelters us, a world escaping. The ultimates that are at the beginning of thought stay incomprehensible as they comprehend *it*. But that about which one cannot speak, that alone the tragics have said, and it must be said.

The ceaseless rearrangements within any given language epoch appear only to a pre-understanding of ultimates. The same is true of the breaks when, instead of Greek, Latin—and later, one or the other modern vernacular—becomes philosophy's *lingua franca*. The originary double bind can be verified as it is put to the test of these historical loci. Its pre-understanding provides, not to be sure a fixed grid, but the dynamics of allocations and dislocations opening each time an epoch. Outside the epochal articulations, these traits remain indeed untreatable. They could solidify into theoretical objects, only at the cost of erasing the language breaks so as to decree some philosophical *volapük*. How could the refigurations and breaks even be investigated as such, unless one possessed a prior knowing that allows one to read both the trait that welds a world together and the one that tears it?

Now if we know ourselves to be so incongruously bound, there is something comical about the urge to force an exit from the ultimate double bind. Comical, inasmuch as that urge looks very much the same whether one seeks to rise to some speculative belvedere towering above one or the other metaphysical terrains, or whether one seeks on the contrary to escape all such terrains on which to speculate so as to gain private consolation and public consolidation. This is also why "anarchy" does not mean and cannot mean to relegate all *archai* among obsolete philosophical tools and to go and settle happily in a place deprived of principles.[19] The phenomenology of ultimates adds an epilogue to hegemonic fantasms, but an epilogue to fantasms as such would be unthinkable. It would be no less unthinkable than not putting universals into the service of some consoling and consolidating name. All common names are capable of so consoling the soul and consolidating

---

19 Jacques Derrida gives an example of anarchy as characterizing an "outside" on which to settle in a resolute "decision." He describes a strategy of "changing terrains, in a discontinuous and irruptive fashion, by brutally placing oneself outside and by asserting an absolute break and difference" (*Margins of Philosophy*, trans. Alan Bass [Chicago: The University of Chicago Press, 1982], 135). I read these lines as a description of events in France at the time the essay was finished ("May 12, 1968," ibid., 136).

the city, inasmuch as we think and speak under the fantasmogenic impetus of natality. It is however possible to enlarge one's way of thinking[20] beyond the common so generated. In our languages, verbs in the middle voice always lead their speaker out of simple nominative rule governance. It is then possible to think for itself the double bind of which we have a prior knowing. After hubristic sufferings—not unlike Oedipus who at Colonus wants his eyes open, wants himself open-eyed—it is possible to love differing ultimates. This, I submit, would be expanding the limits of imagination.

Natality gives and regives us a world in which to dwell. It does this by extolling names or "general ideas" under which to rally. Of these, the best would be the most general, hence also the most simple. It would give us the best of all worlds. As a consequence of its simple bind however—and the West has witnessed those consequences—such a world kills. The thetic thrust mutilates thinking. Just as desire, of which it is the public agent, theticism has no use of remaining faithful to phenomena, which faithfulness is called thinking. It singles out some square meaning, augments it, institutes it as an authority, bestows hegemony on it. Such squaring of thought produces fantasms that are mortal not only in that they perish, but also in that they make perish.

The metaphysician in us is recalcitrant against the insight that the ultimate is not—nor can be—simple; that it becomes so squared, only under blows of thetic denial. The tragics on the other hand did not fear what they knew. Beneath the profusion of plots they show one and the same nomic differing, first cut down for the sake of institutions, then suffered, recognized, accepted, embraced. For them, some blinding meaning was instituted only as a result of a different blinding: of *hubris*.

Thinking becomes urgent, one would like to say easy, once *hubris* has been committed. Then Antigone all of a sudden speaks in the voice of Creon and Creon, in Antigone's.[21] The Furies, avengeresses according to the terrible heroic code, suddenly plead the democratic order; and Athena, the city's tutelary, advocates the *deinon* in

---

20 In Kant, the "expanded way of thinking" (*die erweiterte Denkungsart*) consists in a judgment that takes singulars into account, cf. *Critique of Judgment*, § 40, 77.

21 Sophocles, *Antigone*, lines 504–09 and 734–41.

institutions.[22] This discursive permutation has been praised as the moment of dialectical reconciliation. But not so, since the opposition does not amount to a determinate negation. Rather thinking here stays faithful to disparate ultimates. In the aftermath of *hubris* committed (totalitarianisms lying behind us in Europe, it seems), new questions get a chance such as: how could thoughtlessness ever go so far? Concerning these aftermaths, we enjoy today an indisputable prerogative. At the end of this century in the West, we are rather well stationed to recover—if that were possible—from denial and thoughtlessness. Looking back from hubris toward tragic knowing, expanded imagination may indeed see singulars jar incongruously with their world:

> No one was able to remember when and how long ago Akaky Akakievich had entered the ministry, nor who had given him the job. The directors, department heads, division managers and other administrators came and went; he was always seen in the same place, in the same position, at the very same duty of a copying clerk. No respect was shown him in the office. The porters, far from getting up from their seats when he came in, took no more notice of him than if a fly had flown across the room. The head clerk's assistant would throw papers under his nose without even bothering to say "Copy this." The younger clerks jeered and made jokes at him to the best of their clerkly wit. They would scatter bits of paper on his head and exclaim "Snow falling!" Akaky Akakievich, however, remained impassive. Only when one of them jolted his arm and hindered him from doing his work, he simply said:
> "Leave me alone. What have I done to you?"
> There was something strange in these words. He uttered them in such a poignant tone that one young man, new to the office and who, following the example of the rest, had allowed himself to tease him, suddenly stopped as though cut to the heart. From that moment on, the world appeared to him in a different light.[23]

---

22 Aeschylus, *The Eumenides*, lines 517, 696ff.

23 Nikolai Gogol, "The Overcoat," in *The Complete Tales and Plays*, vol. 2, trans. Constance Garnett, ed. and rev. Leonard J. Kent (Chicago: The University of Chicago Press, 1964), 564–65 (translation slightly modified and abbreviated).

Appendix

Interview with a Young German Writer[1]

Reiner Schürmann is 36 years old. Born in Germany during the height of the war, he has not ceased bearing the burden of the wrongs that he has not committed. In an attempt to escape the past, he throws himself into wandering. A stay in a kibbutz in Israel, studies in Paris, travel in Greece, then a stabilization in the U.S. where he is a professor of philosophy. In a disturbing book, Les Origines, *autobiographical to a great extent, he tells of his suffering from being marked at this point by his "origins." At a time when terrorism has pushed Germany to the forefront of current events, Reiner Schürmann helps make sense of what is happening, and how his people have reacted to the return of violence.*

* * *

Why do you write (and superbly) in French?

Because of the subject. In Germany it is spoken of too much. Or not enough. But badly. Our ears are blocked, offended in advance. I believe that my compatriots don't want to hear it mentioned. So this is a book written for non-Germans. But now that it is out in the U.S. and in France, Germans have taken an interest in it.

The title: Les Origines...

That is a little complicated. First of all, the origins are my national origins, since it is the story of a German born during the war who has not even seen the war and who lives with it a little too much. Not with it, but with its consequences. And next, the origins refer to a search, an attempt to find myself, but this time, very personally, on the level of human relations. A thrust toward what I am, Me, Reiner Schürmann. Why is my life marked at this point by the

1 [With the exception of the final section, the following translation has been produced by Reiner Schürmann himself. Occasional minor edits have been made throughout for grammatical reasons, based on the original French published edition.—Eds.]

obsession with a particular past. There is this originating fact: being born German at the time when my country was committing all these crimes; and then there is the origin in the sense of the individual identity, of the zone preserved in oneself from which a life arises.

Your whole book is a long cry of shocked suffering.

Certain critics, otherwise very kind, have taken this book to be … what was that woman's phrase? … Oh, yes … an "expiation." A German who asks forgiveness of the French people, a kind of international settling of accounts. No, I did not want to set down anything other than a kind of X-ray of my mind, a series of obsessions all focusing on the same problem.

Can you briefly recount the concept of the book?

It concerns a German who begins to travel too young, at the age of 16, around the end of the 50s, and who, wherever he goes, is forced to identify himself with what the Germans had subjected other people to; Poland, Israel, Greece, France, and in the end, America. Everywhere, because I am German, I was identified with a past which I didn't want, which I didn't know, in which I had no hand. In Crete, for example, I was 16 years old … I was with two friends my age and we were refused service in a restaurant. "Nothing for the Germans." At 16 one is not equipped to face this kind of rejection. In the U.S., at 30, I was trying to find a job as an assistant professor in a university. The first thing that I heard was: "Oh, you're from Cologne! Do they still make soap from human bones where you're from?"

The present terrorism

Do you think that there are many young Germans who are traumatized like yourself by this rejection and guilt?

My answer will not be simple. The genius of France lies in the word. In this country one speaks, and the incomprehensible, once it takes the form of a statement, seems to be understood. In Germany the most important things are not spoken of. They are transformed into abstract philosophy or music. This often gives an impression of dumbness, of distance. I am certain, I have seen it, with the help of beer, after midnight, there are outbursts that are not pretty to see. Suddenly a hidden core reemerges. It is concealed under the ordinary facade of life, but that cracks. Then the chinks are patched over. The rigid policing at this time in Germany is the same cover-up at the basis of vertigo: create a climate where all diversities of opinion are impossible. The solidity of a surface where only a single tone is accepted and all the others suppressed, where all obsession and anguish is carefully covered up—such solidity will only continue to grow.

If this were to be spoken about, that would be less unhealthy, more curable?

That is why I write, to heal myself. Here it is necessary to talk about the role of writing. If you listen a little to what people are saying in the sidewalk cafes and restaurants, well, it's always more or less the same thing. They speak of the meal, they recount what is happening in their lives, they talk about films. Writing has the role of piercing the veneer of speech, in which communication is pleasant, not too offensive, where there are conventions, where one only half listens. Writing's task is to say the things that are not spoken of at a restaurant table. That is, to bring out into the open; but it is necessary to have a foundation to make things emerge. One can live very well with jargon, with polemics that the whole world repeats. What I call "the origins" is the effort of plunging much deeper, beneath the mental schematics accepted in our everyday relations with people.

Does the Germany of the Baader gang, of terrorism, have something to do with the disorder of the young Germans? And in the face of terrorism, the general torpor of opulence, of economism, that society of profit, that "life of profit" of which you speak in your book—doesn't all this hide the same disorder?

In fact, I think it is the same confusion, the same flight from a past that must be forgotten at any cost.

Can this terrorism of the young be explained a little to try and understand it?

First it must be located in history. It seems to be spoken of as a new phenomenon. It has its novel aspects, but they have very ancient roots. German unity was imposed by victorious external forces. As President Heinemann said in his inauguration speech: "We have not been able to unify our country ourselves (it needed an external power since this was Prussia), nor to establish a democratic regime ourselves."

The democratic regime was imposed twice by the victorious powers. These remarks were not pleasant! Can you imagine a president of the [French] Republic denouncing the nation's incapacity to establish a republican way of life? There was the impossibility of creating a nation out of regional divisions, and of doing it democratically. The result was that the political conscience of Germany always remained under foreign surveillance. Not only did the allies impose a democratic regime on us, but they again maintained it through their constant presence. The presence and surveillance of the allies remains in effect, and is perhaps indispensable.

So, with so few of our own political moorings, it is understandable that the terrorism be provoked in part by the impossibility of creating a breadth of opinion sufficiently vast to absorb the extremes. As the political voices are weak, for the historical reasons which I have mentioned, the least difference of opinion is felt as a threat. The result: those who withdraw from, say, "moderate," behavior are met with such rigidity that they wind up driven ever further into the margins, and are eventually reduced to taking up arms. Rather than waging violence, it is necessary to speak of counter-violence.[2] It is the necessity behind this counter-violence that may be considered a new phenomenon. But evidently it can take diverse forms. I don't agree with the bloody form of anarchy.[3]

Some of your newspapers complain or regret that for us there aren't any parties of the left that are more solidly formed. This

2 [In the original French the sentence reads as follows: "Plutôt que de parler de violence il faudrait parler de contre-violence."—Eds.]

3 [In the original French, it is "l'anarchisme."—Eds.]

is putting the cart before the horse. Parties cannot be formed, for example, a Communist party, that are stronger than the two that [already] exist, if to begin with there is not the psychological groundwork necessary for accepting divergent opinions or ways of life. In Germany, there is this terrible accord, for the man in the street as for the intellectuals who otherwise I respect, enormously—an accord concerning the directive excluding any extremists from public offices. There is a unity of judgment—I use this as an example—concerning the exclusion of the leftists, in which I can see nothing but the fear of seeing people diverging from a rather mediocre final consensus, but the one which alone reassures.

I will take another example of this tacit consensus. You wonder in your newspaper if we must pardon Kappler, or put him back in prison. But no, the real problem doesn't lie there; it is much vaster, it concerns the method of administering justice. On this point, in Germany, justice is not rendered. Since the end of the war in the courts there has been a continual, persistent, universal abstention—if not actually a constraint—from doing the least bit to punish the war criminals and impose justice on them.

Return to Nazism

Recent films about Hitler and other signs make us think about a resurrection of Nazism.

Resurrection? I would rather say continuation—not of Nazism, but of what makes it possible. There are the neo-Nazis, but they don't have much influence. The true totalitarianism is the intolerance of the forms of life and thought that go beyond an extremely narrow margin, in practice, the margin that you just called economism.

I noticed this phrase in a newspaper: "A society where gold is God..."

That is rather pathetic... Gold, no. That phrase is not only pathetic, it is also a little silly. The German God is actually security. When one has experienced two wars and is turned upside down psychologically as this nation has been for half a century, well, there exists a vertigo, a basis of vertigo on which one solidifies a fantastic dream of being finally tranquil.

You write: "Neither rebellion nor current affairs, but letting be."

Not rebellion, not indignant rejection of my origins, but neither giving way to current events, that is to say, the race after gain and success, the materialism that is now in the back of the minds of my compatriots.[4] Neither insurrection nor submission, but what I call "letting be"—giving everything, in the present, the weight that accords to it. After a period of escapism [*fuite*] spent in a pointless search for a unique and dependable origin—a stable foundation of things, as if that had ever existed!—I ended up discovering the following: it is in the absence of a stable identity, in that dislocation, that our joy must be located. Joy is not a profound rooting or a solidity, which life, my life, has taught me to no longer desire. Letting-be is a wandering joy. What Nietzsche calls the "gay science," that's precisely wandering joy: to accept chaos and plant our joy in it.

And France?

You're living in the USA now. You observe the American youth and you write: "they look only to the future."

I did not write that with admiration! On the contrary, I see in this an immense poverty. The great strength of Americans is specialization. When they throw themselves into something they really go all the way in, they are very strong. But ask them questions of "general knowledge," as we would say, outside of their domain: nothing! This is where their fear of ideas comes from. And also, the poverty of their human relations. They are not really curious about each other. They [*ils*] care about whatever news is trending and their

---

4 [Here the existing English transcript breaks off. The remainder of the text has been translated by us.—Eds.]

careers. I see them entirely focused on things to be realized, at the expense of the present.

You spoke just now of men ["ils"]*? And what of women* ["elles"]*?*

Oh! You know, American women are not very feminine. When compared with Americans, French women seem to me very submissive, unhappy in their skin, and dependent. American women have little charm and a confidence in the material enterprise of life that often makes them into men.

Germany, USA... And France?

France... What bores me with you is your wordiness, and in such poor schemas. In France one expends heaps of energy on debates between right and left, when it's really up to everyone to discover in themselves the resources for a minimum of creativity, rather than to keep repeating the same slogans. When one doesn't know what counts in one's own life, one repeats stereotypical ideas. As for myself, I have so far led a life of escapism [*fuite*]. Who knows? Maybe I will always be a being in flight. But for now, what I flee from resolutely is insignificant life, life lived vicariously. The congestion, the humdrum of massively present things, the immense jumble of words and especially of jargons, the jumble of fears, all that prevents one from seeing, in a pared down present, the life at stake therein. A significant life is not necessarily a grandiose life. It is more enjoyable when it is grandiose, when accompanied by strong emotions, but for me the task that I've set myself is to discover what is most tenuous, most fragile in human situations, provided it is very personal.

On the Philosophers' Release from Civil Service

Gruber:* *Following Heidegger, your work on the relation between "being" and "acting" raises the question of technology within the tradition of philosophical thinking. Could you begin by speaking about this tradition and the particular way you understand how technology has come to dominate our world today?*

Reiner Schürmann: Let me offer an anecdote. Kant begins the second Preface to the *Critique of Pure Reason* saying that in one of its activities reason is burdened with ideas that it can neither resolve nor escape. Two years after publication of the *Critique*, he writes this magnificent little essay called "On Enlightenment," which begins: "What is Enlightenment? It is man's release from his self-incurred tutelage." And what is this "tutelage"? It amounts to reason's self-subjection to *historical* representations set up as supreme by reason itself.

So, in *The Critique of Pure Reason* he would say that slavery to supreme representations is systematic, that it is built into reason inescapably. It is our transcendental fate. However, in "On Enlightenment," he seems to say this bondage is historical. Tutelage is self-incurred and man's *release*, a possibility within history.

The reason I mention this shift in perspective, in Kant, is to suggest that the distinction between systematic and historical which has been so important to the reading of the history of philosophy should perhaps be relegated among those disjunctions that are of rather limited pertinence. Technology has come to dominate our world today because its logic—the systematic grounding or fixing of everything that can become a phenomenon—has remained operative in the West historically ever since classical Greece.

---

* The original gives only the surname of the interviewer. We were unable to establish their first name.—Eds.

So are you suggesting that in order to understand the basic assumptions of our world, we must think about technology as a "supreme representation"?

Yes. And looking at the opposite pole of classical Greece, at our own age, I am also suggesting that the closure of which technology is one figure must be understood as both systematic and historical.

By "closure" you mean that today technology has become so pervasive that it announces the end of tradition of thinking about "being" and "acting."

When Heidegger speaks of an "end of philosophy," one immediately thinks of a kind of a run that comes to a stop. That is, an historical cycle begins with the Greeks and then terminates at a specific point in time. But that is really only part of the story. The other is the systematic closure. What makes it systematic is that from Parmenides on (and Parmenides is the ambiguous founding figure), philosophers have placed themselves under the authority of some one ultimate standard, one supreme principle. Husserl, in the beginning of his book on the "European crisis," says that we philosophers are the functionaries of mankind; and that has been the status of metaphysicians in the West certainly since Plato, and most explicitly in the role Plato gave to the "philosopher king." Whether royal or bureaucratized as civil servants, philosophers are the ones whose task it has been to secure the ultimate grounds on which we can then peacefully live, and construct, and govern ourselves both privately and publicly. That mission of private consolation and public consolidation has been the original technological function of philosophy. The Greek word *technē* means know-how. The philosophers have been the experts in the know-how of rendering safe and secure, of mooring, all that there is—not exactly a minor responsibility.

Thus, regardless of the forms that technology has assumed historically, are you saying that philosophy has been assigned the task of elaborating various relevant value systems-representations?

Philosophers are functionaries who provide not only "various" foundations, but *the* foundation upon which everything else rests. Traditionally, with regard to any organization of the sciences, the philosopher has been expected to define the root of all knowledge. But his foundational expertise has been sought beyond the realm of science. In that sense, the philosopher has been indispensable, not a luxury—an indispensable public official in the West, systematically securing one normative focus. So once again, from the systematic point of view, the closure means that one can characterize the task of philosophy quite *a*historically as the service rendered to Western Civilization of securing a supreme reference point.

But, one must also characterize this historically. And the difficulty is to think the systematic and the historical together, in such a way as not to lapse into the cycles we have learned from Hegel—who is surely the big shadow here—in which everything ends up reconciled. That would be the philosophical operation modeled no longer after the city-state monarchy and not yet after modern-day bureaucracy: the truly imperialistic operation.

Is there a moment within the tradition where the philosopher no longer submits to thinking "foundationally"?

For me, it is quite clear that from Nietzsche onward the function of the philosopher becomes very difficult. If Nietzsche is the closing figure, he is as ambiguous as Parmenides, the opening figure. There is still perhaps a metaphysics—that is, a first philosophy—in the "will to power" and "eternal recurrence." But after Nietzsche, I believe in the later Wittgenstein most clearly, the impossibility of rendering that foundational service to our civilization becomes obvious.

So, for you, the crisis of philosophy is that both its historical and systematic grounds have been rendered obsolete by the power of technology.

I think what is so exciting and certainly awesome about our present situation is that we are on a boundary line as decisive as that which preceded Plato and which one can trace very beautifully in

Parmenides. It is not a wild guess to say something like: "Ours is a time of crisis." All grandfathers have said that! But, if one accepts that somehow philosophers—as Hegel would say—are the mouthpieces of their times, then from Nietzsche to Wittgenstein there is a clear *dispersal* of foci. Except for rare quarters such as Frankfurt, the philosopher's job description today no longer stipulates for him to refer all phenomena to one focal point from which they receive their phenomenality. That philosophers can no longer do. Nietzsche and Wittgenstein are the paradigmatic figures of this dispersal. The philosopher still remains embedded within the tradition, for how could that not be? And yet, he works on it from a situation that is already "other" in nature, more dispersed.

Are you suggesting that this tradition, which is identical to laboring under the sway of a single focus, is now lost?

Yes. It becomes refracted, in Nietzsche's language, into innumerable constellations of will to power, into configurations of domination; or in Wittgenstein's language, it is now equally broken up into innumerable language games and their grammars.

And, this loss of a single focus also means that philosophical inquiry itself becomes less principled.

This is my point when I speak of the philosophers' release from civil service. The closure can thus best be described by what we might think about as the withering of principles. In that sense, we are talking about a culture deprived of an *archē*. *Archē* taken not only as the beginning, but in the twofold sense of the Greek verb *archein*, which means both to begin and to command. *Anarchy* means, if we are to trust the mouthpiece of the philosopher, that culturally we are already in a situation where the *archē* is lost.

I imagine that both socially and psychologically this loss of focus, this anarchy, might induce feelings of anxiety and chaos.

Let me attempt a little piece of socio-psychology which I will surely regret. Perhaps the "mean-ness" of institutionalized brutality and discipline, of which we have seen many kinds in this century, reflects efforts to reinstitute figures of some authoritative First that in fact have been lost for good.

Something like Freud's return of the repressed.
It's not really that principles are repressed. I don't think that is the appropriate image. But rather, it has more to do with mourning. After a death, what do you do? You mourn. That would be our cultural situation: the mourning after foci or supreme referents whose authority went without saying. As I said, the Greek term *archein* carries within itself the ambiguous meaning of both author and authority. So *archē* is both an author standing at the beginning and the principle commanding as an authority. It is the authority that we mourn, and we try to conjure it back by institutionalizing it in various ways: most visibly in totalitarianism, but also—in this country today—for instance by some brand of fundamentalism. This need not be biblical. I am struck by the fierce fundamentalism concerning the Constitution among otherwise highly critical minds.

At the opposite pole of the temporal spectrum from the archē *is a representation of* telos, *an end, as in both a finishing and an aim. You seem to suggest that just as there is a dispersal of* archē, *there is also a dislodging of teleocracy, of an orientation to the future which enframes how we think and act today. I see this as a kind of double movement, and one that in your previous work on Eckhart and your theorizing on Heidegger is best portrayed as "releasement"—as a way in which the original nature of thoughts, feelings, and actions presence themselves and become available to encounter.*

I think the question amounts to something like: What form would releasement take for us? The kind of releasement of which Meister Eckhart speaks has to do with interiority—of which there is still a trace in Heidegger's little text, *Discourse on Thinking.* In Kant, releasement is something quite different. It is the project of Enlightenment with a big E—to trust one's reason as the agent of emancipation from all authorities. The discreet charm of this project consists of course in that it institutes reason itself as the new *archē*.

By the way, Fontenelle describes this same project a few years earlier very beautifully. He says that one does not easily persuade men to place their reason in the place of their eyes. So, with the eyes, the oldest speculative function/metaphor available to philosophers, one sees what is present, but thinking and reason would "comply" with presencing, with the ever changing plies or folds according to which phenomena render themselves present to us. Heidegger makes a notorious pun: *thinking*, he says, is a matter of *thanking*. Thanking what? The way events happen to occur around us, for the time being (this extraordinary phrase in your language, "for the time being"—the symmetrical opposite to Heidegger's attempt at understanding "being as time"). Thinking as thanking means to cease imposing on inner and outer phenomena the stamp of one representation held to be normative. In another well-publicized phrase of Heidegger's: it amounts to letting phenomena be; letting them unfold themselves according to their own economy. When I speak of "plies" or "folds," I have in mind the fabric of interaction that characterizes a time. Think of what you mean when you say: "This film is typically the Fifties"; "That rally was the Sixties all over again." What we mean in expressions such as these is that a decade amounts to something like a fold in the fabric of interaction. Now we always and without question comply with these epochal plies. But in their more modest task—more modest than their civil servants' mission—philosophers have always told us to learn to do explicitly what we do implicitly anyway. They have told us: Become what you are. In this case, that old injunction translates as: Unlearn the normative fantasms that are alien to everydayness. Each age gives a specific responsibility to its philosophers. I believe that our responsibility today amounts to helping people unlearn the "standards" whose grip becomes all the more brutal and irrational as they fade.

In our western countries, releasement may still be the most appropriate term to describe this compliance and the closure of metaphysical representations. I can, however, think of quite a few situations in many countries in the twentieth century where releasement does not bring one very far. For example, in the 1960s, we on the left had heros—and the greatest of them were the Khmer Rouge. And my biggest shock was that when the Khmer Rouge finally came to power, they served us Pol Pot. Now, in such a situation, or in a situation of occupation, releasement is just a luxury that makes too much of interiority. And there, anarchism has to be taken in a very strict and militant sense including acts of terror. Man's release from his self-incurred tutelage is not as serene an undertaking for us as releasement could be under the sway of interiority in the heritage of Augustine. It may take a great variety of forms according to context. *And some of these forms, while attesting to releasement's pliability, may also suggest an acquiescence to the on-going "fitness" of things as they are.*

Yes. It can exactly play into the hands of that of which it is meant to hasten the closure or withering.

Are you speaking of something analogous to what the critical theorists Horkheimer and Adorno term the "dialectic of enlightenment"?

I don't use that vocabulary, but I recognize their inquiry to be addressing concerns that obviously occupied Heidegger as well. I think that what makes the topic particularly complex is that perhaps *the* enduring principle has been subjectivity—man himself. So that when Heidegger says that humanism is as old as metaphysics, what he is also saying is that there are not that many supreme principles under which we have placed ourselves or which the philosopher as the civil servant par excellence has had to secure. The epochal principles always had to do with *man* understood in one way or another. And this remains relevant to the project of Heidegger's major book, *Being and Time,* itself. His project founders on the tip of the iceberg that it was supposed to melt—namely subjectivity. It founders on the tip of this iceberg in as much as the question of time is raised at the end of the book exclusively and very perplexingly in terms of authenticity and inauthenticity—that is, specifically in terms of the self. So one could argue that the book that was to announce the *end* of subjectivity concludes with a further elaboration of subjectivity—of the authentic self!

But if subjectivity is the fundamental problem that confronts us, how does "releasement" inform us about how we might live our lives differently, anarchically?

The French title of my book would have translated as *Anarchy-Principle*. But I do think that people have misunderstood my vocabulary as if it were yet another attempt at dialectics: "anarchy" as the determinate negation of "principle," which negation would then be expected to sublate itself and yield some new principal form of being. In particular, the Italians who call for "weak thinking" have understood the book that way.[1]

That seems to be an obvious oversight about the role that the word "displacement" has played throughout your work. Rather than merely a thought-experiment, my understanding is that anarchy *displaces the distinction between activity and passivity to a more practical dilemma of how one is to orient, to stand or to be disposed toward the world.*

What I intend is indeed something much more concrete than lofty dialectical speculations. It has to do with detecting remnants of those representations we have artificially endowed with ultimacy—detecting them wherever they occur and in whatever shape they take and pointing them out as targets for discursive intervention.

It's interesting that in the United States today, many would claim that anarchy already reigns due to the subversion or displacement of a universal moral fiber; that there are no binding representations.

Voltaire said: "One does not free people easily from the chains that they adore." It is against those principles that continue to enchain us—all the while we run around saying "god is dead, god is dead," or announcing the end of metaphysics—that I am writing. The fantasmatic nature of those chains appears with radicalized enlightenment. Today's possibility of combating them was what I wanted to indicate by the hyphen between Anarchy and Principle. Again, in various contexts this takes many forms. It covers the front pages of newspapers, or happens on the psychiatrist's couch. Foucault, for example, was admirable in sporadic struggles in which he engaged

1 See Schürmann's essay "Deconstruction Is Not Enough: On Gianni Vattimo's Call for 'Weak Thinking,'" *Graduate Faculty Philosophy Journal* 10, no. 1 (1984): 165–77—Eds.

with a force that did *not* come from any preconceived moral system. People here often say we need standards, we need values. I don't think that this is possible. An insight into the fate of the "universal moral fiber" is all it takes to modify one's understanding and practice. But negatively, we can identify those idols that are still around. Remember, this country is the second most religious country after India on the globe! In the U.S., contradictions between the life-world and standards turned hollow and brutal, which I seek to grasp through the phrase anarchy principle, are most blatant. These contradictions are not dialectical since they oppose the real to the fantasmatic. Nevertheless, in my view they account for both the internal and the external violence of this democracy.

The exploration and articulation of this anarchy principle seems to infuse all of your work, including the role of the poetic imagination.

It is meant to be a description that characterizes every possible struggle against remnants of those principles that we in fact mourn: to push into their tomb whatever idols remain. Hölderlin may have lost his mind over this struggle. He said: "I received from the gods more than I could digest." And it seems that what he got from the gods had to do with such a dispersal away from a One, away from an ultimate representation. Hölderlin remains for me the poet who has suffered the flight of the gods into the fake, a poetic experience unequaled in modern times.

So you are using Hölderlin, as you use Heidegger, as a symbol—as a figure who joins the loss of the past with the anticipation of a new beginning?

Hölderlin is the typical figure of closure. He's the mourning figure, and he utters pathetically the incipient dispersal. Those that are far away from the origins are the ones who mourn the source. He is the paradigmatic figure for us because of that distance and that mourning. His language is so moving because it *is* the very wound that opened up in the nineteenth century.

He is a kind of boundary figure, one in transition between having a desire to perpetuate an orientation and already sensing the pervasive uprootedness.

The wound that opened up is the boundary line between what is now called modernity and post-modernity. It's a bizarre fate that mass culture inflicts on our language when the most pertinent terms become written on the sidewalks of SoHo and become so worn out that they become impossible to use. This does not mean, however, that they are not pertinent terms. They must simply be seen as expressions of the historical-systematic lapsing out of order of the *principial game* that we have been playing, that we have lived. That's what I mean by boundary.

Thus, a boundary not only contains our yearnings for order, but simultaneously presents us with the possibility of violating the entire "game" of living according to principles.

The founding figures, those who opened a new focal game, were of course the great transgressors. For example, Martin Luther. One can beautifully show how in Luther the Subject comes to the fore as the ordering principle in place of the preceding ultimate representation, which is not necessarily god, but perhaps nature. Now Luther, in setting up an entirely new arena of thought, cannot but be received as a major transgressor. That is the fate of those who are capable of seeing what is happening to their culture. Perhaps what is happening to us now is that we are displaced out of this principial game altogether, just as Luther and others before him have spoken to their culture as defined by one new authority. Their displacements would be relative ones, viz., to the referent held supreme. Ours would be absolute, the absolute loss of such referents. That loss offers us the chance of gaining a different attitude towards death.

Isn't it your reading that according to Heidegger, it is technology that ends this whole way of thinking?

It *could* end the metaphysical grip by deploying it to the extreme in the form of "enframing." This is an Hegelian remnant in Heidegger that in my book I've simply swallowed and have not criticized. Metaphysics comes to its end because it comes to its completion. The idea is that once it's full blown it also reaches its end. It's nice to say. And when Heidegger is pressed on this point, he can say: Yes, perhaps it may take another three hundred years! That really shows the speculative character of this perspective. Recently, I asked someone who had gone to Taiwan: "What kind of place is it?"; and I got this horrifying answer: "Well, it's just like any other place." And it is probably true. We are tending towards world-wide cultural isomorphism. The completion certainly is global, but it may not at all have reached its peak in terms of comprehension. The extension we have. Technology is extended all over the world. But as to the comprehension or intensity—in this sense, technology may certainly have a few more surprises in store: even more institutionalized brutality as it takes longer for supreme strongholds to fade than they reign.

In your understanding of the epochal shift from modernity to post-modernity, have you "swallowed" that the "completion" of technology announces the closure of an entire way of thinking and being?

The global character of technology is surely one form of completion, but we can become much more disciplined and technologized, still more ferociously set on mastery and domination, than we are even now.

So the whole technology question for you is more open than it appears in Heidegger?

In my book I say that the pertinence of the statements about the possible end that technology would produce has to do with our own site and not with what will happen in fifty or five hundred years. So, Heidegger's excursions back into a not-so-distant past—say to Nietzsche and Kant; and into a very distant past—back to Plato and Heraclitus; as well as the excursions forward where Heidegger speaks about a possible new thinking or the preparation for another thinking, a new "economy" as I would call it—all of these are exclusively made for the purpose of understanding our own borderline situation. The advantage of bringing such heavy historical machinery into play is that it prevents one from following one's neurosis, one's inclination, one's own preferences—which pass as common sense, but really amount to no more than laziness of mind or unstated cultural prejudice. In this sense, philosophy is more closely linked to its own history than to any other social or human science. And here the history of philosophy provides a very useful tool of checks and balances.

I understand how your topological readings of Heidegger reaffirm the historical nature of philosophy, but once again I wonder about the practical implications of the "displacements" inherent in the anarchy-principle that your book espouses. As Nietzsche would ask, what are their uses for life, particularly in light of the infinitely expanding incursions of technology?

The caricature of what I am describing appears in many forms. It can be observed in psychic release, the alibi of the frustrated in need of letting off pent-up resentment. In the political realm it appears as anomy, for instance in the posture of the powerful positioning themselves beyond the law.

The use for life of complying with the modes of presenting lies rather in what I tried to capture in the heading of the last chapter of the book, "From Violence to Anarchy." The clamp of epochal principles—and most of all, of their last but ambiguous form, contemporary technology—has been built into Western life from our origins. Among the sufferings people have inflicted and continue to inflict on each other, the worst have consistently been committed in the name of these so-called substantive standards. Under the epochal rule of "nature" people are stoned for acts against nature. Then these practices fade. Under the epochal rule of the "subject," people get destroyed through inner paralysis. Most recently, under the dominion of what Heidegger calls the "enframing," we claim to have liberated ourselves from the subtleties of the self-destructive psyche; the violence built into metaphysics no longer camouflages itself; it takes open recourse to gas, nuclear fission, the release of the raw market forces. The call for standards, whether its addressee is the philosopher or any other functionary, only amounts to asking for more of the same.

The philosopher's release from civil service is then but the consequence of a possibility built into our contemporary epochal network of interactions: the possibility or potential of releasing life, both private and public, from its submission to ultimate representations. That releasement may well have been going on under our very eyes for quite some time already. We have more to gain from hastening the downfall of value-laden principles than from devising for them life-sustaining equipment. What we have to gain is a sober insight into the condition of mortals. That, rather than hegemonic fantasms, yields for each situation the nonrepresentational standard for answering the question, What is to be done?

Abstraction that Makes the Viewer Think

More than one night has fallen in the twentieth century upon what painters held traditionally to be their specific assignment: to generate visual beauty through pigments interacting on a surface so as to emanate light.

With the devastations that Europeans have inflicted on each other in the first half of our century still on our minds, and with the self-destruction of the planet that mankind is inflicting on itself in its second half already before our eyes, has the night not fallen once and for all on the light of the beautiful in general and on that of painted surfaces in particular?

Many artists think that way. One can only admire an artist like Anselm Kiefer who, marked by his country's history, covers vast canvases with tar and liquid lead because organized exterminations are still ringing in his ears. Others paint doom because they are endowed with an eardrum fine enough to hear the suffocation of a planet about to gas itself to death. Answers to the question, How to paint? always depend on how one answers the prior question, How to think?

Louis Comtois' paintings give witness to a different kind of thinking. They radiate splendor. "I can only put to work my hope," he says, "not my despair." Yet theirs is a radiance that has gone through its own agony of thinking. One need only look closely at the skin of these surfaces. Beneath bright colors that jubilate there is an undertow toward the dark; beneath the darkness, an incandescence. He wants his art to work as cultural therapy. And serenity is indeed what his paintings communicate. One arrives before them as before an open window in a suffocating room. Still, as dark layers shine through the bright—and bright ones, through the dark—serenity remains conquered over threats.

Hence thoughtful splendor. To think is to pause and dwell on the conditions of what one is living. As Comtois tells them in his paintings, these conditions have to do with light not given, but won. Hölderlin may have been right, who thought that creators more than others look face to face at the contortions of their times. Such remains their burden, and such our need for them. Working with his paints—oil or dry pigments and encaustic—Comtois opts for lucidity in every sense of the word: perspicuity, luminosity, translucency, and above all clarity.

The largest among his recent paintings is entitled *The Riddle of the Sphinx: In the Morning on Four, at Noon on Two, in the Evening on Three,* (80" x 234", in eight sections). This riddle was put to Oedipus who solved it, answering: man. The morning of childhood is rendered through dark greens with underlayers of cadmium yellow and red rose; the noon of adulthood, through bluish pinks that reveal a light cobalt blue; and the evening of old age, through various Indian yellows. From dark, to blue and pink, to yellow: life, struggling toward light.

But is the light one brings really an option? Comtois says he never had a choice. Nor are his paintings narratives. They hold together visually by an inner necessity that is proper to each. Since there is no universal criterion for success or failure in abstraction, such strength and coherence proper to each work requires an ever new dialectic of intuition and analysis.

* * *

His recent triptychs (56" x 96") are comparable to nothing currently seen in galleries. They have their sources in art history, yet they stand entirely on their own. Modern abstraction tended toward formalism; post-modern figuration denies abstraction. Comtois' abstraction, while embedded in the modernist tradition, nevertheless transgresses its laws.

His surfaces are composed of elements made of wood, covered with folded jute or muslin soaked with plaster. These two-dimensional volumes of uneven width and height make up the underlying structure of his works. A larger panel serves to give greater weight to one color. Some of the materials used are thicker than others. As they recede or advance slightly, they produce in-depth variations. Additional relief effects result from curved and oblique shapes superimposed on the rectangular elements. They balance the geometry with lyricism. The materials are selected for the diversity of their textures. Each absorbs or reflects light in a particular way. Their natural roughness is enhanced by the multiple uses of wax. The resulting range of tactile qualities brings greater energy to the surface than traditional canvas could ever produce.

These structural elements are painted with oil and encaustic. A white ground of gesso persists through all subsequent strata of color. It accounts for the pervading luminosity of Comtois' paintings. He then applies many translucent layers of pigments mixed with wax. In some sections, broad shapes of contrasting hues are allowed to shine through. The painted surface is never opaque. His purpose in adding layers upon each other is to generate varying chromatic densities. These add their own logic to that of size and shape in distributing weights among colors. Comtois is fond of dermatological terminology to describe his surfaces: the wax produces the skin of a pachyderm; underlayers transpire subcutaneously.

A painting becomes a whole through the balance of its colors. It holds together as it emanates a powerful sense of space and light.

* * *

A beautiful body as well. Beauty here has nothing to do with either estheticism or decoration. Decorative beauty is what pleases immediately, but one cannot live by it. From a life partner one expects a different beauty than from a fashion model. Likewise for Comtois' paintings. They take time to reveal their beauty, and the viewer must in turn be generous with his own time. These are works one has to dwell on before they yield the fullness of their light. But beauty, it seems, has today become something feared. Could it be that it asks too much from us?

"Our age needs visual beauty just as it needs Mozart," Comtois says. Beauty as a cultural therapy, a public service. Can we dispense with it any more than with freedom or with space? Resting in front of Comtois' paintings one somehow comes to one's senses. There could be no greater homage.

A serene yet overcrowded painting would be a contradiction in terms. The struggle for light is a struggle for simplicity. The two are won together or lost together. For Comtois: they were won paradigmatically by Piero della Francesca, Vermeer, Chardin, Malevich, Barnett Newman, Albers, and Rothko. "They show us what we should try to be," he says. Abstraction was born with the Russian constructivists and reborn with the American expressionists. In truth, though, it is as old as the Florentine Renaissance. Whoever is seized by colors and shapes as they interrelate is looking at an abstract painting, whether there be figures present or not.

For Comtois, to simplify and reduce the components of his works—he is now working on diptychs—does not mean making them more facile or glib; nor, more difficult or inaccessible. Rather his abstraction aims at something as simple as an evidence: as when one says, "Now I see." People who claim to understand nothing about abstraction have proven perfectly capable of sensing the rigor of such simplicity. "That color does not fit," they may say. One is more alone here than in front of a picture that spells everything out before the beholder. In addition to time, then, it takes a certain self-confidence to stay with an abstract painting. It frustrates one's expectations of spectacular contents. But Comtois' work rewards the viewer with a beauty that makes him think.

Kieran Aarons and Nicolas Schneider

Reiner Schürmann's Philosophy of Broken Bonds

The essays and interviews collected in this volume span two decades of Reiner Schürmann's thought, from the early 1970s into the final stages of his life. The first five selections were published between 1972 and 1979, and point forward to his philosophy of ontological anarchy familiar to readers of *Le Principe d'anarchie* (1982, trans. *Heidegger on Being and Acting: From Principles to Anarchy*, 1987), while the remaining three belong to the period leading up to the final major work, *Des Hégémonies brisées* (1996, trans. *Broken Hegemonies*, 2003), with its emphasis on the exposure of the "tragic double bind" through a "phenomenology of ultimates." The material gathered here is wide-ranging, and includes a nuanced philosophical theory of symbols, a post-metaphysical reading of poetic language, illuminating engagements with figures such as Heidegger, Hölderlin, Kant and Arendt, as well as focused studies on the problem of evil, the nature of political transformation—including the place of violence therein—as well as rare reflections on aesthetics. In what follows, we wish to underscore and situate a few of the major lines of inquiry from among these various threads, in order to draw out their importance for Schürmann's thought as a whole.

I. Missing Links

Schürmann's theory of "symbolic difference" occupies a strange position in his oeuvre. On the one hand, the attempt to fuse ontology and symbology serves as a recurrent motif in Schürmann's work, beginning already with his doctoral work in the 1960s and continuing through the early 1980s. During this period, each time Schürmann would launch a new major project the theory of the symbol formed either the crux of the inquiry, or was positioned as its culmination point. Yet each time without fail, it would wind up excised from the final product, relegated to standalone articles whose relation to his larger works became anything but transparent, or simply left unpublished. For example, when it was still a *thèse du lectorat* at the French Dominican school Le Saulchoir, the initial plan for what later became the book *Maître Eckhart ou la joie errante* (1972) was to produce a fully-fledged hermeneutic semiology to be titled *Dieu et l'homme, son symbole* [*God and Man, His Symbol*], in which commentary upon Eckhart would play only a secondary part.[1] Although some two hundred typescript pages of this semiology were produced throughout the course of 1968, when the dust settled they were cut out of the final product, which was reframed around Eckhart alone. It was not until 1972 and 1976 that these pages would be published, in the *Cahiers internationaux de symbolisme*, as the essays "Symbolic Difference" (1972) and "Symbolic Praxis," which open the present volume.[2] By this point, however, the focus of Schürmann's work had undergone a shift, and was concerned less with theology than with the deconstruction of political philosophy in the wake of Heidegger's destruction of metaphysics. As the final remnant of his Le Saulchoir work was being published in 1976—the same year he quit the priesthood—Schürmann published a remarkable essay entitled "Situating René Char" which could, perhaps, be interpreted as an effort to peel the theory of symbolic difference away from its residual theological and mythological encumbrances in order to

---

1 Schürmann updated the book for his English translation, which was published as *Meister Eckhart: Mystic and Philosopher. Translations with Commentary* (Bloomington: Indiana University Press, 1978) and later republished as *Wandering Joy: Meister Eckhart's Mystical Philosophy, Translation and Commentary* (Great Barrington, MA: Lindisfarne, 2001). The initial French publication was a revised and expanded version of Schürmann's dissertation at the Sorbonne, itself a revised and expanded version of his *thèse du lectorat* for the French Dominican school Le Saulchoir, entitled *Identité pérégrinale: Le concept de détachement dans les sermons allemands de Maître Eckhart* (submitted in 1969; available online here: https://digital.dombibliothek-koeln.de/ddbkhd/content/titleinfo/523718). On the development of this project through its successive variations, see Francesco Guercio and Ian Alexander Moore, "The Call of the Origin: On Christology, Conversion, and Peregrine Identity in Reiner Schürmann's Early Work on Meister Eckhart," in *Medieval Mystical Theology* 32, no. 1 (2023): 2–17.

2 The table of contents for the proposed work is provided in Guercio and Moore (2023), the first three chapters of which correspond almost verbatim to those of "Symbolic Difference" and "Symbolic Praxis." Innumerable other borrowings and transpositions also take place across these early works. To take but one example, the opening section of "Symbolic Difference" reproduces, in slightly altered form, the opening paragraphs of the *thèse du lectorat*, "Identité pérégrinale."

bring it more in line with the anarchistic deconstruction of politics he was in the process of preparing.

This merger of symbolism and deconstructive thought is visible in the two essays that follow it, "Political Thinking in Heidegger" (1978) and "The Ontological Difference and Political Philosophy" (1979), both of which argue that, in an age in which first principles are withering and receding, the theory of symbolic difference provides the "missing link" allowing us to think an an-archic relation between being and acting, ontology and politics.[3] There is no question that the concept of symbolic difference was envisioned, in these years, as the very crux and culmination of the project that would later become *Le Principe d'anarchie*. This is made clear in the first draft of this work, submitted as a doctoral thesis at the Sorbonne in 1981 under the title *Politique et déconstruction. Heidegger et les fondements de la philosophie pratique*. The argument of the dissertation culminates in a section entitled "Une proposition: Le concept de différence symbolique" that amounts to a *précis* of the first five articles in the present volume.[4] However, when *Le Principe* was finally published in 1982, this chapter was removed, replaced by a brief section entitled "Economic Self-Regulation and its Loci" that aims largely to recapitulate the preceding arguments in the form of several "rules" and consequences.[5] In sum, if the theory of symbolic difference is a "missing link," it is so in several senses at once: as a missing bridge between his early studies of Meister Eckhart and Christian mysticism and his deconstructive an-archaeology of political action in the 1970s; as a missing theory of how, in a positive sense, being and acting fit together an-archically

---

3 In this volume, 109, 113, 135–36, 145.

4 Reiner Schürmann, *Politique et déconstruction. Heidegger et les fondements de la philosophie pratique*, PhD Dissertation, Sorbonne, 1981. The final chapter is divided into two parts. The first half, which concludes the original material of the argument, concerns the theory of symbolic difference, while the latter half is concerned only with clarifications of the overall argument in view of potential objections.

5 Reiner Schürmann, *Le Principe d'anarchie. Heidegger et la question de l'agir* (Paris: Seuil, 1982; reprinted edition: Zurich: Diaphanes, 2013), 405–14. For the corresponding English pages, see Reiner Schürmann, *Heidegger on Being and Acting: From Principles to Anarchy*, trans. Christine-Marie Gros (Bloomington: Indiana University Press, 1987), 282–89.

in practice; and finally, as a fraught ambition within Schürmann's broader philosophical project, the limitations of which can help illuminate the direction of his later work. In this sense, the present volume gathers the materials required for a reconstruction of the place of the symbolic in Schürmann's work.

Over an Abyss

Schürmann's theory of symbolic difference aims to supply a vocabulary for praxis which subverts all references to the One. More specifically, its ambition is to push beyond Heidegger's own account of the ontological difference by identifying the "missing link" or middle term connecting the "anarchic coming into presence" and the "practical a priori," the two pivotal concepts around which the argument of *Le Principe d'anarchie* turns. Since the theory of symbolic difference was initially designed to form the capstone of *Le Principe d'anarchie*, it is worth briefly introducing the essential question around which this project turns before addressing its specific function within it.

Throughout his work, one of Schürmann's central claims is that Western political philosophy has long been content to function as a "secondary" discourse, subordinate to the "primary" discourse of metaphysics. The civil service provided by the philosopher consisted in supplying the grounding principles for earthly political powers, by raising up standard-setting Firsts and positioning them within a general ontological doctrine. As such, the response to the question "what is to be done?" finds itself ensnared within legitimation structures that operate by means of a disjunctive operation whose function is to ensure that action appears *as if* it was a derivative "realization" of principles established at an ulterior and more foundational level. Action is articulated *to* 'being,' as its grounding foundation, yet it remains held apart *from* 'being' as its subordinate expression. Needless to say, in such a schema, if one wishes to truly overthrow a given political regime or institution, it will never be enough to simply critique or disrupt its empirical functioning while leaving its principial foundation intact, since whatever replaces it will only play out a similar pattern. If a deconstruction of politics is necessary, this is first of all because the political tradition depends essentially upon its ability to project its grounding rationale outside of and, as it were, "behind" itself. It is this retrojective operation that must be exposed if we wish "to push into their tomb whatever idols remain" of those ultimate representations allowing ruling powers to continue nourishing and rejuvenating themselves.[6]

By historically *situating* the lineage of these metaphysical first principles in reference to which the authority of political philosophy rests, Heidegger's "destruction" of metaphysics dealt a severe blow to every relation of ecstatic legitimation between being and acting, bringing to a close "the era of derivations between general and special metaphysics, between first philosophy and practical philosophy."[7] Deconstruction's aim, more generally, is (Schürmann writes) to deepen this interruption, by "throwing out of gear" any derivative relation between act and existence according to which practice is intelligible only as the *realization* of something outside of it.[8] If this interruption is liberating, this is because it enables us to rethink action on its own terms, without reference to a reality beyond it. Such a liberation is only conceivable in our historical moment, marked as it is by the collapse of that final principle of hegemonic legitimation, the Subject: "Action bereft of *archē* is thinkable only at the moment when the problematic of 'being'—inherited from the closed field of metaphysics but subject on its threshold to a transmutation, to a passover—emerges from ontologies and dismisses them."[9] At the same time, however, once action is stripped of the linguistic and conceptual schemas that once conferred intelligibility upon it, the "hypothesis of closure" risks leaving practical philosophy dangling over an abyss. Once the principial economies of Western metaphysics that prop up the political begin to falter, what new relation between being and acting takes their place? How is the transition from an archic to an anarchic economy to be conceived, provided that it cannot be represented in terms of

6 "On the Philosophers' Release From Civil Service," in this volume, 251.

7 Schürmann, *Heidegger on Being and Acting*, 1.

8 Ibid.

9 Ibid.

a simple linear move from one to the other? This is the central mystery to which the theory of symbolic difference responds.

To appreciate how it might accomplish this, we must understand how symbolic action is capable of overturning the grounding relation between theory and praxis without succumbing once again to a metaphysical understanding of being. What distinguishes the symbol, such that in it "language gives its own essence over to be explored"?[10] If our participation in symbols attests to a "reception of knowledge" in the form of a lived practice, what type of knowledge is at stake in it, and how is it possible to characterize the latter as "an-archic," plurivocal, and ateleological? As we shall see, these two features—an *a priori* condition of practice and an internal doubling and differentiation of meaning—are joined in reciprocal presupposition.

Double Meaning

Symbols constitute a special class of signs marked by a plurivocal structure of double meaning. Schürmann draws inspiration here from the hermeneutical philosophy of Paul Ricœur. In *Freud and Philosophy* Ricœur defines the symbol as that "region of language that presents itself as the locus of complex significations where another meaning is both given and hidden in an immediate meaning."[11] This duality of the symbol should not be confused with that of the sign/signifier, which allows words to *express* significations (at the level of structure) while *designating* a thing or object (intentionality). Instead, Ricœur argues, the doubling of the symbol is of a "higher degree," since it is added to or "superimposed" over the significations of words as a second latent meaning that withdraws and conceals itself within the first literal and immediate meaning.[12] While relations of the sign to the signified

---

10 "Symbolic Difference," in this volume, 20.

11 Paul Ricœur, *Freud and Interpretation. An Essay on Interpretation*, trans. Denis Savage (New Haven and London: Yale University Press, 1970), 7. The book originates in lectures first delivered at Yale in 1960–1961.

12 Ricœur, *Freud and Interpretation*, 12–13.

are "univocal," the symbolic consists in a relation of one meaning to another (or to many others), and must therefore be defined as "plurivocal."[13] Furthermore, since this latent meaning adheres tightly to the site of the first meaning behind which it withdraws like an "enigma," its exploration must assume the form of a work of interpretation that unfolds or "dis-implicates" it.[14]

From the point of view of formal linguistics, the double meaning internal to the symbol can be approached as a specific order of semantic difference. From this vantage point, symbols differ from myth, allegory, metaphor, images, etc. by the way they make this difference explicit. For example, symbols are distinct from allegory and metaphor, both of which are marked by a *discontinuity* between signifier and signified. Not only do they only operate diacritically within a referential system that confers upon signs determinate rules and operations, but they both generate meaning either by referring to something (metaphor), or by letting us hear and understand something that the speaker left unsaid (analogy). In the case of the symbol, by contrast, the second meaning is enveloped within it, immanently. Whereas the metaphorical use of the signifier exhausts itself in referring to another meaning that surpasses it, the symbol realizes what it signifies. Although it is precisely this immanent continuity of meaning that allows the symbol to be so easily overdetermined by metaphysics and religion, Schürmann is careful not to confuse the symbol with either myths or images. It is true that myths are assembled from symbols, but considered in itself, the symbol is a noun or word rather than a phrase or a narrative, and therefore is not inherently mythic; and unlike images, which merely reflect or resemble what they signify, symbols *are* what they signify.[15] In sum, what distinguishes the doubled semantic meaning of the symbol from metaphor, analogy, myth, or images is the quality of being a concrete object or phenomenon that is at

---

13 Ricœur, *Freud and Interpretation*, 10–11. This difference between univocal and plurivocal regions of language is precisely what Ernst Cassirer's overly broad definition of "symbolic forms" overlooks, by extending the term to include all forms of mediation between consciousness and its objects.

14 Ricœur, *Freud and Interpretation*, 18.

15 See "Symbolic Difference," in this volume.

once itself *and* something else, in which a *referential* difference between multiple meanings is contained or "realized" immanently within the same self-showing and concealing without passing over into an outside or beyond.

Symbolic Praxis

Such semantic typologies only take us so far, however. In spite of their valuable insights, hermeneuticians like Ricœur ultimately come "no closer to an ontological approach to the symbol than the structuralists whom he denounces for having forgotten 'meaning' in language."[16] We find in his work no reflection on the "ontological grounding of human practice that results from its interpretation."[17] In order to pass from a semantic to an ontological conception of the symbol, it is necessary to interrogate the phenomenological relation between the symbol and practice, which exceeds the narrow hermeneutical recognition of an inevitable "work of interpretation." If symbols are a specific class of signs, this is not simply owing to the formal relation between the plural meanings they envelop, but also because their intelligibility depends upon an *act* as its immediate practical condition. In order to understand the symbol, it is not enough to contemplate the object that bears it from a distance, nor is its meaning imposed upon it by a mental operation having its seat in the subject. To grasp the symbol, one must *do* this or that thing. Those who do not do, cannot comprehend:

> Symbols constitute that area of reality whose understanding requires a certain way of existing. To grasp the full meaning of a symbol a certain practice is required. Unless one plunges into the waters, jumps through the flames etc., the rejuvenating, purifying, initiatory effects attached to these symbols will not be comprehended.[18]

---

16 "Symbolic Difference," in this volume, 29 n.46.
17 "The Ontological Difference and Political Philosophy," in this volume, 140.
18 Ibid., 135.

To the extent that the second meaning enveloped within the first can only be explored through an appropriate praxis, symbols announce an inversion of the relation between being and acting that prevailed in Aristotelian or Kantian philosophy. Symbolic action cannot be understood as the application or realization of a theoretical canon or design conceived in advance by reason. It is necessary, however, to distinguish here between two senses of realization. By contrast with Aristotle and Kant, symbolic action is not the realization of a thought or doctrine positioned prior to the act; at the same time, as we have seen, unlike in the case of metaphor or analogy, the exploration of the symbol's double meaning does not refer beyond itself to a meaning ulterior to it—the meaning we explore in the symbolic act is realized here and now in the particular. In this second sense of realization it is not action that realizes 'being,' at least insofar as the latter is understood as a superior or foundational reality that precedes and stands outside of it. According to Schürmann, symbolic difference—this referential opening or spacing emerging between the first and second meanings—must be understood as a clearing or site wherein 'being' simultaneously discloses and withdraws itself, whose call can only be comprehended and concretized provided it is actively received. This circularity between call and reception is neither vicious nor accidental but is an essential element of Schürmann's argument, as it serves to interrupt any unilateral foundation on the side of being or the subject. All symbols gather people for some activity, and incite some behavior (e.g. festivity, accusation and penance, and even combat). In every encounter with the symbol, we experience an incitement to adopt the attitude of existence that would be necessary to rejoin it. If we have not yet adopted the form of existence appropriate to this or that symbol, this prerequisite will therefore take on the form of a call to conversion, a "practical summons to exist originarily" that places us on its path.[19] In other words, reception of the symbol coincides with an awareness that, in order to "explore" the second meaning harbored within it, we must first enact the practical disposition that forms the precondition of its comprehension. In this

19 "Political Thinking in Heidegger," in this volume, 120.

way, reception "establishes a new way of existing in the listener," with the result that comprehension and conversion coincide.[20]

It is this threefold process of incitation, reception, and conversion that allows Schürmann to claim that the theory of symbolic difference offers an advance beyond Heidegger's own notion of ontological difference, since it accounts not only for the difference between 'being' and beings but also for the specific process whereby 'being' renders beings its own, the way in which it appropriates them.[21] The privileged status of the symbol lies in the fact that it explicitly dramatizes the only "all pervading" element in the epochal history of Being's self-disclosure, namely, the "duplicity of concealment and unconcealment."[22] In this step beyond Heidegger, what is at stake is a reciprocal ungrounding of practical philosophy and ontology. If Schürmann associates the etymology of "symbolic difference" with a verb (*symballein*) rather than a noun, this is because it encompasses these two dimensions within a single process: our reception of a call to conversion through the plurivocal incitation of being's releasement in the entity, as well as the enactment of the practical disposition required in order for this ontological difference to be explored in thought. The two halves of the clay tablet rejoined through the *symballein* are, therefore, nothing other than being and acting: action that follows "the pluriform, precarious, unstable appearance, stripped of any *archē*" rejoins itself to being and "becomes originary"—this is the "deconstructed practical *a priori.*"[23]

At the same time, Schürmann's phenomenological reading seeks to strip away all the overdeterminations imposed on the symbol by the philosophies of the sacred, subjectivity, mind, meaning, and man. When given an ontological and no longer merely a semantic interpretation, the symbol is no longer conceived of as this or that celebratory object, poetic element, or mythic narrative, but instead

20 "Symbolic Difference," in this volume, 7.

21 "Political Thinking in Heidegger," in this volume, 124–25.

22 "Political Thinking in Heidegger," in this volume, 110.

23 Schürmann, *Politique et déconstruction*, 628: "Le seuil post-moderne permet cette libération à la condition, en outre, que l'agir se laisse effectivement réunir, *symballein*, à l'apparaître pluriforme, précaire, instable, dépourvu d'*archē;* à condition, autrement dit, que l'agir devienne originaire: voila l'a priori pratique déconstruit."

signifies an "event of appropriation" bereft of any connotation of the proper, propriety, or possession, the auto-deployment of an historical order of presence without any reference to an appropriating subject.[24] With the passage from a principial economy to an anarchic economy of presence, the concept of symbolic difference offers a language to grasp this displacement whereby action and thought become appropriated according to multiple modalities of *phusis* without any ordering First. Understood in this way, the "second sense" of the symbol is nothing other than *phusis* itself. Symbolic difference refers to the difference of a multiple, dispersed event, the theory of which is "essentially hostile to *archai* and principles, to all that commences and commands, that dominates in order to impose order."[25] The world, as the symbolic texture and context that situates the thing in its being, "arrives to the thing in an arriving that is like a gesture," while the thing enters the world "without why" and without reference to any One.[26]

II. Confrontations

If it is true that, in the final analysis, the sole practical imperative Schürmann offers us is to respond to and follow the mutations of the unruly coming-into-presence of our situation, and to do so without maximizing fictive grounds into permanent ones, this simple imperative nevertheless remains complex at the level of its practical instantiation. The reception of the symbol can take a number of possible directions. For instance, we might respond nostalgically in a metaphysical manner, by approaching the double meaning of

---

24 In the 1969 Saulchoir dissertation, an early account of this process—referred to as "peregrine difference"—is defined as "the itinerancy [*itinérance*] under which the existence experiences Being [*l'Etre*] as that which converts itself to it in order to send it on the way of its own conversion. The peregrine difference is the distance that joins man to his origin, in a detached existence." (*Identité pérégrinale,* 134). As Guercio and Moore observe, what is in question is the "ontological difference but experienced by the human as wandering" (Guercio and Moore, "The Call of the Origin," 15).

25 Schürmann, *Politique et déconstruction*, 628.

26 Ibid.

the symbol as a "reverse bridge"[27] linking the entity to an ulterior origin withdrawing behind it. To do so is to engage in what Schürmann describes as *archē*-mourning.[28] Alternately, we might cleave to the singularizing undertow of the anarchic giving of the world, and attempt to camp upon its shifting soil, "without why." Still, even for those who set out in search of a politics of singularity, a temptation to retreat back into metaphysical and mythic mourning continually reasserts itself. In his efforts to resist the "natural metaphysician in us,"[29] Schürmann stages a series of confrontations intended to clarify the perils and pitfalls, but also the beauty and courage that an anarchic life demands. In the next section, we will briefly consider two such confrontations, one poetic and the other transcendental. The first concerns his reading of Hölderlin and René Char, the second that of Hannah Arendt and Kant.

The Now of the Poem

In "Situating René Char," one of the most intriguing essays in the present collection, Schürmann expands his theory of the symbol in dialogue with René Char's poetry, in particular around a poem titled "Le requin et la mouette" [*The Shark and the Gull*] that unfolds around the ambiguous symbolism of water. The ambiguity of the aquatic symbolism lies in the fact that water gives life but also threatens it. Schürmann interprets the poem, which thematizes the communication between a shark and a gull, as bringing together duration and instant, horizontality and verticality. In this gathering are reconciled "weight and lightness, submission and transgression, the dive and the flight, or again the oceanic spread and man's freedom," indicating a union of the opposite dimensions:

---

27 This term is borrowed from Giorgio Agamben, who defines myth as the "engine" by which human subjects attempt to articulate a "reverse bridge" from discourse back to language, abolishing the margin between the semantic and the semiotic and grounding history in nature. Giorgio Agamben, *Infancy and History* [1978], trans. Liz Heron (London and New York: Verso, 1993), 59–60.

28 "On the Philosophers' Release From Civil Service," in this volume, 247.

29 "Conditions of Evil," in this volume, 213.

> The Now of the poem abolishes yesterday's dispersions and separations. [...] The morning is the hour of rising, of innocent beginning, of the gull. Heaviness is of the impenetrable sea, of the house, of the shark. As if a lightning flash, the poem makes me a unifier. Reality is antinomic, but the heart, man, or the poet unites. The language of the poem is the multiple matter in which things diverse and opposite enter into relation.[30]

The importance of this poetic union of opposites lies in the way it realizes the "origin" through its manifestation in language. The origin brought forth by Char's poem is not a mythical one that would designate a First or inaugurate a new history, but one which "founds a world which is inseparable from its speech":[31] if the poem "realizes the unity of the world that it signifies," it does so "only for the moment of its articulation."[32] Put differently, the origin does not exist outside of or prior to its coming into presence in the poetic expression. It is the language of the poem itself that achieves this ephemeral unity.

In this, Schürmann discovers a split between two distinct notions of origin, which he proceeds to illustrate by contrasting Char's poem to Hölderlin's hymn, "The Rhine." While both poets use aquatic symbolism to convey the unity of opposite dimensions, Schürmann sees a radical difference at work in their respective notions of origin. In Hölderlin the origin is elsewhere, outside the poem itself: "What used to be the most powerful presence, the divine, has fallen into oblivion. Only the poet remembers."[33] Hölderlin translates or transmits an origin that is itself absent from the situation of the poem, one that pits the immortal origin against the loss of mortals. Char's poem, by contrast, opens up a world that presents itself in and through its symbolization. Schürmann conceives this difference in terms of the distinction between original and originary, natal and nuptial: while the former invokes the transcendent or the sacred, the latter remains immanent to the poem's situation, to the presence of things. The natal is tethered to a causal notion of origin,

---

30 "Situating René Char," in this volume, 84.

31 Ibid., 85.

32 Ibid., 88.

33 Ibid., 95.

while the nuptial, rather than referring to a past event, occurs in the present.

This break between origins has important consequences for Schürmann's notion of symbolic difference. It allows him to situate Char between, on the one hand, the idealism of Hölderlin, whose "poem speaks of the ideal itself as much as of its loss" and turns away from the visible to the invisible, and, on the other, a structuralist focus "on the order of words and things."[34] Only in Char do the three dimensions of presence—things present, their being-present, the event of their presencing—enter into interplay. In Char's poem, what is achieved is an ephemeral "identity of the non-identical" expressed by a descriptive "there is" that cannot be separated from its moment of being-there. Interestingly, Schürmann connects this difference to the linguistic one between the German ("*es gibt*") and the French ("*il y a*") or English ("there is"). Whereas the German locution contains a "mythical reminiscence" by virtue of its "invitation to silence," the French "*il y a*," as it occurs in poems by Rimbaud and Apollinaire, as well as the English "there is," eliminates any mythical reference.[35] If Schürmann assures us that reading Heidegger in Hölderlinian terms runs the risk of misunderstanding him, these reflections nonetheless point toward a stark fissure between Heideggerian philosophy and Schürmann's theory of the symbol. That this linguistic rift has conceptual implications is also expressed in a remark in "The Ontological Difference and Political Philosophy," where Schürmann notes with regard to Heidegger that "for him theories of the symbol pertain to, and indicate, late forms of representational thinking."[36] Rather than opposing representational thinking in Heideggerian fashion, Schürmann's reading of Char testifies to a reconfiguration of representation in language, expressed precisely by these divergent notions of origin.

But how are we to understand this reconfiguration that puts a distance between Char and Heidegger's "Germanic thinking"? The displacement from ontological to symbolic difference opens up to a reconsideration of the problem of reflection. Instead of reflec-

---

34 Ibid, 94, 99.

35 Ibid., 101.

36 In this volume, 139.

tion occurring between present substances, in Char's poem it takes place between the different levels of presencing that are joined in the symbol. In a 1976 lecture course on hermeneutics at the New School for Social Research, Schürmann again draws upon the work of Ricœur, this time invoking his concept of "concrete reflection":[37]

> To communicate in a symbol requires [...] active reflection. There is no blind communication in a symbol. But there is none, either, which would be 'the spirit speaking purely to the spirit': quite as the symbol itself, communication here has a bodily dimension; it remains concrete.[38]

As concrete, reflection is no longer a reduplication of consciousness but an activity connecting the incongruent elements internal to the symbolic difference.[39] The next section will give a brief overview of this revision of reflection in light of Schürmann's references to Kant in the essays collected in the present volume, before turning to the practical consequences of this confrontation with transcendental philosophy.

Self and Reflection

In "Symbolic Difference," Schürmann introduces Kant's critique of the dogmatic presuppositions of the ontological proof of God's existence to illustrate the limitations of a metaphysical perspective that casts God in terms of a supreme entity, thereby obliterating the

---

37 Ricœur, *Freud and Philosophy*, xii, 54–56, 419–58.

38 Reiner Schürmann, *Hermeneutics*, in *Course Lectures, Volume 6: Twentieth Century Philosophy*, transcript located in Reiner Schürmann papers, NA.0006.01, The New School Archives and Special Collections, The New School, New York City, USA, ts. 87.

39 In the lecture course cited above, which produces an original interpretation of hermeneutics in dialogue with Ricœur's analysis of Freudian psychoanalysis, Schürmann observes that Ricœur's account of concrete reflection implies the irreducibility of "cultural objectivations"—noting that this view stands in contrast to Habermas' attempt to overcome this split. In Ricœur's view, objects (e.g. the body) remain external to consciousness, while Habermas' approach ends up restricting reflection to cognition. See Schürmann, *Hermeneutics*, ts. 71–78.

appearing or coming into presence that conceals itself in present entities. By restricting cognition to operating under *a priori* regulative principles, Kant's solution prevents us from concluding anything about the existence of a supreme entity in separation from human experience of it. Despite this displacement of metaphysics, and notwithstanding the attention it pays to how phenomena present themselves to human beings, Schürmann argues that Kant's transcendental philosophy remains tethered to the world of present entities, which provide the sensible substance that enters into a relation with concepts.[40] The issue reemerges in the later essay "On Judging and its Issue," which offers a critical appraisal of Arendt's *Lectures on Kant's Political Philosophy*. Here Schürmann identifies two discordant concepts of being that appear in Kant as a result of his "discovery" of reflective judgment.[41] Whereas in determinative judgment singular phenomena become subsumed to a compelling rule that transforms them into particular instantiations of a universal, reflective judgment denotes the failure of this subsumption and the assertion of disparate singulars. This "judgmental difference" in Kant's critical philosophy produces a "*différend*" between incongruous claims concerning being as one and being as many.[42]

Whereas in his critical doctrine being denotes a categorial form conferring unity upon objects of experience in general, a second "countervailing" concept of being as givenness or as possibility is found in his pre-critical writings. Between the two, there arises a conflict over the determination of being: "Is 'my existence' the indeterminate content of sensation or the determinate act of consciousness?"[43] Since neither of these two options is workable,

---

40 Cf. "Symbolic Difference," in this volume, 27.

41 In this volume, 163–86. For a more detailed account of Schürmann's reading of Arendt and Kant, see Nicolas Schneider, "Topologies of Judgement: Arendt, Schürmann, and Shell on the politics of Kantian *sensus communis*," in Jussi Palmusaari and Nicolas Schneider (eds.), *Possibilities of Place in Continental Thought: Critique, Politics, Philosophy* (London: Bloomsbury, 2024), 81–103.

42 "On Judging and its Issue," in this volume, 165–66, 183. See also "Conditions of Evil": "In Kant, the 'expanded way of thinking' (*die erweiterte Denkungsart*) consists in a judgment that takes singulars into account, cf. *Critique of Judgment*, § 40, 77" (in this volume, 230, n.20).

43 "On Judging and its Issue," 177.

the self-presence of the subject remains fractured by the conflicting pulls of determinacy and indeterminacy. It is to this fissure, whose incongruous moments position the critical subject at the intersection of the "I think" and "my existence," that concrete reflection pertains. For Schürmann, this fracture in Kant's ontology between the indeterminacy of the given and the act of self-determination is not an unsolved remainder, but in fact forms the heterogeneous ground out of which 'being' arises. What Schürmann had earlier analyzed in terms of the symbolic difference is here recoded into a "transcendental difference": "One has to view that break as a displacement of the old metaphysical difference between *einai* and *on*, or *esse* and *ens*, and one may speak consequently of a transcendental difference in Kant."[44] Although Kant's transcendental philosophy sought to invert the relation between determination and the indeterminate—with determination now falling on the side of the subject, as the "act" of categorizing an indeterminate sensation—the inversion fails, resulting in a *différend* between categorial "representation to the understanding" and givenness as an "act of reception in sensibility."[45] What emerges in its place is the space of symbolic equivocity.

The problem of what we might call "symbolic reflection" therefore cannot be assimilated to that of reflective judgment one-sidedly, but must rather be situated within the conflict or *différend* between reflective and determinative judgment. On Schürmann's original reading of Kant as it is presented in this late text, this judgmental difference binds together the discordant pulls of dispersion and synthesis into an aporetic "*différend* [that] neither consolidates nor consoles."[46] Unfortunately, the practical consequences of this differend remain largely unexplored here, beyond an adumbrated critique of an Arendtian politics of the singular. However, in his earlier essay, "Symbolic Praxis," an explicit connection is made between the theory of symbolic difference and Kant's "theory of the symbol" as it is laid out in section 59 of the *Critique of Judgment*. Here Schürmann reminds us that in the Kantian system, the

44 Ibid., 179.

45 Ibid., 182.

46 Ibid., 184.

symbolic function of the imagination is supposed to "reconcile[] the theoretical and practical discourses of transcendental philosophy," and with it, necessity and freedom more broadly.[47] Of the two activities of the imagination—the schematic and the symbolic—the former pertains to the understanding of empirical realities, while the latter is reserved for non-empirical realities or concepts of the supra-sensible such as God or the despotic State. The symbolic imagination is operative in reflective judgment which, as with judgments of beauty, is unable to subsume that which by definition eludes determination, instead substituting the generally valid for the universal concept.

Just as Ricœur had correctly critiqued Cassirer's conception of the symbol for being excessively broad, Kant's tendency to treat symbol and analogy as synonymous "grants the symbolic realm a breadth which is equal to that of all non-empirical concepts," thereby preventing us from "receiving the symbol as a given."[48] On this point, Schürmann contrasts his "phenomenological" approach with the Kantian transcendental method: whereas "the transcendental method witnesses the empirical presentation of a non-empirical concept that never appears," the phenomenological method addresses "the appearance of the non-empirical *in* the empirical."[49] While Kant sets out to think "the sensible presentation of an essentially mysterious concept," the phenomenology of symbolic difference responds to "the recognition of the essential mystery *in* the sensible present."[50] Contrary to Kant's notion of symbol, which remains restricted to the sensible presentation of a mysterious—that is, *absent*—concept, symbolic practice consists in relating to the appearance or *presencing* of mystery within the givenness of the sensible.

At first glance, this emphasis on mystery might seem at odds with his insistence, in his text on Char, on the elimination of the mythical. However, "mystery" here does not refer to a specific content or meaning (mythic or otherwise), but to the necessary coincidence of presence and absence in all symbols by which their presence allows us to sense *more* than what is empirically measurable by

47 "Symbolic Praxis," in this volume, 45.

48 Ibid., 48.

49 Ibid.

50 Ibid.

the standard of representation. This "more" cannot be reduced to "a metaphysics of *analogia entis*," which would understand it as a "first cause that is both revealed and hidden by its effects."[51] If the symbolic difference accomplishes an anarchistic subversion of metaphysics of representation, this is because the mystery in question is generated not by a lack or absent origin held in abeyance, but by an excess or abundance that defines the very presencing of presence itself: "it is symbolization as such, that in-between the first sense (present) and the second sense (absent), which is both revealed and hidden in the historic constellations of truth."[52] Since this doubling or difference of the mysterious is an immanent feature of all symbolic praxis, the mystery is therefore not in itself mythic; it becomes so only when mythic thinking treats the second meaning as something imposed *upon* actors from without, as an injunction or command. Put otherwise, the mythical use of the mystery arrests the symbolic difference in an original scheme of reference, thereby destroying the specific meaning of the symbolic Schürmann aims to champion. For this very reason, the affirmation of this symbolic mystery can never be enough to eliminate, disprove, or depose either myth or metaphysics as possible *uses* of the symbolic. However, it does allow us to take a slight step to the side, shifting the criteria of responsibility from normative signifiers to what we might call the 'present-keeping of what is absent', an imperative that Schürmann retrieves from Parmenides: "The things that are absent, behold them nevertheless as firmly present."[53]

Although certain aspirations of the essays on "Symbolic Difference" and "Symbolic Praxis" will eventually be abandoned—most notably, the possibility of rescuing a concept of "authentic myth" from its cybernetic instrumentalization for the purposes of control or manipulation—continuities with Schürmann's later work are still visible at other levels.[54] Considered in this light, the move from a

---

51 "Political Thinking in Heidegger," in this volume, 111.

52 Ibid.

53 "Technicity, Topology, Tragedy," in this volume, 204.

54 On the relation between symbolism and myth in Schürmann's thought, see Kieran Aarons, "The Ambivalence of Myth in Reiner Schürmann's Phenomenology of Symbolic Praxis," forthcoming in *Philosophy Today* 68, no. 4 (2024).

Kantian theory of the symbol, as that which is essentially absent or external, to one in which the symbol denotes a process of coming to presence, may be read as an effort to think the relation between the mutually irreducible elements that come together in the symbol. In this sense, although the specific notion of "symbolic difference" will disappear from Schürmann's later work, the problem of difference as it emerges in these discussions will persist throughout all of his subsequent work. For example, in a later text, Schürmann notes that the specific difference so circumscribed "can no longer guarantee any tranquility of order," without for that reason implying a loss of all need of justification.[55] The theory of symbolic difference offers an early iteration of his 'philosophy of broken bonds': a thinking that unfolds as the reconstruction of a three-tiered difference.

Omnilateral Activity

As we have seen, Schürmann's inversion of the Kantian theory of symbol allowed him to broaden our concept of practice beyond the problem of positing. However, the flip side of Kant's excessively broad notion of symbol is an excessively *narrow* understanding of action which, on Schürmann's reading, limits practice to "the imagination in the act of giving itself laws" or, more specifically, to "a *mental* 'doing'" that unfolds "under the authority of something absent."[56] As noted already, this critique entailed a parting of ways with Ricœur, since what reflects itself in the symbolic difference is not a posited self, as Ricœur affirms following Fichte, but a coming into presence realized in practice: "It seems to me, [...] contrary [to Ricœur], that the symbolic domain takes reflection out of 'positing of the self'; that reflection does not refer to a judgment at all, but to practice and interpretation."[57] In this, Schürmann plays on the countervailing concept of being in Kant: practice is solicited not by a concept that remains absent from experience, but by the empirical reality of the symbol. This becomes most tangible in the powerful descriptions of

---

55 "Technicity, Topology, Tragedy," in this volume, 203.

56 "Symbolic Praxis," in this volume, 48–49.

57 Schürmann, *Hermeneutics*, ts. 89.

the symbols feast, song, dwelling, and work in "Symbolic Praxis," in which Schürmann illustrates the symbolic difference at work in joining together transgression and rule, individual and totality, memory and promise, the terrestrial and the divine, the worker and the product of their labor.[58] Common to all of these examples is the way they join together humanity and nature; it is only in the symbol of work that the conflict between the incongruous elements cannot be reconciled. While the other symbols can be understood in terms of a "life without why," the form of life that corresponds to detachment (*Gelassenheit*), work presents a greater difficulty:

> Work is always subject to a Why: one works for a salary, for comfort, for food ... The why opens onto a not-yet, a far-off state of things that praxis strives to bring closer. This is the genuinely symbolic part of work: the internal coherence of the universe has not yet been achieved, and existence itself has not yet become alive in all of its fractions. Human needs still need to be met. The ancient harmony between man and nature is no longer, and the new one is not yet.[59]

This rift created by need, which imposes on human beings the appropriation of objects, remains unbreachable in capitalist society. Schürmann traces this to a "perverted symbolism" in which the human being does not meet nature as a subject but "no longer encounters anything else but himself in what he does."[60] Under the conditions of industrial-capitalist civilization, the joining together of human beings and nature remains suspended.

While these rich pages contain an original and provocative critique of Marxism, they also rely on an approving reference to the Marxian demand to abolish alienated labor. On the one hand, Schürmann is clear that historical materialism cannot provide an adequate starting point for a theory of the symbol, both because it eclipses the event for the sake of history and because it operates with a concept of matter that precludes what is at stake in symbolism: "The life of the earth is precisely that in things which resists

58 "Symbolic Praxis," in this volume, 49–75.

59 Ibid., 71–72.

60 Ibid.

the reduction to primary matter."[61] On the other hand, he agrees with Ernst Bloch that what obstructs the reconciliation between human beings and nature is "the typically modern ailment of not-yet concretely mediating the materials subject and the human subject in production."[62] Contrary to Marxism, Schürmann seeks to formulate the overcoming of the "not-yet of work" not (only) as a future achievement but as something that is "already-there" in the symbol of work. It is work as an "'*omnilateral*' activity,"[63] a term Schürmann attributes to the young Marx and through which human practice would recover a form of action that is properly singular and not determined by the compulsion to execute a rule that relates cause and end for the benefit of surplus value.[64]

III. Anarchistic Strategies

If an an-archistic politics is to be thinkable today, it must be rooted in a critical understanding of the relation between action and singularity. In this regard, two distinct yet complementary lines of argument cut across Schürmann's thought which, when combined, can be read as a single "counter-strategy" with two prongs, each adapted to specific circumstances. On the one hand, following Arendt, Schürmann highlights the importance of those "rare" moments in history in which mass political insurgency succeeds in momentarily interrupting and suspending the course of history, in which the absence of the constraining truths of political life flashes up before our eyes allowing the radiant singularity of acts "without why" to assume centerstage. On the other hand, precisely because since such moments remain fleeting and exceptional, a strategy is necessary for negotiating the violence of everyday life under

61 Ibid., 71. For his reading of Ernst Bloch, see the passages on 59–61; also 63, 65, 72.

62 Ibid., 72.

63 Ibid., 73.

64 For a more detailed discussion of Marx, see Schürmann, *Heidegger on Being and Acting*, 44–60, and Reiner Schürmann, *Reading Marx. On Transcendental Materialism*, ed. Malte F. Rauch and Nicolas Schneider (Zurich: Diaphanes, 2021); see also Nicolas Schneider, "The Place of Marx in Reiner Schürmann's Work: On the Tenacious Life of Ghosts," *Graduate Faculty Philosophy Journal* 42, no. 1 (2021): 117–48.

"normal" circumstances, those in which the singular remains submerged by the "tragic denial" on which hegemonic politics depends. Along this second line, it will be a question not of "turning away" from the reign of hegemonic principles in search of an "outside," nor of taking up residence in the margins, but rather of *assuming* and inhabiting the "fissured ground" of being-there as a terrain of conflict. Rather than reading these two approaches as contradictory or mutually exclusive, we wish to suggest that a political outlook adequate to our historical moment—one marked, let us recall, by a vast concussive wave of revolts across the globe—must avail itself of both dispositions: it must be capable not only of engaging with singularization events in their pure state, but also of recognizing and retrieving their submerged persistence beneath the fantasms of archic order.

Intermittent Liberty

By introducing a demarcation between a mythic and a non-mythic use of symbols, "Situating René Char" signaled a reorientation within the theory of symbolic difference. Char, Schürmann tells us, is engaged in a "battle" against any "mythological origins, against any reference to ancestral incipiencies."[65] If the poem realizes the unity of the world's dimensions that it signifies (lightness and gravity), it does so *only* for as long as it is articulated. There is a kind of communion in the poem, but it amounts at most to an "ephemeral victory over dispersion and dislocation," one which appears suddenly before swiftly dissolving. In the final analysis, the world united through poetic language remains an "unhabitable element."[66]

This ephemeral victory of the poem finds its political analog in Schürmann's discussions of revolutionary councilism in Hannah Arendt's thought. From the mid-1970s until his final works, Schürmann continually returns to the handful of pages in *On Revolution* and *Crises of the Republic* in which Arendt describes the spontane-

65 "Situating René Char," in this volume, 89.
66 Ibid., 88–89.

ous emergence, during revolutionary waves of mass self-activity, of councilist forms of organization operating at various levels of society, from neighborhoods and workplaces to housing blocs, etc.[67] Of chief importance for Arendt's argument is the near-total "absence of continuity, tradition, and organized influence" overdetermining these forms: the councils, she claims, "never came into being as a result of a conscious revolutionary tradition or theory, but entirely spontaneously, each time as though there had never been anything of the sort before."[68] Unlike party programmes, which are "'ready-made formulas' that demand not action but execution," councils are "spaces of freedom" that "spring from the very experience of political *action*," and as such challenge the hierarchical basis of the party system as such.[69]

Following Arendt, Schürmann interprets these rare moments as instances in which "an absence of any principle of legitimation has at times invaded the political field and for brief lapses, before one ontic origin could replace another, has set action free."[70] Although they might occasionally be subject to "revival" by later sequences of struggle, allowing us to speak of a liaison from one singular point to another, such events are first and foremost breaks or caesurae in historical time, sufficiently powerful to bring epochs to a close. While both associate intermittent liberty with the suspension of reigning principles, they interpret this absence differently. For Arendt, the singular remains associated with the moment in which a new political continuity is established, carefully calibrating the rela-

---

67 Examples include the citizens' unions during the American revolution, the "popular societies" of Paris in 1789, 1793, the Paris Commune (and its "revival" in May 1968), the Russian soviets in 1905 and 1917, as well as the 1918 Arbeiter- und Soldatenräte in Berlin and the Bavarian Räterepublik of 1919 ("revived" during the Hungarian uprising of 1956). Hannah Arendt, *On Revolution* (NY: Penguin, 1990), 262; For Schürmann's treatment of these passages, see "On Judging and its Issue," in this volume; *Politique et déconstruction*, 632-33; *Heidegger on Being and Acting*, 91; *Broken Hegemonies*, 678 fn. 68; *Modern Philosophies of the Will*, ed. Kieran Aarons and Francesco Guercio (Zurich: Diaphanes, 2022), 122–23. On one occasion, Schürmann adds to this list the movements of the Free Spirit during the twelfth century, which some saw as being revived during the Paris Commune (*Heidegger on Being and Acting*, 332 fn. 61).

68 Hannah Arendt, *Crises of the Republic* (NY: Harcourt, 1972), 231.

69 Hannah Arendt, *On Revolution*, 264-65; *Crises of the Republic*, 231–32.

70 Schürmann, *Heidegger on Being and Acting*, 91.

tion between the old (the political tradition) and the new. By contrast, Schürmann emphasizes the essentially singular or *singularizing* character of these events. Although Arendt is right to emphasize their rupture with history, it is a mistake to look to them to supply political judgment with a realizable common end, or to extrapolate from it a formal norm or principle of government applicable at all times.[71] If there is a generic truth that these rare moments express, it lies less in the specific content of the actions undertaken therein than in the absence of any overarching principle guiding it. Instead of focusing on the "direct democratic" character of how power is arranged during such intervals, Schürmann emphasizes the liberated quality of the relation between words, things, and deeds that is unleashed once the *princeps* and *principium* finds itself destituted:

> We could describe these diverse and precarious realizations of the communal idea as moments of direct democracy, when power is exercised by all. But it would be more precise to describe them as anarchic intervals: for a time, the epochal *principium* whose power secures each being in its place is eclipsed.[72]

If the Paris commune, the Russian soviets, etc., are of relevance to Schürmann's notion of the symbolic, this is because they were moments in which "action turned away from principles," leaving "the 'event of appropriation' (*Ereignis* or *symballein*) as the sole economic law."[73] The philosophical significance of the "intermittent liberty" afforded by such interregnum periods resides in their verification[74] of our an-archic condition. The collapse of ontic polit-

---

71 Here Schürmann appears to take leave of Arendt, who sees in such rare moments precisely the germinal form of a "council-state…in which the principle of sovereignty would be wholly alien," and which would be "admirably suited to federations of the most various kinds, especially because in it power would be constituted horizontally and not vertically." Arendt, *Crises of the Republic*, 233.

72 Schürmann, *Politique et déconstruction*, 632.

73 Ibid., 633.

74 "'The interregnum—during which one principle has receded and a new one is not yet in place—forms the only conjuncture we are aware of wherein we can verify the Heraclitean expression (as Heidegger sums it up) *poiein kata physin*, to 'produce by following the coming-into-presence [of beings]'" (ibid.).

ical regimes allows the ontological singularity of action to shine forth. The truth of the origin—"the simple event in which all that happens to be present"[75]—suddenly pierces through the political, stripping away the fantasms on which it rests. The liberated quality of collective insurgent action reveals that, if there is an origin linking words, things, and deeds, it cannot be traced back to any substantial entity, whether God or subjectivity, nor to any organizing social principle. The *scandalon* exposed by the ontic event of revolt is that "the origin 'establishes' nothing."[76] Such a truth is by nature precarious, however, and tends to be forgotten the moment that insurgents direct their newfound liberty to issuing revolutionary decrees, which "turn against our liberty as soon as they are taken to be charters for statist organization in perpetuity."[77]

The communion of the poem founds nothing, and does not endure. It opens a space wherein words and things belong to each other and lets them be, held together in the identity of the non-identical. The principial suspension ushered in by revolt gathers together not only words and things but also actions, freely arraying and arranging all three "without why" into expressions of communal potential that make *flagrant* the tragic denial of existence on which the servility of our social and political arrangements depends. However, the truth of the origin revealed by these rare moments is precarious, perpetually threatened by the constituent impulse to issue decrees and legal charters that the rarified ontological vision afforded by revolt has generally proven too weak to forestall. For this reason, while it is good and well to champion the intermittent liberty of revolt, to seize upon and embrace these openings, and even to deepen them where possible, Schürmann's focus will increasingly be drawn to understanding the roots of the "thetic relapse" to which they so often give rise. Is there a more general vantage point through which the interaction of these two dynamics, singularization and legislation, can be grasped? What drives the constituent impulse, and how might its historical unfolding inform our understanding of power today, including during the "normal" time of everyday life?

---

75 Schürmann, *Heidegger on Being and Acting*, 91.

76 Ibid.

77 Schürmann, *Politique et déconstruction*, 633.

Tragic Ultimates and the Pull of the 'No'

A politics of singularity cannot rest upon fleeting or intermittent suspensions of order alone. Where "intermittent liberty" is not on offer, other tasks still present themselves, to which Schürmann's focus is increasingly directed during the final decade of his life. One way to distill the strategy at work in essays such as "Technicity, Topology, Tragedy" and "Conditions of Evil" is as a phenomenological practice of *recentering our attention* upon the "conflictuality glimpsed, then infallibly repressed, at the inception of every single epoch in our past."[78] This emphasis on the phenomenological displacement of our attention was already announced in *Le Principe d'anarchie*: here we are told that to become free is to "shift one's attention" since, by "retraining" our hearing, we can retrain our "allegiance" so as to "abide by presencing without recourse to ultimate representation."[79] In the period leading up to *Broken Hegemonies,* Schürmann will pair this phenomenological emphasis on attention with an original theory of a "tragic double bind" according to which the human condition is riven by the two incongruous "ultimate conditions" of natality and mortality. Whereas natality leads us to elevate or "maximize" singular deictic experiences into universal signifiers treated as normative grounds for judgment, thereby stabilizing strategies of speaking and hearing on a "steady focal point" signaling what we are to do and not to do, the countervailing pull of mortality effects a singularizing withdrawal that disturbs the tranquility of order and interrupts worldly contextualizations, without for all that constituting a "determinate other" to it.[80] What Schürmann calls "hegemonic fantasms" are "fixations of attention" that emerge wherever the maximizing function of natality obliterates the unspeakable singular by smothering it beneath directive ideas on which this or that culture comes to rely "as if

---

78 "Technicity, Topology, Tragedy," in this volume, 206.

79 *Heidegger on Being and Acting*, 92.

80 *Broken Hegemonies*, 9, 16; As Schürmann insists, "death joins life without, however, forming a tandem with it [...] it does not reflect life symmetrically nor oppose it with a determinate negation" (23).

[they] provided that in the name of which one speaks and acts."[81] If Schürmann's phenomenology of ultimates is fundamentally tragic, this is because the elevation of fantasms that guarantee "certainty in knowledge and rectitude in acting" cannot help but come at the expense of a broken link to the manifestation of the singular: this is the price we pay to "render the world livable."[82]

A confirmation of these disparate ultimates that condition human experience can already be glimpsed in the brokenness of the Kantian transcendental subject discussed above: as equiprimordial ontological moments of being, indeterminate presence and self-determination exhibit the "double bind" that marks our tragic condition, pulled at once toward *synthesis* and thetic maximization on the one side, and toward dispersion and singularization on the other. As Schürmann summarizes it, "the human condition is to stand under the twofold law of collocation and dislocation, without recourse to any supreme locus from which would proceed all allocations."[83]

One of the defining features of Schürmann's deconstruction of action lies in his unwavering conviction that there is an immanence of the practical discourse in the phenomenological one.[84] If philosophy's negative task lies in "hastening the downfall of value-laden principles," its positive task proceeds from the assumption that "sober insight into the condition of mortals" is capable of generating "for each situation the nonrepresentational standard for answering the question, 'What is to be done?'"[85] In this sense, if the phenomenology of ultimates carries an imperative within it, its political content will be measured by its phenomenological capacity to redirect our attention toward the insoluble agonism that grips our lives intimately, to ensure that we no longer deny it by looking elsewhere. In a word, the imperative that forms the second "prong" of Schürmann's political strategy is to *inhabit* the conflictuality of givenness, which is only possible provided we first "undeny" the grip of the twofold pull of the ultimates that operate within all prin-

---

81 *Broken Hegemonies*, 7.

82 Ibid., 8.

83 "On Judging and its Issue," in this volume 183.

84 See "Conditions of Evil," in this volume, 215.

85 "On the Philosophers' Release from Civil Service," in this volume, 255.

cipial economies.[86] By pulling apart the dislocating strategies, the phenomenology of ultimates assists us in cultivating the ability to *see* mortality in natality, without conflating their conflict with dialectical or metaphysical schemas: "The most enlightened insight is into that double bind. There is no greater sobriety than to recognize and live that conflict, without dreamt-up sublation."[87]

Confronted by the progressive exhaustion of Western hegemonic metaphysics, our strategy cannot be to flee toward some imagined "outside" of the West, nor to "attack the texts from their margins"; instead, we must dive "straight into the thicket," i.e., into the central matrix of power's apparatus of legitimation, train our attention upon the cracks in its main edifice, and conflictually inhabit them.[88] An anarchistic politics of singularity cannot mean to "settle happily in a place deprived of principles," but must rehabilitate the "pull of the No" that lies under the thetic "Yes," as one of its deferred possibilities.[89] This entails a combat against the reigning fictions of our time, as against everything that mutilates our capacity to rejoin the manifestation of the singular:

> [T]o enter fully into an anarchic economy, we must first precipitate the decline of everything in public life that stands in the way of the 'without-why' and 'letting-be.' All that functions as a screen between the thing and us must be cleared away.[90]

---

86 "Technicity, Topology, Tragedy," in this volume, 208.
87 "On Judging and its Issue," in this volume, 184.
88 *Broken Hegemonies*, 14–15. "What field outside the terrain must one occupy in order to affirm rupture? I know of no other place than the one whereupon the waning twentieth century has planted us" (ibid., 14).
89 "Conditions of Evil," in this volume, 229; "Technicity, Topology, Tragedy," in this volume, 200.
90 Schürmann, *Politique et déconstruction*, 630. In "'What Must I Do?' at the End of Metaphysics" (*Tomorrow the Manifold*, 52), Schürmann writes: "What must I do at the end of metaphysics? Combat all remnants of authoritative Firsts [...] dethrone the many idols with which we still adorn public and private life [...] unlearn the nomos as an artifact of reason and follow the sole nomos as the 'injunction' contained in the ever new 'dispensation of being.'"

In sum, the practical orientation of Schürmann's philosophy leads in two directions at once. During the exceptional moments of revolt, when the singular twists free of the principial regimes and appears for itself, fidelity to the intermittent liberty afforded by such moments demands a struggle against the reappearance of the constituent legislative impulse, dependent as it is upon a forgetting of the origin. In such a struggle, "'protest' recovers its primitive meaning, which is to 'testify' to truth."[91] On the other hand, when such liberty is unavailable, we must patiently cultivate a shared sensibility capable of attending to and *inhabiting* the conflictuality that engulfs the singular, of living with open eyes in the tragic truth of our condition, riveted to the manifold origin of our situation. To "bring about a generation detached from metaphysics" in this way cannot be accomplished overnight or suddenly, but constitutes a long term task.[92] Yet it is only by contributing to this task that philosophy can succeed in canceling the civil service contract that has secured its servility to the state for all too long.

IV. Displacing Action

Rather than freezing practical philosophy into a ready-made doctrine or set of practices frozen into constant presence, Schürmann insists that the liberation of action and gesture must "take a great variety of forms according to context."[93] The ground of our existence is marked by a conflictual interplay of activity and passivity, of a "there is" and an "omnilateral activity" as inseparable as they are irreducible. Riven by this irascible dynamism, the enactment of freedom can therefore only flow from a sensitivity to, and compliance with, the givenness of our situation as an historical constellation of presence. In his rare text on fine art, "Abstraction that Makes the Viewer Think," as well as the two remarkable interviews from 1977 and 1988 reprinted in the appendix to this collection, Schürmann

---

91 "Political Thinking in Heidegger," in this volume, 123; *Heidegger on Being and Acting*, 269.

92 "Political Thinking in Heidegger," in this volume, 123.

93 "On the Philosophers' Release from Civil Service," in this volume, 248.

powerfully suggests how a deeply situated and "released" conception of anarchistic practice sensitive to this combination of contravening moments should be understood politically and aesthetically.

Written on the occasion of an exhibition of paintings by his partner Louis Comtois in 1989, "Abstraction that Makes the Viewer Think" analyzes the interplay of abstraction and the splendor of colors in Comtois' works. By contrast with the darkness and doom prevalent in artists such as Anselm Kiefer, who capitalize on the depth and obscurity of mythic representation, Comtois' "chromatic densities"[94] allow the origin to shine forth as fundamentally non-original and present, rather than as shrouded in the opacity of a purportedly primordial past. In the "thoughtful splendor" produced by Comtois' work, a poetic moment asserts itself: "To think is to pause and dwell on the conditions of what one is living. As Comtois tells them in his paintings, these conditions have to do with light not given, but won."[95] There are clear parallels between this "winning of light" and the poetic practice of René Char, as well as the concept of concrete reflection traced above: in each case, the abstraction of the artistic gesture does not abolish the incongruence between the elements it relates, but preserves and accentuates it. Moreover, this process is not guided by any criterion external to itself, which would reintroduce a mythical notion of origin as a past present to be recuperated, but produces sense through the confrontation with a violence that it resists: "Since there is no universal criterion for success or failure in abstraction, such strength and coherence proper to each work requires an ever new dialectic of intuition and analysis."[96]

---

94 Schürmann, "Abstraction that Makes the Viewer Think," in this volume, 259.

95 Ibid., 257.

96 Ibid., 258. It is interesting to note that Schürmann describes this process in terms of a "dialectic" here, given his explicit rejection of dialectical thinking elsewhere. For instance, in "On the Philosophers' Release from Civil Service," he laments that "people have misunderstood [his] vocabulary as if it were yet another attempt at dialectics: 'anarchy' as the determinate negation of 'principle,' which negation would then be expected to sublate itself and yield some new principal form of being" (in this volume, 249–50). Yet if his critique of dialectics is due to its reliance on standards of representation for thinking and acting, the emphasis here is precisely on the lack of such guiding criteria of determination.

What is true for aesthetics is even more so for politics: there is no single method or principle that can guide us. Although it is certain that "to enter the play of freedom means to struggle," what this struggle entails can and must differ depending on our concrete historical circumstances.[97] Schürmann's sensitivity to the essentially *situated* character of tactical and strategic considerations is evident in the two remarkable interviews included here, which adopt quite distinct positions on the justification of political violence at different moments. In his 1977 interview with the French Catholic newspaper *La Croix*, Schürmann rejects the "bloody form of anarchy" waged at the time by the Red Army Faction to free imprisoned members of their group, emphasizing the link between "letting be" and the political significance of embracing the "absence of a stable identity."[98] In the 1988 interview, by contrast, Schürmann underscores the danger of a narrowly interior understanding of releasement that would reduce it to a spiritual ethic, rather than a worldly politics: if one finds oneself living under a dictator such as Pol Pot, or "a situation of occupation" more generally, "there, anarchism has to be taken in a very strict and militant sense including acts of terror."[99] In view of the obvious limitations of a Nietzschean celebration of joy in the face of political repression, the historical struggle for "man's release from self-incurred tutelage" must take on different shapes in divergent situations.

At the same time, in both interviews, the "situatedness" of action is understood not merely in terms of its concrete factical givens, but always at the same time as a relation between our historical and our ontological condition. Since the givenness of our situation is itself given only in accordance with this or that historical constellation of presence, "regional" political strategies must comply with epochal lines of fracture that form the proper object of *thought*, and which, prior to taking on the status of theoretical or imaginary universals, emerge through "multiple originary acts" that cannot themselves be planned or foreseen in advance.[100] In this respect, that our

97 Schürmann, *Heidegger on Being and Acting*, 93.

98 "Interview with a Young German Writer," in this volume, 240.

99 "On the Philosophers' Release from Civil Service," in this volume, 248.

100 Schürmann, *Heidegger on Being and Acting*, 53.

epochal situation is marked by an "absence of a stable identity," the displacement of a "wandering identity,"[101] means that all regional political strategies in which "appeal is made...to the humanistic quest for self-identity, self-possession, resolution of alienation, etc." amount to little more than *archē*-mourning, "efforts to reinstitute figures of some authoritative First that in fact have been lost for good."[102] That we stand in a site deserted by the successive representations of an unshakable ground is cause neither for intoxicated jubilation nor mourning. It may, however, be hoped that with sober thinking and a bit of courage, we might finally face the conflicts that grip us with open eyes.

---

101 Reiner Schürmann, *Wandering Joy: Meister Eckhart's Mystical Philosophy* (Great Barrington, MA: Lindisfarne Books, 2001), xx.
102 "On the Philosophers' Release from Civil Service," in this volume, 246.

Acknowledgments

The essays assembled here were first published in the following journals and essay collections:

1) "Symbolic Difference," trans. Charles T. Wolfe, *Graduate Faculty Philosophy Journal* 19/20, nos. 2/1 (1997): 9–38. First published as "La différence symbolique," *Cahiers internationaux de symbolisme* 21 (1972): 51–77.

2) "Symbolic Praxis," trans. Charles T. Wolfe, *Graduate Faculty Philosophy Journal* 19/20, nos. 2/1 (1997): 39–72. First published as "La praxis symbolique," *Cahiers internationaux de symbolisme* 29/30 (1976): 145–70.

3) "Situating René Char: Hölderlin, Heidegger, Char, and the 'There Is,'" *boundary 2* 4, no. 2 (1976): 513–34. An earlier version of this text was published in French as "Il y a dans le poème...," *Cahiers internationaux de symbolisme* 24/25 (1973): 99–118.

4) "Political Thinking in Heidegger," *Social Research* 45, no. 1 (1978): 191–221.

5) "The Ontological Difference and Political Philosophy," *Philosophy and Phenomenological Research* 40, no. 1 (1979): 99–122.

6) "On Judging and its Issue," in Reiner Schürmann (ed.), *The Public Realm. Essays on Discursive Types in Political Philosophy* (Albany: SUNY Press, 1989), 1–24.

7) "Technicity, Topology, Tragedy: Heidegger on 'That Which Saves' in the Global Reach," in Arthur M. Melzer, Jerry Weinberger, and M. Richard Zinman (eds.), *Technology in the Western Political Tradition* (Ithaca: Cornell University Press, 1993), 190–213.

8) "Conditions of Evil," in Drucilla Cornell, Michel Rosenfeld, David Gray Carlson (eds.), *Deconstruction and the Possibility of Justice* (New York and London: Routledge, 1992), 387–403. The text has been translated from the French by Ian Janssen.

Appendix

1) "Reiner Schürmann. Entretien avec un jeune écrivain allemand," *La Croix*, September 30, 1977, 2. Translation based on an English transcript from the Reiner Schürmann Archive, Reiner Schürmann Papers, 1958–1993. NA.0006.01, box 1, folder 11. The New School Archives and Special Collections. New York: The New School, no date.

2) "On the Philosophers' Release from Civil Service," *Kairos* 2 (1988): 133–45.

3) "Abstraction That Makes the Viewer Think. About the Last Paintings of Louis Comtois," *C Magazine* 29 (1991): 6–7.

Reiner Schürmann
Selected Writings and Lecture Notes

Edited by
Francesco Guercio, Michael Heitz,
Ian Alexander Moore, and Nicolas Schneider

This edition aims to provide a broader perspective on the prolific, multi-faceted, and still largely unrecognized body of work produced by Reiner Schürmann (1941–1993). It brings together a selection of Schürmann's as yet unpublished lecture notes, written for the courses he delivered at the New School for Social Research in New York between 1975 and 1993, with previously uncollected essays.

These works offer an additional avenue into the repertoire already available—including recent re-editions of his major philosophical works and of his only novel. The printed works will be complemented by a digital edition of Schürmann's typescripts, along with transcriptions and an extensive critical apparatus.

We hope that the *Selected Writings and Lecture Notes* will contribute to a renewed appreciation of the scope of Schürmann's philosophical endeavor and help to establish him as one of those thinkers who are indispensable for the understanding of our present—or, rather, to show our present as the moment of legibility for Schürmann's work. We are grateful to the Reiner Schürmann Estate for entrusting us with the responsibility of this work and for their full endorsement.

Ways of Releasement. Writings on God, Eckhart, and Zen
Edited by Francesco Guercio and Ian Alexander Moore
Paperback, 424 pages

Modern Philosophies of the Will
Edited by Kieran Aarons and Francesco Guercio
Paperback, 192 pages

Reading Marx. On Transcendental Materialism
Edited by Malte Fabian Rauch and Nicolas Schneider
Paperback, 160 pages

Neo-Aristotelianism and the Medieval Renaissance
On Aquinas, Ockham, and Eckhart
Edited by Ian Alexander Moore
Paperback, 144 pages

The Philosophy of Nietzsche
Edited by Francesco Guercio
Paperback, 176 pages

Tomorrow the Manifold. Essays on Foucault, Anarchy,
and the Singularization to Come
Edited by Malte Fabian Rauch and Nicolas Schneider
Paperback, 184 pages